I cannot forget so k[...]
as he was to me & I s[...]
he is well & prosperious, it is a
great comfort to me to think the
cruel war is over & that there is
no bloodsheding now - but every
thing is dreadfully dear in this
country & there does not appear
any chance of things getting cheaper
at present, our house stands quite
alone but there are some more
large farms very near us, our
neighbours are very friendly
which is nice to think in a
country place. is any of Mrs White's
family living at Chevington now
or who have you for a minister
I heard the Clerk's name was Mr
Jonathan Cooper & I was quite pleas[ed]
to hear it hope he may continue in it
for many years tell him with my love
I must now conclude my Husband joins me
in best love to you all ever believe me dear Brother
your most affect Sister Sophia Whydel

CHEVINGTON

A Social Chronicle of a Suffolk Village

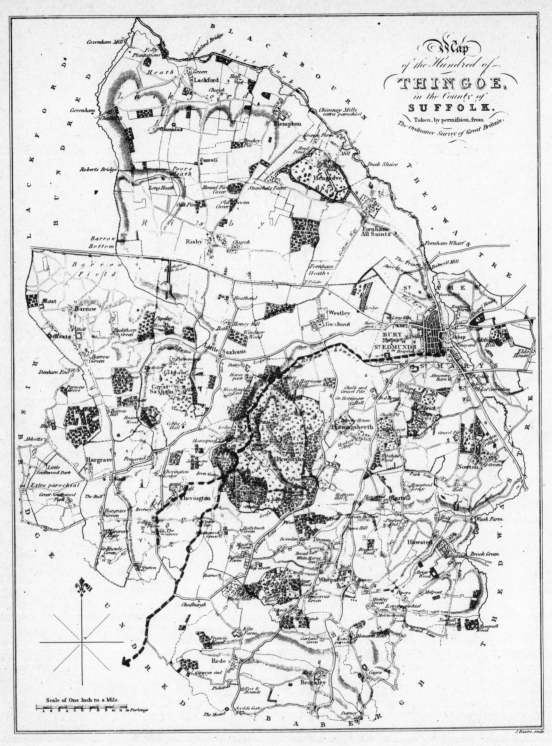

Frontispiece: *The former Thingoe Hundred from John Gage's* History and Antiquities of Suffolk, *1838, reproduced from the Ordnance Survey, c.1830. Chevington Way has been indicated here by a broken line.*

Chevington

A Social Chronicle of a Suffolk Village

Frank Cooper

Phillimore

1984

Published by
PHILLIMORE & CO. LTD.
Shopwyke Hall, Chichester, Sussex

ISBN 0 85033 558 2

Typeset in the United Kingdom by:
Fidelity Processes - Selsey - Sussex

Printed and bound in Great Britain by
THE CAMELOT PRESS LTD.
Southampton, England

CONTENTS

In grateful memory of the people of Chevington, past and present, and in particular, of my father, William Henry, who spent his life in the village, 1880-1947, and of my mother, Ada Elizabeth, who lived there for fifty years, 1902-52.

O come, blest Spirit! whatsoe'er thou art,
Thou rushing warmth that hover'st round my heart,
. . .
Bear me through regions where gay Fancy dwells;
But mould to Truth's fair form what Memory tells.

Live, trifling incidents, and grace my song . . .

— Robert Bloomfield, Suffolk poet, 1776-1823

LIST OF PLATES

(between pages 12 and 13)

LIST OF TEXT ILLUSTRATIONS

ACKNOWLEDGEMENTS

IT WAS ALWAYS an ambition of mine to write a history of Chevington. Thanks to many very helpful friends, who have made my task a happy one, I have fulfilled my ambition during the years of retirement from teaching.

I thank the people of Chevington for their patience and good humour in answering many detailed questions and for allowing me to see their houses. The members of the history of Chevington steering committee have worked sacrificially, but a special word of appreciation is due to the Pettit family and to Job Willis for their unfailing encouragement.

I am indebted to David Dymond, Resident Tutor in Suffolk for the University of Cambridge Board of Extra-Mural Studies, for his wise advice in the preliminary stages of the work and to Geoffrey Clements, A. C. (Gus) Edwards, Eric Reed and my brother, Henry, for reading either the entire MS., or parts of it, and for their pungent comment. Sylvia Coleman, Advisor on Historic Buildings and Phillip Aitkins, an Historic Buildings Inspector, both for Suffolk County Council, have helped generously with Chevington's buildings and Howard Dove and Donald Simpson have accompanied my wife and me on a number of delightful visits to Chevington to take photographs. However, many of the photographs have been kindly provided by local residents, but I regret that it has been impossible to include them all.

I have been heartened, too, by the ready help that Mr. Nigel Underwood has given me about his forbears who were rectors of Chevington in the 17th century. Miss Joscelyn, grand-daughter of the Reverend John White III and Mr. A. J. Keble-White, grandson of the Reverend A. Keble White, have given strong support. Mr. Raymond Smith, the great-grandson of W. H. Smith I, has been an enthusiastic and reliable source of information. The account of the ecclesiastical unrest of 1926 would have been impossible without the kind co-operation of Mrs. P. Nottage and Mr. Christopher Nottage.

It is a pleasure, too, to express my deep appreciation of the guidance of Mr. R. G. Thomas and his staff of the Suffolk Record Office at Bury St Edmunds, particularly Mr. K. C. (Ken) Wright for his patience during my many frenetic telephone calls and for his constant courtesy during my many visits.

In conclusion, I thank the members of my family, my three daughters who have been an inspiration in their specialised fields: Rachel, for her prudent advice on all matters of historical material; Anne, for meticulous help with translations and for archival matters generally; Susan, an environmental planner, for her frank and relevant comments and Andrew, my son-in-law, for his plan of the Church of All Saints. I am indebted to them all.

However, most of all, I thank my wife, Jean, for her cheerful forbearance, encouragement and constructive criticism in all matters of detail far too numerous for me to mention and for her line drawings of the flowers of Chevington. Without her support, this social history of my homeland would not have seen the light of day.

I should like to thank the following persons and institutions for permission to

xi

reproduce illustrations. In the plate section: Nos. 4, 5 and 7, the National Trust; No. 6, the Tate Gallery; No. 15, Donald Simpson; Nos. 36 and 37, the *Bury Free Press*; and for permission to reproduce illustrations in the text, the following: No. 1, the General Editor of the *Victoria County History*; the frontispiece and Nos. 2, 8, 9, 10, 11 and 13, reproduced from Ordnance Survey maps by permission of the Comptroller of Her Majesty's Stationery Office (Crown Copyright Reserved); No. 4, Suffolk County Library; No. 5, Gonville and Caius College, Cambridge; No. 20, drawn by the late R. Morris, reproduced by permission of Mrs. E. Morris; No. 21, Peter Steer of Chelmer Valley High School.

PREFACE

Visitors to East Anglia are quick to acclaim the merits of Suffolk. The traveller will recall many distinguished churches such as Long Melford, Blythburgh, Lavenham and Mildenhall; the great houses of Ickworth, Kentwell, and Hengrave; the timber-framed cottages and the Georgian houses; the river valleys, the undulations overlooking large, extensive fields, the village greens and, moreover, the villages themselves.

Whether linear, scattered over a wide area, or nucleated around a green, most villages retain something of their earlier character which stimulates the imagination and, perhaps, a concern for the people who lived there in past centuries: their occupations, their domestic and social life, their triumphs and, maybe, their disasters.

However, in spite of the widening interest in local history, some parishes have been passed by and remain, as a consequence, relatively unknown. They lack the features necessary to make an impression on the sightseers. Furthermore, if they are remote from the accustomed track, only the dedicated pilgrim will arrive. In spite of such ancient parishes remaining unhonoured and unsung, they have been the homes and sources of livelihood of countless people down the years — and people matter. When the social history of those villages is explored, much of permanent significance is often revealed. Chevington, a village in Suffolk, is such a one.

Chelmsford, 1984   FRANK COOPER

BIBLIOGRAPHY

These books have been included because of their likely appeal to the general reader.

Dymond, David: *Writing Local History*, Bedford Square, 1981.
Hoskins, W. G.: *Local History in England*, Longman, 2nd edn. 1972, 2nd impression in paperback, 1974.

Fairbrother, Nan: *New Lives, New Landscapes*, Penguin Books, 1972.
Hyams, Edward: *The Changing Face of Britain*, first pub. by Kestrel Books under the title: *The Changing Face of England*, 1974, pub. in 1977 by Paladin.

Clifton Taylor, Alec: *The Pattern of English Building*, new edn., Faber & Faber, 1972.
Girouard, Mark: *Life in the English Country House*, Yale University Press, 1978.
Hervey, Manners W.: *Annals of a Suffolk Village*, University Press, Cambridge, 1930.
Strong, Roy *et al.*: *The Destruction of the Country House*, Thames and Hudson, London, 1974.

Briggs, Asa: *A Social History of England*, Weidenfeld and Nicolson, London, 1983.
Dymond, David and Northeast, Peter: *A History of Suffolk*, Phillimore (forthcoming).
Trevelyn, G. M.: *English Social History*, 1st edn. in Great Britain, Longmans, Green & Co., 1944.

Davy, David Elisha: *A Journal of Excursions Through the County of Suffolk* (ed. John Blatchly) *1823-1844*, Boydell Press, 1982.
Fincham, Paul: *The Suffolk We Live In*, George Nobbs Publishing, 1976
Jobson, Allan: *Suffolk Villages*, Robert Hale, 1971.
Scarfe, Norman: *The Suffolk Landscape*, Hodder & Stoughton, 1972.
— : *Suffolk, A Shell Guide*, Faber & Faber, 1976.
Smedley, Norman: *Life and Tradition in Suffolk and North-East Essex*, J. M. Dent & Sons Ltd., 1976.
Thirsk, J. and Imray, J. (eds.): *Suffolk Farming in the 19th C.*, Suffolk Records Society, vol. I (1958).

Cautley, H. M.: *Suffolk Churches and their Treasures*, 1937, 4th rev. edn., Boydell Press, 1975.
Gage, John: *History and Antiquities of Suffolk, Thingoe Hundred*, John Deck (BSE), 1838.
Gage, John: *History and Antiquities of Hengrave*, London, 1822.
Pevsner, Nikolaus (rev. by Enid Radcliffe): *Suffolk (Buildings of England)* 2nd edn., 1974.
Sandon, Eric: *Suffolk Houses*, Baron Publishing, Woodbridge, Suffolk, 1977.

Whittingham, A. B.: *Bury St Edmunds Abbey*, Department of the Environment, H.M.S.O., 1971.

Agate, John: *Benches and Stalls in Suffolk Churches*, Suffolk Historic Churches Trust, 1980.
Clauston, R. W. M., and Pipe, G. J. W.: *Bells and Bellringing in Suffolk*, Suffolk Historic Churches Trust, 1980.

Childe-Pemberton, William S.: *The Earl Bishop* (2 vols.), Hurst and Blackett, Ltd., 1924.
Erskine, David (ed.): *Augustus Hervey's Journal*, William Kimber, 1953.
Fothergill, Brian: *The Mitred Earl*, Faber & Faber, 1974.
Halsband, Robert: *Lord Hervey*, Oxford, 1973.

An asterisk* in the text at the first appearance of a word indicates that the term is included in the glossary on pages 138 and 139.

Abbreviations

BL	— British Library
BRO	— Bedfordshire Record Office
BPP	— British Parliamentary Papers
CROC	— County Record Office, Cambridge
CUL	— Cambridge University Library
CUP	— Cambridge University Press
ERO	— Essex Record Office
GLL	— Guildhall Library, London
NRO	— Norfolk Record Office
PRO	— Public Record Office, Chancery Lane, London
PRO (Kew)	— Public Record Office, Kew, Richmond, Surrey
PSIA	— Proceedings of Suffolk Institute of Archaeology
SRO BSE	— Suffolk Record Office at Bury St Edmunds
SRO I	— Suffolk Record Office at Ipswich
WN	— Wickhambrook and Newmarket.

CHAPTER ONE

THE PARISH OF CHEVINGTON
AND ITS LIFE IN THE MIDDLE AGES

'... toward thyn herytage
Hast on thy weye, and be of right good chere,
Go eche day onward on thy pylgrymage.'

John Lydgate, born in Lidgate, Suffolk,
poet and monk at St Edmundsbury, 1370(?)-1450.

THE NAME CHEVINGTON was drawn from Cifongas,[1] the name of a very early tribe; the —ing place names are usually the place, farm, or clearing, belonging to a man of a certain name.[2] Chevington, a hamlet two miles from Pershore, Worcestershire, owes its origin to 'Cifa's farm', or 'tun'.[3] Chevington in Suffolk and Chevington in Northumberland both owe their patronymic name, Anglian in origin, to Ceofan,[4] the leader of that tribe. Chevington, the place, clearing, farm, or 'tun' of Ceofan appears as *Ceuentuna* in Domesday Book in 1086. About two hundred years later the name is written 'Chevintun', 'Cheventun',[5] or 'Cheveton'. It was not until the 14th century that the 'g' appeared in the name of the parish[6] and the spellings of 'Cheuingtone' and 'Chevyngton' are both common from the beginning of the following century. By 1450 the variant of 'Chevyngton' was in frequent use[7] and it remained so[8] until the late 1500s, when the spelling was stabilised as Chevington.

The parish and village of Chevington in Suffolk is situated about seven miles southwest of Bury St Edmunds in the administrative district of St Edmundsbury. Before the reorganisation of local government in 1974, Chevington was one of 18 parishes in the Thingoe Rural District which formed part of the County of West Suffolk and which was coterminous with the ancient Thingoe Hundred. This relatively large and rambling village is accessible from Bury St Edmunds on the A143 to Haverhill via Horringer and past the National Trust property of Ickworth, or from the minor road to the west of Bury St Edmunds leading to Little Saxham Church with its round Norman tower and to Hargrave, a friendly neighbour, with which Chevington has been closely associated for centuries.

Some indomitable travellers have succeeded in finding their way to Chevington. In the period 1732-34 John Kirby,[9] of Wickham Market, Suffolk, in writing of the Thingoe Hundred in his *The Suffolk Traveller*, referred to the Bury St Edmunds environment:

It has a most beautiful enclosed country on the south and south-west and on the north and north-west the most delicious Champaign fields.

In 1827, an unknown explorer of villages described his visit to Chevington from Bury:

The road from Bury lies through the beautiful village of Horningsheath (or Horringer), the ground rising into gentle hills and, being well wooded, occasional openings are seen, which afford some good distant views over a very rich country.[10]

1

On Friday, 26 August 1831 the outspoken David Elisha Davy arrived at Hargrave and Chevington:[11]

> We at length reached Hargrave, which may do very well in summer, but I should be very sorry to have anything to do with it in the winter: the land undulates a good deal, but appears very wet and stiff, and wants more wood to make it agreeable in my eyes. The church stands rather high, but contains nothing to produce any interest. It had just been repaired; we had before heard that this had not been done before it was needed.
>
> From Hargrave we went on to Chevington; still upon high and wet ground: this place, however, appears much more habitable than its neighbour which we had just left.

To the west of Chevington there rises a range of chalk hills, the northward continuation of the Royston Downs, extending from Haverhill in the south, by Newmarket and Bury St Edmunds to Thetford and which reaches the Wash in low chalk cliffs at Hunstanton on the Norfolk coast. This ridge serves as a corridor between the flat lands of East Anglia and the rest of the country, terminating at the Marlborough Downs in Wiltshire. For over 4,000 years the Icknield Way has followed this ridge, connecting East Anglia, including Chevington, with south-west England. From Lackford, a village six miles north of Chevington, the Icknield Way cut south-west to Cavenham, to Newmarket and beyond. In 1916 its history and course were narrated by the poet Edward Thomas who made reference to Chevington Way, the ancient route from Bury St Edmunds to Chevington and to the villages further to the south-west. There are very early references to the track. Between 1297–1300, William de Westley was granted land 'on the Way leading to Chevington' and on 15 August 1466 Ralph Holdernesse obtained land in Little Saxham 'adjoining land of the abbot . . . on the Way leading from Chevington . . .'.[12]

Chevington Way, sometimes in its history referred to as Abbot's Way, left Westgate in Bury and, passing down what is now Hospital Road, followed the course of the river Linnet to what is currently named Westley Bottom overlooking three sweeping brecks to the south. The Way is still traceable here and there. Entering the parish of Ickworth, the former road flanked Mordebois, now an isolated thatched cottage but, until the early 19th century, the centre of a village community. Keeping close to the line of the river Linnet, Chevington Way joined the present road in Ickworth Park, wound its course to what is now Iron Gates and then climbed steadily to Chevington Hall, a distance of over seven miles from the Norman Gate of the Abbey at St Edmundsbury. Today an unhurried walk to Chevington will take about two hours.

Drift of glacial origin frequently overlies the chalk formation. This is of crucial importance for boulder clay forms very fertile soil, constituting the stiff, 'heavy' land for arable farming for which villages in the locality are renowned. Chevington is situated on the western edge of the boulder clay plateau and has the characteristic heavy soil, but the depth of clay covering the village fluctuates considerably. Its greatest depth is usually found in relatively low-lying areas, the hill slopes being more chalky.[13]

On the east and north-east, Chevington is bounded by Ickworth Park, the ancestral home of the Herveys. In 1956, Theodora, the late Marchioness of Bristol, presented the property to the National Trust. To the north, south and west, presenting an undulating environment of large, sweeping fields, are the farming villages of Great Saxham, Whepstead, Hargrave, Depden and Chedburgh most of which formed part of the original Bristol estate.

The highest land in Chevington is in the south reaching 375 feet on the Bury St Edmunds road near the old blacksmith's forge. This higher land continues through the villages of Chedburgh and Depden and reaches 425 feet near Elms Farm, Depden, which is regarded as the highest point in Suffolk. The land slopes gradually to below 250 feet in the north-west of the parish, the lowest level being 238 feet near the little Linnet on the edge of Oxpasture Grove.

Although Chevington winters often bring sharp and penetrating winds from the north-east, the climate is very favourable to tree growth and, because of the moisture retentive soil, there can be little doubt that, in prehistoric times, the parish was completely forested. Jennison's Grove, Oxpasture Grove and the 19th-century woods, Park, Twist, Stoney Hill, Downter's and Lownde, still give a quiet charm to the landscape. Four of those woods flank the western side of Ickworth Park, most of which was planted by John Hervey, First Earl of Bristol, early in the 18th century,[14] although many considerably older trees remain which warrant close investigation.

The strategic ancient trackways and other important routes, most of which crossed East Anglia in a north-easterly direction, did not touch the villages to the south-west of Bury St Edmunds. However, for centuries, and indeed well into the 1930s, many footpaths edged the fields, meadows and woods. They were used extensively by villagers who lived in remote corners of the locality and by pupils of the village school who had to walk tedious distances even when snow had drifted over the land.

Chevington and the Abbey of St Edmund

During the reign of William I (1066–1087) Chevington, a former part of the Saxon estate of Britulf, was given to the Abbey of St Edmund at Bury,[15] one of the richest Benedictine abbeys in the country. Founded in 1020[16] to shelter the remains of St Edmund, the former East Anglian King who was murdered by the Danes (probably at Bradfield St Clare), the abbey church was partly built by Abbot Baldwin (1065–1097). It was Baldwin who was responsible for the acquisition of Chevington. From his Hall there, to the north-east of the Church of All Saints, Abbot Thomas in 1309 wrote to King Edward II apologising for not attending the King's Parliament.[17] Less than twenty years afterwards, on the death of the King, the suppressed townspeople of Bury plundered the Abbey. The Abbot, Richard of Draughton, took refuge at Chevington Hall[18] pursued by a crowd of militants,[19] led by one de Bouten. According to the historian Gottfried,[20] some members of the group returned to Bury where they ransacked the Abbot's house. Richard of Draughton was thrust into a sack, conveyed from Chevington to London and eventually exiled to the continent, returning to his Abbey two years later. Many local manor houses, including Great Horringer Hall, were destroyed by the insurgents of 1327 and it is probable that the Hall at Chevington suffered some serious damage.

Chevington Hall, a 17th-century farm house (a Grade II Listed Building) but containing work of the previous century, occupies a site of great historical importance and beauty. The earthworks could well date from the Romano–British period, or even earlier. The site warrants a visit even if such an occasion is confined to the area of the 'moated' driveway which leads to the house and farmyard. The present buildings[21] are surrounded by a very ancient camp site, the western and northern sides being angular, the latter being protected by a fosse, or deep trench, 60 feet wide and 14 feet deep,

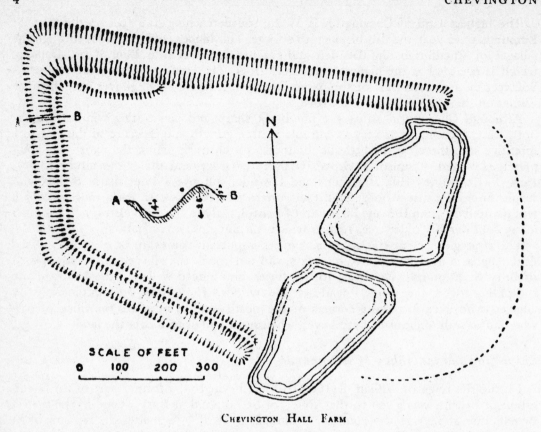

CHEVINGTON HALL FARM

1. Plan of the fortified site of Chevington Hall. Note that the ramparts originally extended to the east. The two ponds were dug later.

which increases in size to the north-west. This section of the fortification includes a vallum, or rampart, which rises to approximately nine feet. In the front of the present house the trench and rampart, originally semi-circular, have virtually disappeared although slight traces remain here and there. Chevington Way cuts into this eastern area. Two large ponds, erroneously styled 'the moat' and separated by a causeway, were later constructed inside the original camp. The area, fortified by fosse and vallum, exceeded four acres. The entire stronghold was adapted at an unknown date, possibly as early as the 12th century, as a protection for the Hall, one of the country seats of the great Benedictine abbey at Bury which after the Dissolution became a manor house for the Kytsons and Gages of Hengrave who were then the Lords of the Manor and chief landowners of Chevington. On the north side there was formerly a small mound which could have been an observation post commanding an uninterrupted view of the country to the north and west of the camp. Later, to the north-west in Chevington Park, stood the hunting lodge parts of which remain as the present Lodge cottages.

Moats, which are numerous on Suffolk's boulder clay country,[22] provided a ready supply of water and a useful means of drainage. There were a number of moated sites in Chevington: at the former Rectory, the College Farm, the Moat Farm, Tan

Office Farm, and the Lodge, although sparse evidence remains of their former extent and significance.

At the time of Domesday (1086)[23] the abbot held Chevington (*Ceuentuna*), a manor of six *caracutes*,* approximately one and a quarter square miles, or 800 acres; *Ceuenta tenuit Sanctus Edmundus pro manerio 6 carracates terrae*. There were 13 *villeins*,* or unfree tenants, and six slaves. On the manor there were 140 sheep, 40 goats and three hives of bees.

At that time there was only one free tenant, or *sokeman*, who probably farmed about 30 acres. As a tenant he would pay rent and would attend the lord's manorial court when required. Such tenants may have had their homesteads a mile or so from the centre of the Manor and, as such, were relatively free from the close surveillance of the abbot's authority. If the *messuage** and *tenement** of Henry de Ruffyn were sited in the area of the present Ruffin's Farm, which is likely, he was far removed from the centre of manorial management at Chevington Hall. As the manor of Chevington was a retreat for the Lord Abbot and his staff who, according to local tradition, visited the Hall merely to fish and hunt, the manor would probably be let to a tenant who was subjected to the authority of the lord's representative, the steward, or bailiff.

According to his chronicler, Jocelin of Brakelond,[24] Abbot Samson (1182-1215) forgave a debt of one of his tenants, but no less than four of the malefactor's manors were forfeited. He forgave Walter de Hatfield £19 of arrears of rent, in return for receiving from him the four manors in which he had been confirmed as tenant by Abbot Hugh, namely, Hargrave, Saxham, Chevington and Stapleford. An indication of Abbot Samson's thoroughness in managing his estates, such as Chevington, is given by Jocelin?[25]

> ... the abbot caused inquest to be made in every manor belonging to the abbacy as to the annual revenues of the free men, and the names of the villeins, and their holdings, and the services due from each, and caused all these details to be written down. Then he restored the old halls and ruined houses, through which kites and crows flew; he built new chapels, and rooms and seats in many places where there had never been buildings, save perhaps barns. He also made many parks which he filled with beasts, and had a huntsman and dogs. And whenever any important guest arrived, he used to sit with his monks in some retired grove, and watch the coursing for a while, but I never saw him interested in hunting. He made many clearings and brought land into cultivation ...

In 1268 the Abbot, John de Norwold, owned 460 acres of arable land in Chevington,[26] eight acres of meadow, 40 acres of wood and a windmill. A field, named Little Mill Field, was marked on the 1815 Enclosure Map and the mound on which the medieval mill probably stood was still in existence at the top of Great Days, then pasture, at the end of the Second World War. In addition to owning the land, the abbot held the patronage of the Church and continued to do so until the Dissolution of the Monastery of St Edmund in 1539 when it passed to the merchant, Sir Thomas Kytson, of Hengrave.

John de Norwold's villeins held 322 acres of arable land, over two acres of wood, and three acres of pasture. In return for holding land, the villein was forced to perform services on the lord's lands and to pay certain fines such as *heriot** and *merchet.** The *cottars*,* on the lowest level of the social hierarchy, had to provide labour on the abbot's lands, usually at a fixed rate and they held between them 18 acres of arable land. This land was divided into a few smallholdings each of about six acres. At the time of the survey, Adam and Robert de Seburgh were listed as free tenants. It is of interest to recall that in the early 19th century, two large fields known as Seburgh's existed on the Bury Road on what is now known as Poulter's Lane. The cottages at Brooks's Corner, long inhabited by the Wallace family, were originally styled Seburgh's Cottages and the land immediately in front of them was Seburgh's meadow. The Pinchbeck Register[27] (1330) records that Adam had a house and 47 acres of land, four acres of woodland — '*iiij acras bosci*' — and four acres of meadowland — '*iiij acras prati et pasture*'. They were held 'in socage tenure', *de sokagio*, indicating that Adam de Seburgh, the father of the then Rector, Robert, held free tenure without the obligation of military service, but there would be other compulsory services to the Lord Abbot: '(he) renders freely to the same Abbot for each tenement and for the other tenements which his tenants hold from him, 24 shillings'.

The lord of the manor, i.e. the abbot, or his main tenant, the free tenants ('*liberi tenentes*'), the villeins and the cottars, shared the produce of Chevington's lands. All were dependent on each other for co-operation, thereby enabling them to perform their individual duties but, at the same time, they were acutely aware of social differences. The villein was bound to the soil, *adscriptus glebæ*. For a specified number of days a year he had to work on the abbot's lands — his *demesne** — without pay. Only when the abbot had no further need of labour, were they free to cultivate their own strips on the open field.

The *villein** could not allow his daughter to marry without the payment of a fine. When he died, his best beast was seized as heriot by the lord of the manor. During the rule of Abbot Cratfield (1390–1415), one Solomon Milk of Chevington gave a beast for a heriot and, in addition, paid *childwyt.**[28] According to Gage, Solomon Milk was a villein within the manorial organisation of Chevington in about the year 1400. In return for his loyal services he received protection from his lord, the Abbot of St Edmundsbury. He can be regarded as typical of all the rural workers who followed him.

The Black Death of 1348-9 resulted in the deaths of between a half and a third of the country's population causing a rapid rise in costs, shortage of labour, an accelerated demand for wages and opposition to compulsory work on the demesne. According to Professor Hallam in *Rural England 1066-1348* there were 32 deaths in the Suffolk village of Worlingworth in 1348-9 and 70 in Redgrave in 1348-50. Knowles and Hadcock in *Medieval Religious Houses in England and Wales* tell us that in the late 13th century there were 80 monks at St Edmund's Abbey; only 47 remained after 1349. Some villages were wiped out, others resettled in a different area of the manor or parish. Such could have been the case in Chevington's neighbouring villages of Depden and Hargrave. Although figures are not available for Chevington, it is reasonable to conclude that the village was not immune from the effects of the pestilence.

Control over land was the main source of power in the Middle Ages: a prerequisite of authority over people which was to last for centuries. There are many known land transactions for Chevington. In 1381, John Brett and six others acquired 'tenements, rents and services' from Edward Fitz Lucas of Bury.[29] Those monastic tenancies were again transferred to one John de Staverton in 1401. The greed for land was insatiable.

The Lord Abbot's senior manorial officer, the High Steward, was a powerful figure, but there is reference to a late 15th-century conflict[30] between the abbot and his 'Chevyngton' steward who had taken no action when, not far from Bury, 'a servaunt and a sermonre' from the Abbey Church, was beaten to death:

all the good rewle that sumtyme was withinne ... is at this day turnyd upsodown to our great hurt and hindrance ... the steward executeth nought his office dewly as he oweth to do.

'Certeyn personys' of Chevington were determined to ensure that the King's writ be executed against 'swich mysdooeris' of the steward, but 'they were take owght of owre place at Chevyngton ... and led in to the gildable and there enprisoned'. The public-spirited people of Chevington were released by the abbot's staff at great cost and labour. It is not known whether they were rewarded for their initiative or whether, in the course of time, the negligent steward was brought to justice.

From the late 13th century, the family of Paman became prominent in the parish. They rose to the status of yeomen, freeholders owning their land with the virtual right of occupation. In the 17th and 18th centuries some members of the family were designated 'gentlemen', others remained 'husbandmen'. A study of a selection of 16th-century Paman wills reveals that the family were generous benefactors of the parish and its church. Two centuries later one became a distinguished doctor, a friend of the Archbishop of Canterbury and the Public Orator of the University of Cambridge. No graves or memorials are known to exist although, because of their prominence, most of the family would have been interred in the chancel of the Church of All Saints.

During his first year of office Abbot Curteys (1429–1446), a shrewd administrator, directed a survey of his manor in Chevington to ascertain the value of his demesne lands: *ad cognoscend' valorem terrarum dominicalium ibidem*.[31] A translation of the written survey reads:

There is one enclosed pasture called 'Le Exeleswe' which is well able to fatten up 40 young oxen per year, and which is worth £4 per year.

And there are three open fields which are well able to fatten up on estimation 70 young oxen, and which are well worth £6 per year.

And further in the aforesaid three open fields 200 sheep can graze well in the period from the feast of All Saints to the feast of the Holy Trinity, which are worth, during that period, £6 13s. 4d.

And further, in the aforesaid fields, from the said feast of the Holy Trinity to the feast of All Saints, there can graze well 300 young sheep which during that same period are well worth 100 shillings at 4d. a head.

And in the park there 24 young oxen can graze well (worth) 53s. 4d.

Total Sum of value per year = £24 6s. 8d. [£24.33p.]

According to Rackham[32] a park was an area of land, consisting of wood pasture enclosed by a pale which was a deer-proof and, as in Chevington, an oxen-proof, fence. The abbot's parkland lay to the north-west of the Church of All Saints in the vicinity of the New Road and the present Chevington Lodge. Sometime after 1528, Sir Clement Heigham, of Barrow, having been granted a lease of monastic lands in Chevington, was appointed to the office of Keeper of the Park at Chevington with a ground rent of 45s. 6d.[33] (£2.27½). Sometimes parks had the extra protection of a deep ditch which was dug inside the pale, but I have yet to discover a trench, or a remnant of one, along the fields and remaining hedgerows of the Lodge. It is interesting to record that a wood known as Park Wood exists near the Great Saxham boundary, but this appears to consist mainly of 19th-century woodland. It could have replaced, of course, a much older wood, or copse. To the west another small wood is clearly seen from the New Road which helps the observer to reconstruct imaginatively the likely appearance and extent of the deer-stocked Chevington Park, most of which probably continued as parkland, with the hunting lodge to the north, well into the 17th century. Although it is possible to identify the location of the park in the abbot's manor, it is difficult to be decisive about the situation of the enclosed pastures and open fields which Abbot Curteys's '*perambulatio*' revealed.

However, in 1585, Sir Thomas Kytson II of Hengrave Hall, surveyed his manor at Chevington.[34] He was the son of the Sir Thomas Kytson, the merchant, to whom Henry VIII had granted the manor of Chevington at the Dissolution of the Abbey at Bury. Throughout the Middle Ages, although some enclosure of the strips had taken place, the parish remained mainly unenclosed. It is, therefore, reasonable to infer that the survey of 1585 revealed the basic field organisation that had existed in Chevington during the abbatial rule. In spite of the obscurity of the Latin inscription, it is clear that the tenements* and other lands lay between the Church of All Saints and the Great Saxham boundary.

> The first area contains all the tenements and lands lying and being between the Royal Street,[35] leading from Chevington Church to Bury from the South and the lands called Saxham Lane dividing Chevington and Great Saxham, starting from the north at the site of the manor and thus by going east to Bury Way aforesaid.

The manorial lands extended from the Park in the west to a point towards Ickworth on Chevington Way and there was 'one hillside pasture land lying nearby called the Mill Close' which, presumably, was the present Great Days. The survey, translated from Latin, continues:

> Thomas Kitson [*sic*], Knight, lord of the aforesaid manor, possesses the site of the demesne manor called Chevington Hall with its gardens and one dovehouse enclosed within the moat . . . The same man holds in that place a certain park with a beautiful house built at the top called a Lodge with other necessary buildings lying nearby, i.e. granaries and stables.
> Remember that inside the said park are 2 copses of woodland and underwood . . . one is called the Steppe . . . and contains 29½ acres, the other is called the Hay and lies next to the manor of Hargrave in the west, part of the said park, and it contains 24 acres and 1½ rods.

Thus it is possible to construct a likely organisation of the manor which existed certainly until the 16th century. The manorial life was centred around the Church of All Saints and its neighbour, Chevington Hall. The park was a little to the west and north, but the fields, pasture, commons and mill were concentrated to form what was the economic and social hub of the manor. The arable land was divided into three great fields lying towards Great Saxham and the holdings of individuals were possibly concentrated under the tenemental* system in areas of the fields. Solomon Milk may have held as much as a virgate, or 30 acres. He was free to graze his cattle on his fields and on the commons, and to share the common meadow, but was compelled to use the lord's mill on the Great Days field.

Throughout the Middle Ages some areas of the country had 'open' fields. They consisted of strips of land cultivated by different tenants, each tenant holding strips in more than one field. The Lord Abbot, as Lord of the Manor of Chevington, would have his own strips which were probably larger than those of his tenants. The common fields were not separated by hedges, but the strips into which they were divided were separated by uncultivated paths, or 'balks'. It is probable that the Lord Abbot possessed an additional area of land some distance from the three fields which could be let as an entity to a prominent tenant such as a Paman. This important part of the arable system would probably lie to the east of the three fields, that is, along

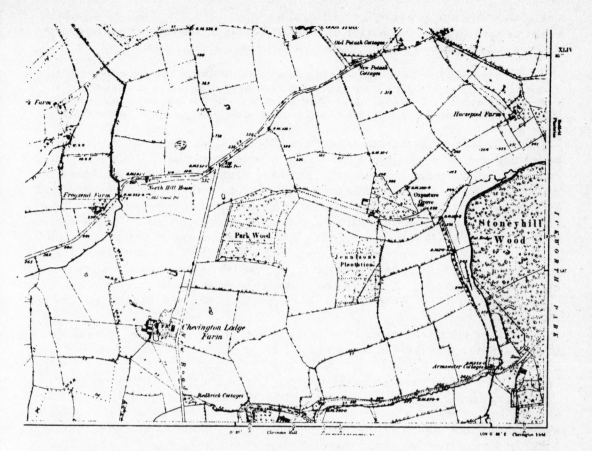

2. Ordnance Survey map, 1902. The medieval fields of Chevington were in the area from Chevington Lodge Farm to Oxpasture Grove, and extended northwards to the Potash Cottages. Chevington Park lay to the west between New Road and the Hargrave boundary.

Chevington Way towards Ickworth. Hurdles would protect the crops from stray cattle. To the south-east there was the pasture, to the west the park and, possibly, beyond that, near Broad Green, the waste. The Survey of 1585 refers to 'tenements',* a system characteristic of the East Anglian field organisation, which could have been operative in Chevington from the 12th century.

The tenants worked strips of land in the great fields. Sometimes the strips would be far apart, and the rotation of crops used on them would be that agreed for the entire field. However, as indicated by Professor Hallam,[36] a group of tenants in west Suffolk could have their strips concentrated in one area of the field where they could choose their own two-, or three-year, rotation independent of that followed elsewhere. As there were wide variations in the open field system, it is impossible to state with certainty the organisation followed in a particular village although, according to the historian J. S. Titow,[36] the East Anglian system was of the tenemental type which led to more independence in the choice of rotation of crops, traditionally wheat, barley or rye, then fallow. It is reasonable to suggest, therefore, in the absence of specified evidence, that the system of cultivation in Chevington followed those general principles.

Professor Postan[37] writes of the relative affluence and efficiency of the ecclesiastical landlords such as the Benedictines of Bury St Edmunds. Chevington was one of the Abbey's manors and was probably typical of the monastic organisation:

> ... the Benedictine monks enjoyed what by medieval standards were high and rising levels of sustenance. ... Hence their tendency to maintain functioning demesnes on as many estates as were necessary ... By the middle of the fifteenth century, very few demesnes — mostly home-farms of Benedictine abbeys — still functioned under the direct management of their lords ...

Hallam states that on eight manors of the Abbey in 1250, wheat was the chief crop, barley and rye were less prominent and peas were unpopular. Suffolk was mainly arable and barley became the chief grain, providing a ready supply of ale and bread, the main necessities in the diet of Solomon Milk. In the 14th century beans and peas became more acceptable and 'the nitrogen-fixating properties increased the fertility of the soil'. The Abbey at Bury started sheep farming on a large scale in 1303–4 and, in 1429, when Abbot Curteys surveyed his lands at Chevington, it was held that 300 young sheep could graze on the three open fields 'from the Feast of the Holy Trinity to the Feast of All Saints'. In all probability, the number of sheep in Chevington would exceed 300. Although Hallam is of the opinion that wool production in Suffolk was at its highest level in 1307–8, there is no available evidence of such activity in Chevington.

The villeins lived in cottages, some of which were no doubt hovels, possibly along Chevington Way between the Church of All Saints and Farrow's. The free tenants — *liberi tenentes* — had houses. Both would have their small enclosed gardens and the occupants worked for the lord on certain days. The customary conditions under which they served had been fixed by the manorial court since time immemorial and it was those understandings that lay at the core of the organised rural structure. In order to maintain vigilance and to ensure that the abbot's instructions were carried out, the bailiff would live close by, perhaps near the present Malting Farm.

The *Valor Ecclesiasticus*[38] listed all the rents paid by the tenants of the manors owned by the Lord Abbot of Bury. The total income of the Lord Abbot from manorial buildings and lands was £549 7s. 8¼d. (£549.38p.) to which Chevington contributed £37 0s. 3d. (£37.01p.). In addition, there were sources of income free from any 'secular restriction'. From the total of £16 11s. 11d. (£16.60p. approx.), 4s. 0d. (20p.) was derived from the manor of Chevington, and a further 16s. 0d. (80p.) was Chevington's contribution to the Infirmary of the Monastery. Thomas Manning,[39] the abbot's bailiff at Chevington, collected 40s. 0d. (£2) in unspecified fees from the people of the manor.

The Church of All Saints in the Middle Ages

The Rectors of Chevington were appointed by the Abbot of St Edmundsbury who received dues. When William of Diss[40] petitioned Abbot Samson (1182–1215) for the Vicarage of Chevington the Lord Abbot answered:

> Your father was master of the schools and, when I was a poor clerk, he allowed me to enter the school without terms and of his grace, and to have the opportunity of leaning. And I, for the Sole of God, grant you that which you ask.

As early as 1291, at the time of the taxation of Pope Nicholas IV, the value of the benefice of Chevington was £16 13s. 4d. (£16.66p.) from which the Pope granted one-tenth to the King, Edward I. In c. 1330[41] Robert de Seburgh, Rector of Chevington son of Adam, held the church in the gift of the Abbot of St Edmund's. There were 20 acres of land with appurtenances from which the church was endowed in various ways. According to the *Valor Ecclesiasticus*, when John Talbot was Rector of Chevington in 1535, the value of the living based on tithes and glebeland was still £16 13s. 4d. (£16.66 approx.) from which small payments were paid to the Archdeacon of Sudbury and the Bishop of Norwich when they visited the Church of All Saints.

In about the year 1300, in the reign of Edward I, the powerful sacrist* of the Abbey of St Edmund, William of Hoo,[42] appointed Alan of Freston Rector of Chevington. Specified church income was to be paid to the Abbey with the exception of certain tithes. There was a further obligation: he was held responsible for preserving the books, vestments and ornaments given by a Richard of Freston and held, presumably, at Chevington.

Throughout the Middle Ages, the Church of All Saints fulfilled a number of diverse functions. In addition to worship, it served as a store, a place of refuge and, probably, at times, a prison. It was the scene of revelry at important fund-raising feasts. Gage[43] asserts that there were a number of ales, or feasts, in the parish: plough-ale at the time of ploughing, bride-ale at weddings, lamb-ale at lamb shearing, and leet-ale at the time of the Lord Abbot's court. Two customary tenants, William Redenhale and Philip de Kedynton, were obliged to plough on the lord's demesne at the time of the plough-ale when the Solomon Milks could have been cavorting in the nave.

At other times, serious and more urgent, the Church of All Saints probably served as the courthouse. As the abbot's representative, the steward would normally preside over the Manorial Court held in the nave of the church, or in Chevington Hall, and keep all records. The allocation and administration of the land were clearly the right of the Abbot as Lord of the Manor. At the Court Baron, after the homage* was sworn (see below), the customs of the manor of Chevington would be defined, the allocation and surrender of lands decreed and the rights of lord and tenant authoritatively enforced. Two typical *cartularies** record that Abbot Hugo (1157–1182) granted various lands in Chevington to William Leo and that, in 1353, Abbot William (1335–1361) leased Richard le Parker, his wife, Christiana, and their heirs a house, without outbuildings and yard in Chevington for a specific rent.

The Court Baron was presided over either by the Lord Abbot himself as Lord of the Manor, or by his steward. If fines were imposed, they were collected by a reeve appointed by the Court and particulars were recorded in the Court Rolls. A study of the Chevington Court Rolls shows that the main work of the Court Baron involved matters concerning the rights of the lord and his tenants, the customary use of the wastes and common land and the allocation and surrender of tenants' holdings. Less serious offences, such as neglecting the clearing out of ditches, misdemeanours concerning brewing ale, making bread without permission and allowing cattle to stray on the lord's lands, were matters for the Court Leet, a less important court than the Court Baron.

Both courts had a Jury, or Homage, which consisted normally of three, or four, free tenants, although at a Court Leet held on 28 October 1517, there were no less than 11 members of the jury, four of whom were Pamans and two members of another prominent Chevington family, the Goodays.[44] Courts do not appear to have been held more frequently than twice a year.

In February 1414, Abbot William Cratfield's Court met in Chevington when some tenants were fined for damaging the lord's fields:[45]

Fine 40d.   John Mellere of Saxham made trespass in the Lord's fields with his cattle.

Fine 9d.   Three women, including Alice Wykham and Margaret, brewed beer and sold it contrary to the Assize.

Fine 4d.   William Osteler and Robert Cros were fined 2d. each for not performing their duty as 'aletastors'; (a William Osteler was serving on the Jury).

In 1420, in the reign of Henry V, during the abbacy of William Excetre,[46] John Mylk (probably a kinsman of Solomon) served on the jury as he had in 1416.[47]

Fine 40d.   Agnes de Ickworth illegally made a roadway over the Lord's lands . . . with her carts.

Fine 2d.   John Osteler senior damaged Page's tenements and John Bakere did the same to Dye's tenement and it is ordered that they must repair them before the next court on pain of 40d.

At the same court, the Lord Abbot granted Thomas Prow 15 acres . . . to hold for 20 years, rendering (i.e. giving as fixed rent) 16s. 0d. a year with usual services, including harvest services. Richard Deldere was granted a piece of meadow called Honeyshill for six years, rent 7s. 0d. per year and the usual manorial services.

The Paman Family

After the Dissolution of the Monasteries, the Manorial Court of Chevington met before Sir Thomas Kytson and his wife, Margaret. At a court in 1540 four members of a jury of 14 were Pamans.[48] It was brought to the lord's notice that John Harvie Esq. had overturned two boundary stones . . . on the customary land of the manor at Chevington in the tenure of Thomas Fletcher. John Harvie Esq., presumably of Ickworth, was ordered to speak to the lord.

Previously of Thurleigh in Bedfordshire, the Herveys had inherited Ickworth in 1467 through the great Suffolk landowners, the Drurys. The parish of Ickworth lay to the north-east of Chevington and the village there was centred between the church and the present rotunda. At the time of Sir Thomas Kytson's castigation of John, the Herveys, as Lords of the Manor of Ickworth, lived as country squires in a house, now demolished, near Ickworth church. They were an ancient family and some members had received knighthoods. However, it was not until the early 18th century that they added to their fortunes, became powerful landowners in Suffolk and Lincolnshire and were elevated to the peerage.

In the 16th century the Pamans of Chevington were substantial yeomen* and copyholders.* In 1539 a Henry Paman bequeathed his copyland called 'Brokkys' to his wife, Joan, who also received all his 'goods, chattels, grains, implements, utensils, jewels and household stuff'. He left 20s. 0d. to the mending of Chevington Way, 'where most needs is' and 5s. 0d. to the 'poor people of the said town on my burial day'.[49] In 1558 yet another Henry Paman left his wife, Mary, his 'free tenements' of Cookes, Overgreene and Somertons as long as she remained a widow.[50]

1. Chevington Hall, built on an ancient site protected by a fosse (moat) and a rampart, both obscured here by trees. The two ponds (one temporarily filled in) in the foreground were dug later, possibly in the early years of monastic rule.

2. Chevington Hall, 1907. The building has a late 17th-century appearance, but it contains parts of an earlier structure.

3. (*left*) Sir Thomas Kytson I, mercer, owner of Chevington after the dissolution of the monasteries, 1539. The builder of Hengrave Hall, 1525-38.

4. (*above*) John, 1st Earl of Bristol, by Van Loo. He purchased the manors of Hargrave and Chevington from Sir William Gage of Hengrave in 1716. He died in 1751.

5. (*below*) The Earl Bishop in Rome by Hugh Douglas Hamilton. He commenced the building of the rotunda at Ickworth in 1795, and was lord of the manor of Chevington for 24 years. His monument is in the parish of Chevington.

6. Lady Elizabeth Kytson, 1573, wife of Sir Thomas Kytson II. The daughter of Sir Thomas Cornwallis, of Brome, Suffolk, she became owner and benefactress of Chevington on the death of her husband in 1602. Oil on wood, by George Gower c.1540-96.

7. The south side of the rotunda at Ickworth, completed by the 1st Marquess of Bristol, the Earl Bishop's son, 1821-9. It was intended as the residential area, but later contained the state rooms for entertainment and the various collections.

8. Moat Farmhouse, 15th-century.

9. The remaining house of Dr. John Battely's estate in Depden Lane. The house, of 16th-century origin, was acquired by Dr. Battely in the late 17th-century. He died in 1708 and is buried in Canterbury Cathedral.

10. (*above*) The original clothing factory, 1852, at Stonehouse (formerly Factory) Farm. Later the building was used as a granary and it is now a general store.

11. (*right*) William Henry Smith I, owner of the second Chevington clothing factory, 1874-84. The factory was built in 1862.

12. (*below*) Some workers in the second clothing factory, Hargrave Road, *c*.1908.

13. Chevington Rectory *c*.1900. The lady with the parasol is probably Mrs. John White, the wife of the Reverend John White III. Croquet, to which parishioners were sometimes invited, was played on the lawn.

14. Flint and stone cottages at Brooks's Corner, built *c*.1840. Simon Last with members of the Wallace family, 1911. There were formerly similar vernacular buildings in the village.

15. The church of All Saints from the south, 1983.

16. The chapel, built in 1799, at Tan Office Green c.1930.

18.   Jonathan Cooper. Born in Depden. Lived in Chevington, *c*.1854-1904. First Clerk of the Parish Council, parish clerk and builder.

17.   James Plumb, d.1903. A survivor of the Indian Mutiny, 1857. He received a medal and a special pension from the commissioners of the Chelsea Hospital. His great-grandson, Leslie Turner, was living in Chevington in 1983.

19.   James Nunn and his 'carriage', 1913. He and his father, Edward ('Nimbly'), had a carrier's cart in which they conveyed passengers from Chevington to Bury St Edmunds on market days. They put up at the *Rising Sun*. The carriage, however, was reserved for special bookings, such as meeting trains at Saxham.

21. The Reverend Arthur Keble White, M.A., Rector 1908-26. The last of the Whites. (Photograph by Howard Dove from the original in the church of All Saints.)

23. William Henry Cooper, 1880-1947. Builder. Clerk of the Parish Council for over thirty years.

20. Joseph Bradfield. Farmer of Chevington Hall Farm, 1902-20. A Primitive Methodist local preacher and a Parish Councillor.

22. Peter Bowers, blacksmith from 1900-28.

24. (*left*) Sam Pettit, *c.*1928, farmer of Broad Green and College Farms, an eminent Forester and Parish Councillor.

25. (*above*) Alfred C. (Alf) Rolfe, contractor, motor engineer, proprietor of the village garage, *c.*1919-77, and Parish Councillor.

26. Harold Avis, builder, 1967- . He followed his father, W. F. (Billy) Avis, builder, 1947-67.

27. Pupils of Chevington School, 1906, with Fred King, headmaster, and two teachers.

28. The village officials of the Chevington Flower Show, 1907.

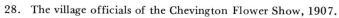

29. (*above*) The marriage of Louise Plumb (daughter of James) with Charlie Turner, horsekeeper, *c*.1900.

30. (*left*) Sam Pettit, farmer, his wife, Alice, and their children, Irene, Herbert and Oliver, 1908.

31. Chevington concert party, 1923. 'Rene' Pettit (*seated right*) b.1897 still lives in the village.

32. The village football team, 1923-4.

33.   The Roosters Dance Band, *c*.1932.

34.   The Chevington Women's Institute with their prize winning banner, 1938.

5. (*above left*) Dick Clarry and 'Hub' Pettit drilling, 1922.

6. (*above right*) Dorothy and ack Stuteley at the bar of the *reyhound* before their retirement, 1979.

7. (*right*) Joe Spurling, wheelright, outside the former blacknith's shop, which he adapted s his workshop, *c.*1977.

38. Harvesting at College Farm, *c*.1930.

39. Farm workers and friends resting in the fields during the Second World War.

40. Harvesting, late 1940s.

The whereabouts of Paman's tenements are unknown but, perhaps, Overgreene, where he lived, was the present Broad Green, or the green afterwards known as Tan Office Green, which extended from the present house to the land lying between the Post Office and Michael McCormack's Stonehouse Farm. In his will Paman decreed that his wife should keep the lands free from 'strip and waste' and, on reaching the age of 20, her son, Clement, was to inherit them. Until that time the young Clement was to remain at school, but he acquired some land before he was 20. Saving the lord's right, the copyland 'Lanes', 'Farrowes', a name which lingers today, and 'Lylyes' were left to the young Clement. It was customary to name fields after previous holders and it is of interest to recall that a John 'Lelye' was living in Chevington in 1420,[51] and a Robert Somerton in 1445.[52] Henry Paman was of some affluence for he bequeathed 12d. to each of his godchildren and 20s. 0d. to each of his servants. He gave money for the re-leading of the roof of the Church of All Saints. He left his son, Clement, sufficient money to provide his daughter, Anne, with £10 a year for life. In conclusion, Henry Paman, yeoman, ordained:

> Residue of goods not bequeathed, moveables and unmoveables, utensils and stuff of household whatever to wife, Mary, she to receive my debts and pay my debts and to bring my body honestly to the earth . . . my body to be buried in [the] churchyard of Chevington.[53]

In the registers of the Church of All Saints there is evidence of close association between the Herveys of Ickworth and the Pamans of Chevington. A baptism took place on 3 March 1590:

> Ambrose Paman, the sonne of Kateryn Paman, the sonne of Ambrose Harveye, gent., as she sayeth, als' [alias] the sonne of the people.

A second baptism was noted on 4 December 1593 — 'Edmund Harveye, the sonne of John Harveye of Ickworth, Esquire.' The families appear to have been on friendly terms, the one rising in the social scale during the 17th and 18th centuries, culminating in a marquisate in the early 19th, the other fading entirely from the local scene from the early 1800s.

The Gild of St John the Baptist

It is certain that by 1532 the Gild of St John the Baptist[54] existed in Chevington and it is likely that it had been in existence for at least a 100 years. A gild was a religious fraternity with the main objective of maintaining brotherhood and concord between its members but, more mundanely, of keeping the Church of All Saints in efficient repair. Referring to Suffolk, V. B. Redstone comments:[55]

> There is little doubt that all villages and towns had a gild, or fraternity, under patronage of saints whose days of dedication were among those of chief festivals in the Church, e.g. the nativity of St John the Baptist.

The members of the Gild had to pay certain dues in order that the gild could fulfil its objectives of keeping the Church of All Saints in good repair, and of providing candles and lights for the altars and various images.[56] An acknowledged advantage of gild membership was the assurance that, after death, there would be prayers and observances for one's 'departed soul'. The members of the gild, in furtherance of their general purpose of mutual help and brotherhood, gave money and, in some cases, goods to the poor of the parish. Such generosity and goodwill charactised the feasts which the gildsmen held from time to time, supposedly in the neighbouring gildhall.

In a glebe terrier* of the Church of All Saints, dated 1729, the following detail is noted:[57] 'a nouse called the Guildhall [sic] situated on a little green near the church-yard, now made into 4 tenements'. The terrier then lists the four poor inhabitants, two widows and two poor husbandmen, of the gildhall. At present (1984) the house, recently restored, is known as Church Cottage but, on the Enclosure Award Map of Chevington 1815, the site in front of the building is clearly referred to as the Work-house Yard. There is little doubt that the medieval gildhall, subjected to considerable alteration after its dissolution in about 1550, became the townhouse, or workhouse, for the parish, and that it was there that, in the Middle Ages, the gildsmen would meet, conduct their business and organise their banquets. The gildhall was regarded as a meeting place for all townspeople and it is likely that the parish feasts, or 'ales',* were sometimes held there. Most of the present building, a timber-framed construction, apparently dates from the 17th century, but it is conceivable that closer examination would reveal some earlier features: there are certainly many exposed beams and an early double brick, open fireplace exists in the reception area.

In the reign of Richard II there was a proclamation that all returns of gilds should be completed before 2 February 1389. There are many omissions: e.g., there was no return from Clare where there was a gildhall and no return from Chevington.[58] Similarly, no certificate of a gild was returned from Chevington in the reigns of Henry VIII (1509-1547) and Edward VI (1547-1553).[59] The gildhall at Chevington would certainly have been dissolved no later than the Inquisition of 1550.

The church reeve would have acted as a deputy to the rector and it was to him that the gildsmen would pay their dues. He had the combined function of secretary and treasurer of the Gild of the Nativity of St John the Baptist at Chevington. In the book of accounts kept by the reeve for 1511-1534, previously among the Kytson family papers at Hengrave and now in the Cambridge University Library,[60] are lists of payments made by the members of the gild:

> William Paman the younger held the Gild A.D. 1521 and gave for increment, 3s. 4d. Edward Neche A.D. 1524 gave 6s. 8d.

> In the yer of our Lord MDxxxij William Paymo dyde hold the Gylde and gayff for increment ijs. viijd.

The essential provision of lights and candles for the church made payments necessary and bequests were often made clear in wills. Candles and beeswax were expensive items. Cows were bequeathed in order to provide a source of revenue for the provision of lights before the many church images, or for the constant repair of the Church of All Saints which occupied a central place in the lives of the Pamans, Goodays and Solomon Milks.

> Henry Yorke has a cow given by John Paman and pays an annual rent of 12d. to the common light of the sepulchre.

> Reginald Paman has a cow for keeping up of 2 lights burning before St Mary.[61]

The gild had its own possessions, certainly some cattle and probably its own flock of sheep which could have grazed on the pasture of Great Days, a little farther down

Chevington Way from the gildhall. It is likely that the gild had its own banners and torches for ceremonial occasions in the Church of All Saints and plates, cups and various cooking utensils for the banquets. To provide ale for the feasts, it is likely that there was a special nearby brewhouse; if not, a particular outhouse at the gildhall may have been used for the purpose. In 1523, the church reeve[62] listed the value of the 'goods' of the Gild of St John the Baptist at Chevington and the names of the brethren and sisters of the gild to whom that particular item of value was entrusted. The following examples occur:

In the hands of John Hartee 5s. 0d.
In the hands of Robert Cryspe 3s. 4d. (surety Robert Wythyng)
In the hands of William Turner 5s. 0d.

'Pots',[63] probably brass, were given to the church and sold as a source of revenue. It is likely, of course, that the reeve himself was responsible for the reception and disposal of such gifts. In his account the following items were recorded:

Item: Henry Paman resayryt [received] of William Paman for hys chyrch pott, xvij d.
Item: Robert Gudday [Gooday] delyvert [delivered] for his chyrch pott, xix d.

In 1543 the reeve listed 71 members of the gild — *Nomina frati et sororum gilde sancte Jonis Baptistæ* — including 17 Pamans, five Goodays and five Sparrows. Twenty-seven members were women and of those eight were Paman wives, or widows. Travellers to and from St Edmundsbury passed down Chevington Way just in front of the gildhall and, when the Lord Abbot and his retinue visited the hall, no doubt they worshipped in the Church of All Saints. To the south-east was the wide expanse of Great Days pasture, with the lord's windmill overlooking the immediate country and the parish of Chedburgh a mile or two over the fields. In spite of the enclosures at the beginning of the 19th century, the scene has remained essentially unchanged for 400 years.

The 'College' of Chevington

In the church registers there is an entry[64] for 1595: 'buried Mary Paman, widow (late wife of Henry Paman of the College, deceased)'. The administration of Mary Paman's estate was granted to her daughter, Margaret Spenser, of Chevington, who was the wife of Richard Spenser. It has been impossible to trace the wills of Mary Paman and her husband Henry of the College. The College Farm and College Green still exist in Chevington, the earliest known reference being on a 1725 map of the farm and of the surrounding fields, highways, and houses.[65] In a recently revised list[66] the Department of the Environment classifies College Farm, of the 16th or early 17th century, as a Grade II building. It is a timber-framed, rendered house with axial and gabled chimneys of red brick and consisting of two storeys and attics. The map indicates a large orchard, surrounding ponds, and two extensive crofts, Great and Little Cherry Crofts. Ol Pettit, who worked on College Farm for about 50 years, recalls being informed many years ago that there were formerly some buildings to the east of the farm in an area known as Sheepyard Meadow. Although one large pond has been filled in, the siting of the remaining ponds suggests that they are residual of a complete moat which could have enclosed a complex of buildings. The site was certainly prestigious, overlooking open country, with College Green and the more extensive Broad Green to the west.

Approaches to the University of Cambridge have not resulted in establishing any possible link between the 'College' and the University. Moreover, there is not the slightest evidence for suggesting that a 'College' existed elsewhere in the parish, or that the present buildings were ancillary to it. Manners Hervey,[67] in writing of College House in Horringer, previously known as College Farm, states in *Annals of a Suffolk Village*:

> as to the name of the house I have not been able to ascertain more about it than the College referred to (i.e. in Horringer) was a College of secular priests. Though rebuilt, the house was therefore of considerable antiquity.

There is some circumstantial evidence, therefore, for concluding that the present College Farm in Chevington is on the site of a college of secular priests, and, moreover, that the farmhouse could be a fragment of the medieval collegiate building. Further research is clearly necessary before that hypothesis is established as fact.

Secular priests lived and worked in the world as distinct from the so-called regular clergy who were bound by the vows of their religious order and were members of a distinct religious community. The Suffolk colleges include one founded in Mettingham in 1350 for eight secular priests and one in Stoke by Clare in 1415, now an independent school. The college at Wingfield was founded by Sir John Wingfield in 1362 for one provost, or master, three other priests, later increased to nine, and three choristers. The last visitation of the college before its dissolution was in 1532, but the college's original timbers are still embedded behind the façade of 1700.[68] The College Farmhouse at Chevington may still have secrets to disclose.

Other medieval buildings

There are, of course, older domestic buildings in the parish than what is at present apparent at College Farmhouse. Moat Farmhouse at Brooks's Corner, the only Grade II* domestic building in the village, is early 15th century with later alterations and extensions. It is an example of a three-cell open hall house with a late 16th-century first floor and attics. There is evidence in the hall of soot blackening, deposits which have probably been there for well over five hundred years. It is likely that the rear wing of the house, formerly moated, was added at the same time as the first floor of the hall. According to Eric Mercer in *English Vernacular Houses*, when the wings were added, the house was turned into cottages.

A somewhat later house, but still in the 15th century, is at Ruffin's, a name which has lingered since Henry Ruffyn helped to survey the Chevington manor for Abbot Cratfield prior to 1415. The house is an open hall house of the Wealden type with later extensions as late as the 17th century to the east. The date 1656 appears in plaster on the gable of the later buildings. Alec Clifton-Taylor writes:[69]

> Of the 'standard' types of timber-framed house, the Wealden is easily the finest; most of them were built by well-to-do yeoman-farmers.

Chevington Hall is timber-framed of the mid-16th century. As Sir Thomas Kytson I died in 1540, it is highly probable that his widow, the then Countess of Bath, modified the Abbot's Hall, but retained the general plan of the original house. On her death in 1562, when her 21-year-old son became the owner of Chevington, the executors issued an inventory of her possessions in the hall and the names of the rooms in which various items of furniture and other effects were to be found. Some components of the present house, with its early 18th-century hipped, steep roof and mullioned windows, could belong to the original pre-Dissolution house.[70]

In 1875 when the 3rd Marquess of Bristol consented to the building of the present Lodge, it is known that a neighbouring site was chosen, but that none of the material was taken from the medieval hunting lodge, a few yards to the west. The original lodge, now converted into two cottages, is timber-framed of the mid-16th century. There are two main storeys and attics and, previously, there were large cellars. An impressive remnant of the moat remains. There appears to be sufficient evidence, both historical and architectural, to draw the conclusion that the building is part of the original hunting lodge of the Lord Abbots and their successors, the Kytsons and Gages of Hengrave. It is reasonable to suggest that, during the time of the deparking of the land surrounding the Lodge and the subsequent enclosures, the house became a farmhouse, certainly after 1716 when the 1st Earl of Bristol purchased the manor of Chevington. Farm buildings were built near the house. Perhaps one of the earliest was the timber-framed barn of four bays which was built in about 1650 when Sir Edward Gage was Lord of the Manor and an occasional resident at Chevington Hall.

There are other timber-framed houses of 16th-century origin at David Clarkson's Garrod's (named, perhaps, after an earlier occupant); Broad Green, although much altered in the 19th century; Batley's, with a 17th-century axial, red-brick chimney; Horsepool Farmhouse, a house in three stages, the earliest portion being at the centre; Tan Office Farmhouse, with a cross-passage entry and jettied upper floor which was rebuilt in the 16th century in two bays; and, finally, the rear range of the Old Rectory, the earliest part of the partially moated house which could be early 16th century.

The Dissolution of the Monasteries and its effect on Chevington

King Henry VIII's quarrel with the Pope because of his refusal to grant him a divorce from Catherine of Aragon and his desperate need for money precipitated the religious, social and economic upheaval of the mid-16th century. The King declared himself Supreme Head of the Church and, after a cursory inspection of the monasteries by Thomas Cromwell, his Vicar-General, he proceeded to their Dissolution. The effect of such revolutionary change resulted in the severance of virtually all west Suffolk, including Chevington, from the power of the Benedictine Monastery of Bury St Edmunds to which it had been subjected for almost five hundred years. The possession of land had meant power over all the people who lived on it: the freeholders, copyholders, yeomen and Solomon Milks.

Relics and images were removed from the abbeys and churches. It is probable that the rood screen* and its statues in the Church of All Saints were destroyed about that time. At the decree of the King, the English Bible was placed in every parish church and priests had to teach their congregations the Lord's Prayer, the Commandments and the Articles of Faith. Perhaps Solomon Milk noticed some differences, but daily life in Chevington continued more or less as before. He would well have heard the Act of Supremacy declared in the Church of All Saints, but he was still expected to attend Mass on Sundays and on Holy Days. He was allowed to read the Bible and, perhaps, think his own thoughts about religion.

In his report on the misrule of the Abbey, John Ap Rice reported:

> As for the abbot, we finde nothing to suspect as touching hys livyng, but it was detected that he lays moche forth in hys Granges; that he delited moche in playing at Dice and Cardes, and therein spent moche money, and in buyldinge for his pleasure. . . . Also that he converted divers fermes into copieholders, whereof poore men doth complayne.[71]

In 1538 Sir John Williams and three other officers visited Bury:

> . . . we have been at Saynt Edmund's Bury, where we founde a riche shryne which was very cumberous to deface. Wee have takyn in the seyd Monastry in gold and silv. 1m. 1m. 1m. 1m. 1m. marks [i.e. 5,000 marks which is about £3,500 (1984)] and above; our and besyde, as well as a rich crosse, with emerald, as also dyvers and sundry stones of great value. And yet wee have lefte the churche, Abbot, and Convent very well furneshed, wythe plate and silvr. necessary for the same.[72]

The annual income of the monasteries of the time was £140,000 and they owned one-eighth of the cultivated area of England. Founded in 1020, the Benedictines of Bury St Edmunds — the Black Monks — received just before the Dissolution a net income of £1,656.[73] For some time the last Abbot, John Reeve, resisted the investigators who accused the Abbey of malpractices and injustices but, in 1539, he finally yielded to the King's power. Together with the prior and 42 monks he signed the official surrender. By order of the King the Abbey and the immediate grounds were sold for a little under £413. Although Abbot John Reeve received a handsome pension, the monks fared far worse, and the Abbey's servants and labourers were ejected from their work as were thousands of their fellows throughout the land. Asa Briggs writes in *A Social History of England*[74] that 'the freed lands passed for the most part not into the hands or pockets of new men and speculators, but into the hands of existing local landowners, the peerage and the gentry'.

It would appear that Henry VIII presented the manor of Great Saxham to Sir Richard Long and Margaret, his wife. Sir Richard was a Gentleman of the Privy Chamber, Master of the Buck Hounds and Hawks and Captain of the Islands of Guernsey and Jersey.[75] Another neighbouring parish, Whepstead, was sold to Sir William Drury of Hawstead[76] for £819 11s. 0d. (£819.55p.); Horringer was sold originally to Sir Thomas Darcy who received a grant from the Crown[77] but, shortly afterwards, it passed into the hands of the Jermyns of Rushbrooke. In 1540, Sir Thomas Kytson of Hengrave Hall was granted the manor of Hargrave.[78] At the same time, he became the Lord of the Manor and landowner of Chevington.[79] Trevelyan reminds us that 'besides the gentry another class that benefited by the Dissolution of the Monasteries were the citizens of towns like St Albans and Bury St Edmunds, now released from the stranglehold of monastic lordship, against which they had been in fierce rebellion for centuries past'.[80] The Lord Abbot and the Black Monks of St Edmundsbury would not be seen again down Chevington Way. The townsmen of Bury and the Solomon Milks of Chevington had other masters.

Ox-eye Daisy: Chrysanthemum leucanthemum.

CHAPTER TWO

POLITICS, PARISH AND PEOPLE

> *The Moving Finger writes, and, having writ,*
> *Moves on: nor all your Piety nor Wit*
> *Shall lure it back to cancel half a line,*
> *Nor all your Tears wash out a Word of it.*
>
> Edward Fitzgerald, Suffolk poet, 1809–1883.

The Kytson Family

ON THE DISSOLUTION of the monastery of St Edmundsbury in 1539 King Henry VIII granted the manor of Chevington to Sir Thomas Kytson of Hengrave[1] who had already purchased estates in Devonshire and Northamptonshire. The son of Robert Kytson of Warton, in Lancashire, Thomas was a rich clothing merchant who had acquired his fortune by his European contacts, mainly in Antwerp. As early as 1521, he had purchased the Hengrave estate from Edward, Duke of Buckingham who, in the following year, was accused by Henry VIII of high treason and beheaded.

Kytson, 'citizen and mercer of London', in addition to the manor of Chevington, acquired the manors of Westley, Risby, Hargrave and the three Fordhams: St Genevieve, St Martin and All Saints, together with the advowsons* of those parishes. However, he did not live long to relish his nucleated acquisitions, for he died in 1540 at the age of 55 when his wife, Margaret, was expecting their sixth child, another Thomas. From 1540, until he attained the age of 21 years, the young Thomas was in the wardship of the Lord Chancellor of England and afterwards in that of his mother. She herself had inherited magnificent Hengrave Hall, built by her late husband in the years 1525–38. Later she married Sir Richard Long of Great Saxham and, on his death, was married for the third time to John Bouchier, Earl of Bath. She died at Hengrave in 1561.

In her will[2] dated 10 days before she died, Lady Kytson, then Countess of Bath, bequeathed to her son, the young Thomas:

> his father's best chain of gold and his best turquoise ring of gold, and fifteen pieces of hanging tapestry work and all the household stuffe whatsoever and all the harnesses and ammunition of wars remaining and being at her houses of Hengrave, Chevington[3] and Newington, plate and jewels except one cyprus chest, with all the linen clothes therein contained . . . to her son, Thomas Kytson, she gave the deer, horses, cattle and stock on the manors of Chevington and Hengrave.[4]

The schedule of possessions which Thomas II inherited on reaching his majority in 1561, is described as:

THE KYTSONS, GAGES AND HERVEYS

The Lords of the Manor and principal landowners of Chevington are in italics

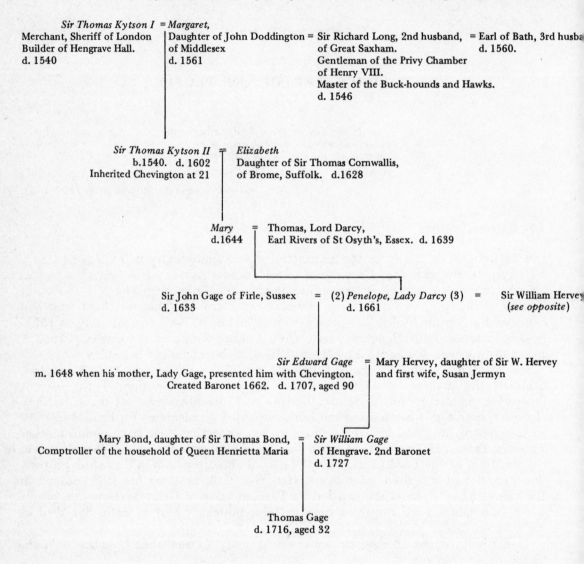

Sir Thomas Kytson I = *Margaret,*
Merchant, Sheriff of London | Daughter of John Doddington = Sir Richard Long, 2nd husband, = Earl of Bath, 3rd husba
Builder of Hengrave Hall. | of Middlesex | of Great Saxham. | d. 1560.
d. 1540 | d. 1561 | Gentleman of the Privy Chamber
 | | of Henry VIII.
 | | Master of the Buck-hounds and Hawks.
 | | d. 1546

Sir Thomas Kytson II ╤ *Elizabeth*
b.1540. d. 1602 | Daughter of Sir Thomas Cornwallis,
Inherited Chevington at 21 | of Brome, Suffolk. d.1628

Mary = Thomas, Lord Darcy,
d.1644 | Earl Rivers of St Osyth's, Essex. d. 1639

Sir John Gage of Firle, Sussex = (2) *Penelope, Lady Darcy* (3) = Sir William Hervey
d. 1633 | d. 1661 | *(see opposite)*

Sir Edward Gage = Mary Hervey, daughter of Sir W. Hervey
m. 1648 when his mother, Lady Gage, presented him with Chevington. | and first wife, Susan Jermyn
Created Baronet 1662. d. 1707, aged 90

Mary Bond, daughter of Sir Thomas Bond, = *Sir William Gage*
Comptroller of the household of Queen Henrietta Maria | of Hengrave. 2nd Baronet
 | d. 1727

Thomas Gage
d. 1716, aged 32

In 1716 he and his father, Sir William Gage, sold Chevington to
John Hervey, 1st Earl of Bristol,
and the advowson to Dr. Edward Grove, Rector of
Chevington. The Marquesses of Bristol have remained principal
landowners but, in 1956, five years after the death of the 4th
Marquess of Bristol, part of the estate (including Ickworth Park)
was handed over to the National Trust. The 4th Marquess was
succeeded by his brother who died in 1960. The 6th Marquess
of Bristol succeeded his father and his heir is his son, Earl
Jermyn.

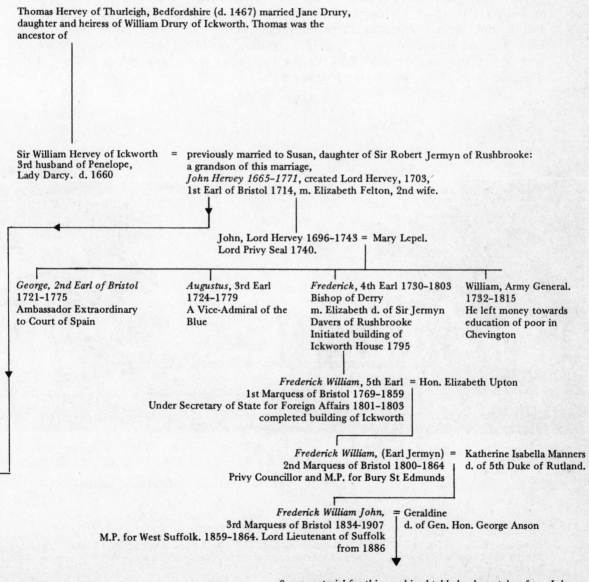

Thomas Hervey of Thurleigh, Bedfordshire (d. 1467) married Jane Drury,
daughter and heiress of William Drury of Ickworth. Thomas was the
ancestor of

Sir William Hervey of Ickworth   = previously married to Susan, daughter of Sir Robert Jermyn of Rushbrooke:
3rd husband of Penelope,   a grandson of this marriage,
Lady Darcy. d. 1660   *John Hervey 1665–1771*, created Lord Hervey, 1703,
                                      1st Earl of Bristol 1714, m. Elizabeth Felton, 2nd wife.

                          John, Lord Hervey 1696–1743 = Mary Lepel.
                          Lord Privy Seal 1740.

George, 2nd Earl of Bristol   *Augustus*, 3rd Earl   *Frederick*, 4th Earl 1730–1803   William, Army General.
1721–1775   1724–1779   Bishop of Derry   1732–1815
Ambassador Extraordinary   A Vice-Admiral of the   m. Elizabeth d. of Sir Jermyn   He left money towards
to Court of Spain   Blue   Davers of Rushbrooke   education of poor in
                                                               Initiated building of   Chevington
                                                               Ickworth House 1795

                                   Frederick William, 5th Earl = Hon. Elizabeth Upton
                                   1st Marquess of Bristol 1769–1859
                              Under Secretary of State for Foreign Affairs 1801–1803
                                      completed building of Ickworth

                                   Frederick William, (Earl Jermyn) = Katherine Isabella Manners
                                   2nd Marquess of Bristol 1800–1864   d. of 5th Duke of Rutland.
                              Privy Councillor and M.P. for Bury St Edmunds

                                   Frederick William John, = Geraldine
                                   3rd Marquess of Bristol 1834-1907   d. of Gen. Hon. George Anson
                     M.P. for West Suffolk. 1859-1864. Lord Lieutenant of Suffolk
                                          from 1886

                          *Some material for this combined table has been taken from John
                          Gage's Thingoe Hundred 1838 and the Hervey Family Tree
                          in Ickworth 1978, by kind permission of the National Trust.*

The value or extent of all the manors, lands and hereditaments* which were late of Thomas Kytson, Knt., deceased, and after his death descended to Thomas Kytson, his son and heir, in possession or reversion, which Sir Thomas died on the eleventh of September 32, Henry VIII, Thomas Kytson the son not being born, Margaret his mother, being then big with child; which Thomas Kytson attained his age of twenty-one years on the ninth day of the present month of October.[5]

From the Hengrave papers, we learn much of the furniture of Chevington Hall at the time that Thomas Kytson II succeeded to his father's estates.[6] In the hall itself, which was the most important architectural feature of the building, there were two long tables, 'the longe formes', a pair of trestles, one livery cupboard, and hangings of 'steyned cloth'. In the New Parlour, there were one old Turkey carpet, cushions of Turkey work, and one long cushion for the window, embroidered with letters of gold and silver. 'My Lady's Chamber' could boast of 'paynted clothes of the story of Judith, one turned bedstead, three pillowes, wherof one is very greate'. The Inner Chamber was another room of apparent significance. There was 'one chiste, covered with lether and bounde with iron, having two locks and a ship chiste, bounde with iron; one other chiste, with two wrought feet'.

A View of the South Front of Hengrave Hall the Seat of Sir Thomas Gage Bart. To whom this Plate is most Respectfully Inscribed by his Obedt. Humble Servt. J. Kendall

Hengrave Hall was built Anno 1538 By a Grant from King Henry 8th & is near St. Edmunds Bury in Suffolk.

Publish'd according to Act of Parliament by J. Kendall at St. Edds. Bury.

4. *Hengrave Hall c. 1770, before it was reduced in size in 1775. The hall was built by Sir Thomas Kytson I, Lord of the Manor of Chevington, in 1538. Originally there was an outer court which was demolished in the 17th century.*

In Mr. Kytson's chamber, surely the room of the young Thomas, the bed was 'of black velvet and grene Bruges satten'. Mr. Longe[7] had his own chamber where 'the bed was of russet velvet'. There was a 'scutcheon of Mr. Longe's armes' in the kitchen and, among the napery (table-linen), there appear the somewhat inappropriate items of 'yeomen's shirts'. In the extract of the inventory there are many items of cloths, curtains, hangings and fustian. It is reasonable to think that many of those items had been collected by Sir Thomas Kytson I, the merchant, during his continental visits and taken either to his great house at Hengrave, completed two years before he died, or brought direct to Chevington as soon as he became its owner in 1539.

Chevington Hall and its park to the west with the hunting-lodge, now in reduced form and divided into two large cottages, were prized possessions of the Kytsons.[8] They provided a welcome retreat from all the demands of running the large estate and house at Hengrave. There was the opportunity of hunting in the park or, perhaps, strolling in Great Days, or down Chevington Way, the track on which they returned to Hengrave through Ickworth, along Westley Bottom and into the villages of Westley and Fornham All Saints.

In the 16th century Suffolk was a land of large estates and it is important to realise the effect of the rural economy on the lives of the Solomon Milks of that time. In the neighbouring village of Little Saxham, Sir Thomas Lucas, Solicitor General to Henry VII, commenced the building of the Hall.[9] He would have been well known to the Kytsons of Hengrave. When Lucas died in 1532, he left £49 'for amending of high waies and specially for the waie called Cheverton Way'.[10] John Eldred, a great traveller to Tripoli and Babylon, bought the manor of Great Saxham in 1597. The Spring family, rich clothiers, owned large estates in Lavenham and Pakenham. In 1578 Anne, the sister of Thomas Kytson II, married Sir William Spring of Pakenham, High Sheriff of Suffolk. There were the Herveys of Ickworth, the Drurys of Hawstead, the Jermyns of Rushbrooke and Great Horringer, and the Blagges of Little Horringer. Further afield lived the very powerful Bacons of Redgrave, the Cordells and the wealthy Cloptons of Long Melford. Such an emerging and landed aristocracy gave a social framework in which the yeoman and Solomon Milks well knew their place. That hierarchical society was destined to last in Suffolk for nearly four hundred years.

In 1578, Queen Elizabeth I made a grand visit to Suffolk, including a stay with Thomas Kytson at Hengrave, who solemnly feasted Her Majesty. Sir William Spring, Kytson's brother-in-law, was an influential figure in the county's celebrations. On her return from Norwich the Queen called at Hengrave 'where the fare and banquet did so exceed a number of places that it is worthy to mention'.[11] Among those honoured with knighthoods after the Royal Progress was, understandably, Thomas Kytson of Hengrave. Undoubtedly, ripples from these royal visits appeared on the quieter waters of Chevington.

For many years a board hung in the Church of All Saints listing the names of nine Chevington men who, in the year of the Spanish Armada 1588, were trained for military service. With other Suffolk bands, composed of men between the ages of 16 and 60, their duty was to defend their country against invasion. Chevington contributed three archers, two 'byllman', two 'shottes', and two 'pykemen' whose armour, probably stored in Chevington Hall, was provided by three Pamans: Edward, Henry and Martin. Among the militiamen were John Gooday (presumably of Seburgh's, on the site of the present Hollybush Stud), and Robert Norman, who were armed with light muskets, or calyvers, and John Petit whose German light armour ('almayn ryvet'), head piece and black bill were also supplied by the Pamans. Prominent Chevington families such as the Goodays, Sparrows and Pamans were required by statute to purchase armour and 'furniture' for the band. Of the 13 suppliers of Chevington's armour, four were Pamans.

In August 1588, Sir John Heigham of Barrow Hall, Sheriff of Suffolk, was in charge of a Suffolk contingent encamped at Tilbury Fort in readiness for the invasion. It is interesting to speculate that among his men were the soldiers of Chevington. In 1595 at a muster, or inspection, by Sir John, armour and light muskets were again supplied by the leading landowners and tenants who were statutorily required to maintain equipment in readiness for an emergency, but the 'bowmen and billmen were not called for neither was it then proposed to call for them any more'.[12]

In his will of 1601, Sir Thomas Kytson II bequeathed £5 to each poor person in Chevington[13] and in each of the other 10 manors which he had acquired after attaining his majority in 1561. To his wife, Elizabeth, daughter of Sir Thomas Cornwallis, of Broome, he left 'the residue of his effects'. In her will of 1627 Elizabeth Lady Kytson left many legacies to her daughter, Mary Lady Rivers, and to her grand-daughter Lady Penelope who, it is important to note, married as her second husband, Sir John Gage, of Firle, Sussex and, as her third, Sir William Hervey of Ickworth. Those early associations with the Gages and the Herveys directly influenced the future of Chevington, as will be shown later.

Elizabeth, Lady Kytson, presented gifts to the people of Chevington. As late as the 1930s a set of new hymn books in the Church of All Saints was worded 'Lady Kytson's gift'. Instructed by my father who was a trustee of the charity, I remember in the 1930s distributing gifts of four shillings (20p.) (discreetly enclosed in envelopes) to the eight oldest born persons in Chevington and an extra eight shillings (40p.) to the very oldest. This Christmas distribution was warmly anticipated by all eligible parishioners. The second benefactor to the village was Dr. Henry Paman, a member of the distinguished family who had lived in Chevington since the 13th century.

Dr. Henry Paman

The name Paman frequently occurs in the church registers of Chevington. The Pamans were originally customary tenants of the manor but, as members of the family were often referred to as 'gent.', or as owning lands, or estates, it may be inferred that the tenancies were converted into estates, virtually independent of the Lord Abbot. A Paman was certainly living at Ruffin's at the end of the 16th century and such impressive houses as the Grove and the Old Rectory were also likely early Paman possessions.[14] Henry Paman, 'son of Robert Paman of Chevington in the County of Suffolk, gentleman',[15] entered Emmanuel College,[16] Cambridge, in 1643 where William Sancroft, subsequently Archbishop of Canterbury, was his tutor. They remained friends for life. Later, Paman transferred to St John's College. He became an M.A. in 1650 and, in 1656, submitted a thesis entitled *Morbis acutis convenit dieta tenuissima* ('The slenderest diet suits acute illnesses')[17] resulting in the award of Doctor of Medicine. In 1662 he was elected to travel abroad:

> to obviate and prevent those forraine dangers which too often ensnare unwary youth both in matter of Morality and Religion.[18]

Further honours followed: Public Orator of Cambridge University in 1674,[19] Professor of Physics at Gresham College, Fellow of the Royal Society in 1679,[20] and Fellow of the Royal College of Physicians, 1687.[21]

In 1677 Paman retired from Cambridge life to live with Archbishop Sancroft, his great Suffolk friend. Later he went to live in the fashionable district of Covent Garden where he died in June 1695. His grave cannot be found in St Paul's church, but his burial is recorded in the Register of Deaths for Westminster. Dr. Paman, a Chevington boy who had travelled many a mile from his boyhood haunts left, among his many legacies, £50 to the people of Chevington: 'having lived frugally, he died rich'.[22] Dr. Paman's name, with Lady Kytson's, is inscribed on the list of parish charities which hung for many years on the south wall of the Church of All Saints. As recently as 1942, an entry in the Chevington Charity Book[23] shows that there were three payments for rent in that year for the Charity Cottages (purchased from the Paman Funds), near the former Stonehouse Farm, now The Oaks. After payment of insurances, land tax and tithe the balance of the Dr. Henry Paman Account was £10 17s. 0d. (£10.85p.). The Chevington charities continue and awards are still made to eligible parishioners.

The village in the 17th century

The Hearth Tax Returns of 1674[24] gave the name of each single householder in Suffolk and the rest of the country and the number of hearths, or stoves, each house contained and on which the tax was based. From the Chevington returns of 119 hearths it is possible to infer some important information concerning the domestic economy of the village in the 17th century. Thirty-eight householders were charged with tax, but 13 were 'certified' as being too poor to pay, i.e. they were unable to pay church rates, or their house was worth less than £1 a year, or they possessed less than £10 worth of goods. One in four of the Chevington householders were impoverished, a proportion typical of the local villages, although the figure was higher in Horringer and, in Little Saxham, there was no evidence of poverty. A Mr. Parker of Chevington possessed 10 hearths which indicated a squire's house; Simon Kemp four, a moderately-sized house; Mr. Underwood, who was Rector, also had four and Thomas Harrison, one of the 13 official poor, one.

At the time of the Hearth Tax, the Lord of the Manors of Chevington and Hengrave, Sir Edward Gage, a staunch Royalist, created a baronet in 1662 by King Charles II, would have been well acquainted with Sir William ('Madcap') Crofts of Little Saxham Hall, a mile or two from Chevington Way. Sir William was the guardian of the King's natural son, 'Captain Crofts', later the ill-fated Duke of Monmouth, who may have visited his guardian at Saxham. The King was certainly there in 1670. 'Madcap' had built a special apartment in which to entertain his Majesty when there was unbridled revelry and drinking. Although there were no official poor in Little Saxham at the time of the Hearth Tax of 1674, a deep chasm existed locally between the deprived, a significant element of rural society, and the social *milieu* of the Hall at Saxham.

The Reverend Augustine Underwood, formerly of Preston in Suffolk, became Rector of the parish of Chevington in 1580. The Ecclesiastical Census[25] held in 1603, the first year of the reign of James I, declared:

Mr. Augustinus Underwoode rector ibidem dicit. Number of communicates there are 120.
No recusants, neither anye that refuseth the Holie Comunion. He hath but the Rectory of
Chevington. Ladye Kydson, wedowe, patron.

Lady Kytson, the widow of Sir Thomas Kytson II of Hengrave, often visited her
manor of Chevington and stayed either at the Lodge in Chevington Park, or at
Chevington Hall itself. Among the Hengrave papers a 1607 inventory[26] gives particulars
of 'remnants of household effects' at Chevington Lodge 'where there was kept a large
stock of deer'. There were particulars of wheat, rye, oatmeal, barley, malt, beer (sent
from Hengrave), haberdines (large cod for salting), fowls and calves 'wened at
Chevington'. At the neighbouring dairy there were quantities of cheese and butter.
The contents of the front parlour, the front hall and 'my lady's chamber' were sold in
the following year to a Lady Wingfield. For some years the benevolent Lady Kytson
had supported her grandchildren whose parents were estranged: to young Thomas
Darcy, her grandson, she gave a 'black cloke lyned with black velvet' and some Holland
lace 'to make him shirtes' and to his sister, Penelope, who inherited Chevington in
1644, she gave money for a 'frenche peticot'.

On Lady Kytson's death in 1628 the manor of Chevington, including the advowson,
became the property of her daughter, Mary, Countess Rivers, who lived at Hengrave,
retaining her Chevington possessions until her death in 1644. The Reverend Augustine
served as Rector during the reigns of Elizabeth I, James I and Charles I. He was the
father of four sons: Augustine, who was born in Preston, and John, Anthony and
Robert, who all first saw the light of day in Chevington. They were scholars of the
King Edward VI Grammar School, Bury St Edmunds, and later, members of Caius
College, Cambridge, where they graduated. All four were ordained in the Church of
England and became rectors of parishes in Suffolk or Norfolk, as did at least three of
Augustine's grandsons. After the 50-year incumbency of Augustine, his son Robert
succeeded as rector of Chevington.

Following a time-worn precedent, Charles I re-introduced Ship Money in 1634 in
order to establish his Treasury on a surer footing. Thirty-seven people of Chevington
paid Ship Money[27] to the King in 1640, two years before the outbreak of the Civil
War, the great contest for religious and political principles. The total levy amounted to
a little more than £21. Robert Underwood, the rector, paid £1 10s. 0d. (£1.50p.).
Four Pamans, including Robert, 'gent.', probably of Ruffin's, three Sparrows and a
Gooday, almost certainly of Seburgh's, were listed in the official return.

Robert was the Rector during the Civil War. Although, as far as is known, Chevington
remained unscathed during those years of strife, it is of importance to note the impact
that the war made on the life of rural West Suffolk. The eastern half of England,
constituting the counties of Essex, Suffolk, Cambridgeshire, Hertfordshire and Norfolk
formed the Eastern Association which strongly supported Parliament in its pursuit of
parliamentary government, independence and toleration. As Everitt writes, 'Few
English shires played a more decisive or distinctive role in the Civil War than Suffolk'.[28]
The Earl of Manchester, Cromwell's powerful lieutenant, supreme in East Anglia as
the organiser of the Eastern Association, was single-minded in his commitment to the
defeat of the King's cause and 'to place orthodox and holy men in every parish'.
Ipswich, not only the largest and most influential town in Suffolk, was one of the most
important centres of the Puritan cause in the entire country. Bury, too, in spite of some
wavering which was effectively suppressed, strongly supported Parliament and the

Puritans, and a committee of the Eastern Association, which controlled the county, met there regularly.

In spite of the strong parliamentary grip in which the locality was held, loyalties were strained occasionally and the Solomon Milks of Suffolk parishes were often mere pawns in a contest between the rival squires and competing landowners. Manners Hervey cites the example of the Blagges of Little Horringer Hall who raised the standard for the King in opposition to the local Lucas family of Horsecroft, near Saxham, who were strong parliamentarians.[29]

As far as is known, Chevington was free from such internecine strife. It is important to state, however, that the daughter of the late Sir Thomas Kytson II of Hengrave Hall, Mary, Countess Rivers, who had inherited the manor of Chevington, was a known royalist. John Gage, a descendant of the Countess, writes:[30]

> Hengrave did not escape the jealousy of the Republican party during the ownership of Mary, Countess Rivers, whose arms were seized under an order of the House of Commons, 1641.

No doubt an insurrection was anticipated from Hengrave, but Chevington remained uneventfully in the background. Long Melford Hall, however, the home of Countess Rivers' daughter, Elizabeth, a Roman Catholic, was violently ransacked by the Parliamentarians in 1642 as indeed was Sir Francis Mannock's home at Stoke-by-Nayland. In the summer of 1648, there were serious risings in Bury, Newmarket, and Stowmarket.[31] In the same year 500 horse and foot assembled at Linton, in Cambridgeshire, from Newmarket, Exning, and Lidgate where Captain Sparrow of Wickhambrook defeated and dispersed the supporters of the King.[32]

During the years 1645–47 statutory changes in church government were enacted, the crucial innovation being the establishment of presbyteries, ecclesiastical courts which had jurisdiction over defined areas. A presbytery consisted of the minister of the Church assisted by elders, deacons and, in some cases, widows. Each parish had its own presbytery, the unit of ecclesiastical control, whose main task was the appointment of the minister. According to V. B. Redstone[33] the ministers of 12 parishes combined to form a type of presbytery, known as the classis,* in order to consider matters of control and government which were common to the constituent parishes. If doctrinal differences occurred each parish accepted the democratic decision of the classis. Such an organisation was supported by all the leading Suffolk families, such as the Bacons, Springs, Barnardistons[34] and, presumably, the Herveys, of nearby Ickworth. Episcopacy had been abolished by Act of Parliament in 1643 and, in the same year, the Solemn League and Covenant, pledged to the reformation of the Church of England and the abolition of episcopacy, became obligatory for all men over the age of 18. If an incumbent of a church living refused to affirm the Covenant, he was certainly evicted from his living as indeed were Richard Hart, Rector of Hargrave, and Robert Goodrick, Rector of Horringer, who 'was turned out with his wife and children'.[35]

The Reverend Robert Underwood, formerly Rector, and then Minister of Chevington, had a happier fate. In 1646, he signed the petition of the Suffolk ministers in favour of Presbyterianism and was appointed Minister of the local classis.[36] It is impossible to discover how long the Reverend Robert maintained his offices but, with the rise of Cromwell, the Independents ousted the influence of Presbyterianism largely as a result of Independence claiming the stronger allegiance of the serving soldiery and, more importantly, of Cromwell's personal religious commitment to it. The main features of Independence were the autonomy of each church congregation and an evangelical emphasis which, from the beginning of the 18th century, inspired many Chevington families to break away from the Church of All Saints in order to worship in their own homes and, ultimately, to build their own 'conventicle', or chapel, on Tan Office Green.

The Act of Uniformity re-established the Church of England and clergymen who refused to conform with the Prayer Book were evicted. Those who refused to agree with the new order were styled 'Nonconformists' regardless of whether they were Baptist, Quaker, Presbyterian or Independent, and they all became separate denominations outside the Church of England. About two thousand Presbyterian ministers in the country, who refused to comply with the enactment, were removed from their livings. As the Reverend Robert remained Rector of Chevington for another 30 years it is evident that, in spite of his previous Presbyterian leadership, he had decided, perhaps prudently, to change his views and to take the oath of loyalty to Church and King. Even had his Presbyterian supporters in the parish wished to build a chapel at that time, they were forbidden to do so by the terms of the Conventicle Act of 1664. The Compton Census[37] of 1676 revealed that there were 150 'conformists', or communicants, in Chevington. There were no papists and only one nonconformist. It is probable, however, that the conformists included parishioners who were, at heart, dissenters, but who qualified as conformists by only occasional church attendance. Dissent was stronger in the towns than in the more conservative rural areas. There were 167 nonconformists in the parishes of Bury St Edmunds, but only 17 in the remaining parishes of the Thingoe Deanery of the Diocese. Twelve of the 19 parishes had no declared nonconformist at the time of the Census. Later in the reign of William and Mary, the Toleration Act of 1689 granted freedom of worship to nonconformists, so any dissenting group surviving in Chevington at that time, wishing to worship according to their faith, was free to do so.

Having served Chevington for 60 years as Rector and Minister, the Reverend Robert Underwood died at Chevington on 24 January 1690 in his 91st year. He had witnessed a long succession of momentous national events: a Civil War, the execution of a King, the reign of Oliver Cromwell, the restoration of Charles II, the deposition of James II and the Revolution Settlement of 1689. He was buried in the Church of All Saints, probably in the chancel: the grave is no longer identifiable. His son, Abraham, already the Rector of Ickworth, now succeeded Robert as Rector of Chevington. He died two years later, a little over forty. Unobtrusive and neglected, with its lettering almost illegible, the Reverend Abraham Underwood's grave is now in the churchyard to the immediate east of the chancel.

The growth of nonconformity

In the early 18th century, dissenters, who were unable to conform to the principles and practice of the Church of England as presented by the Reverend Doctor Edward Grove of the Church of All Saints, met in certain houses for their mode of Christian worship. Those courageous nonconformists were associated with the early worshippers of the Bury St Edmunds Independent Church who themselves had met in private houses in the town as early as 1662. They had encouraged the formation of other worshipping communities, not only in Chevington, but in the villages of Rede and Hargrave.[38] It was Thomas Milway, appointed minister at Bury in 1674, who encouraged many people from Chevington and the surrounding villages to become members of the main Church at Bury.

This zealous work was continued by the Reverend John Beart who became pastor of the Bury Independent cause in 1701:[39]

> He possessed very considerable pulpit abilities and [was known] to have been greatly blessed in his work. A lecture which he preached at Chevington . . . is said in particular to have been attended with happy consequences and to have given Mr. Beart great pleasure. 'My Chevington walks', said he, 'are pleasant walks'.

As the dedicated preacher walked along Wesley Bottom, through the fields and pastures by the bank of the River Linnet down Chevington Way, he would have known something of the transformation of the village of Ickworth. At about that time Lord Hervey was creating his park and planting some of the trees which wayfarers can see today. John Beart died in 1716 at the age of forty-three.

In 1701, Mr. Kirby and Mr. Kemp of Chevington were received into the church and, two years later: 'Simon, the son of brother and sister Kemp, was baptized, some of ye Church being present and some others'. In August of the same year the 'experience' of 'Goody' Bailey of Chevington, who had some time before been 'propounded'* at a church meeting, was read in the church. Mrs. Mayhew of Chevington is recorded on 1 May 1712 as having sat down at the Lord's Table which should have been sooner 'only ye small-pox being in town, she was kept off 'thro fear from coming'.[40] The number of adherents continued to increase so that, a few years later, Chevington became an important centre of nonconformist belief. According to Duncan, during 1702–16 licenses were issued for Independent worship in the villages and, in May 1712, worship in Chevington took place in the home of John Kemp. On 13 May 1713 a parishioner, Henry Last, 'a poor cripple from the womb', was received into the Bury St Edmunds community. In the following year, Susan Coe, servant to Brother Brook, was propounded at Communion.[41] 'Formerly given to vanity and sin', Mary Brook was received into the 'holy Fellowship' in 1733.[42] Throughout those early days of dissent, the Independent minister from the Mother Church in Bury preached at Chevington, and many people from the parish relinquished membership of the Church of All Saints in order to join the developing Independent cause at Bury, the precursor of the present Whiting Street United Reformed Church.

Houses continued to be 'set apart' for worship. On 28 April 1731 'it was certified by Ambrose Harrison of Chevington, yeoman, that the dwelling place of the said Ambrose Harrison "is set apart"'.[43] Similar domestic arrangements continued throughout the century. In the summer of 1788, Thomas Waldegrave, 'clerk, minister of the Gospel', empowered a staymaker, William Prick (Pryke?), to hold services in an apartment in his dwelling house at Chevington.[44] On 21 September 1772, Robert Brook, of Chevington, died: ·

> a member long standing among us, a good old man, strong in faith, went off triumphing in a Covenant . . . God had made him many years before.

The Reverend Thomas Waldegrave of Bury continued his zealous work. In 1799, a barn situated at College Green, Chevington, and belonging to William Last, farmer, was officially certified as the worshipping centre for the local villages. Families such as the Lasts, Kemps, Brooks and Mayhews were prominent in this evangelical fervour throughout the 18th century, names which recur not only in the ensuing century but which, in the case of the Lasts and Kemps, lingered in Chevington until relatively recent times.

1 August 1799 heralded an important event in the history of Chevington. On that day the Reverend Thomas Waldegrave of Bury St Edmunds, 'minister of the Gospel', who had laboured to further the Independent 'cause' in the village, certified that 'a newly erected building, or house, called the Meeting House now vested in Mr. Simon Kemp and other trustees, situate at Tan Office Green in Chevington, be set apart'. Chevington again became the centre of Independent worship for Chedburgh, Rede, Hargrave, Ousden, Lidgate and, because of contention there, Wickhambrook. Nothing more is heard of the barn on College Green. The small village chapel, first Independent, or Congregationalist was, certainly by 1844, leased to the Primitive Methodists and finally bought by the Methodists. It stood at the junction of Factory Farm Lane and Chedburgh Road, opposite the lane to Depden. Its roof was thatched and it was built in stone and flint with some brick dressings, the windows elegantly arched. There was an uneven brick floor, some box pews, a large, deep gallery occupying the entire width of the building and a plain, but prominent, pulpit flanked by tall paraffin lamps which flickered precariously during the winter services. Part of the interior was heated by an old cylindrical coal stove, marked 'Tortoise'. The rest of it was cold and draughty. The chapel was the centre of evangelical worship, an alternative to the Church of All Saints, for 160 years.

Thomas Waldegrave did not make regular entries in the church book but, in 1802, he wrote a letter to his congregation at Chevington:[45]

> And now having finished my pastoral labours among you nothing remains but to say: Now, Lord, lettest then thy servant depart in peace for mine eyes have seen thy Salvation — even so, come, Lord Jesus, come quickly. — O pray, pray for me your aged brother and may you richly increase with the Increase of God. Amen. Amen.

The Reverend Thomas Waldegrave, builder of the nonconformist citadel at Chevington, died on 27 December 1812 in his 81st year. His successor at Bury and Chevington, the Reverend Charles Dewhirst, said in the funeral oration:

> Never, my hearers, did death appear to me less terrible or more desirable than it did in connection with this event. Let me die the death of the righteous and let my last . . . be like his.[45]

The Hervey family (I)

Mary, Lady Rivers, the daughter of Sir Thomas Kytson II and Lady Kytson, who was the heiress of the Kytson estate including Chevington, bequeathed the manor of Chevington in 1643 to her daughter Penelope,[46] who had married Sir William Gage of Firle, Sussex, as her second husband. He died in 1633. In 1648 Lady Penelope gave the manor to her third son, Sir Edward Gage, on the occasion of his marriage[47] to Mary Hervey. Until the early years of the 18th century, Sir Edward wielded great power as the landowner of Chevington. In 1660, on the death of Lady Penelope, the sum of £20 was distributed among the local poor, including those of Chevington, at the discretion of the executors. Sir Edward Gage's eldest son, Sir William, and his eldest grandson, Thomas, sold the manors of Chevington and Hargrave in 1716 to John Hervey, 1st Earl of Bristol, whose home was at Ickworth Lodge and who had already inherited from his first wife large estates in Lincolnshire. The long reign of the Earls — later the Marquesses — of Bristol had begun.

In his diary[48] the Earl gave full details of the purchase of the two manors:

I paid ye principal & interest money to ye purchase of ye mannours of Chevington and Hargrave as followeth, viz

	£	s.	d.
The purchase money being	10942	08	05
Ye interest thereof from			
24 June 1715 to 25 July 1717	1140	13	09
	12083	02	02

	£	s.	d.
By mortgage I made of			
ye premises to ye D. of Marlborough	7000	00	00
By a bill I drew on Messrs Wanley & Cradock	3760	11	10
By a note of Sir Robert Child & Co for	892	10	00
By four hundred guineas paid Guidott			
in specie	430	00	00
Total =	12083	01	10

Although by repute irascible, the Earl was meticulous about the management of his estates, exerting a kindly leadership in his affairs with tenants and accepting responsibility for furthering their interests and welfare. Ault,[49] in alluding to the Earl's protection of tenants, cites cases of his trying to save his Lincolnshire tenants from having soldiers billeted on them in Sleaford and those of Bury St Edmunds from having two troops of dragoons quartered there.

A loyal supporter of the Crown and Member of Parliament for Bury from 1694, John Hervey had been created a Baron at the time of the succession of Queen Anne. On 23 March 1703, he recorded in his diary:[50]

My patent be as date for creating me and my heirs male a Baron of England. My motto, *je n'oublieray jamais*. *(I shall never forget)*.

In 1714, in recognition of his loyalty to the Hanoverian cause, Lord Hervey received an earldom when he adopted the style of the first Earl of Bristol.

Two years after this honour, Lord Bristol recorded an incident in his diary indicative of his benevolence which, in spite of his intention to extend the Ickworth parkland into his recently acquired parish of Chevington, characterised his kindly attitude towards all sorts and conditions of men.

June 7th 1716.[51] Thursday: several drunken officers of ye Guards with their servants attacked my coach (dear wife being in it very big with child) my self and servants in ye strand; for which affront his Majesty had ordered Lord Cadogan to call a Court Martial to have them all broke; but they coming all in my house and submitting themselves and severally asking pardon for ye same in ye presence of ye said Lord Cadogan and I humbly besought King George that their prosecution might be stopped.

Lord Bristol was clearly on close terms with his majesty, King George I. On 2 October 1717[52] he recorded in his diary:

Ye King came to Newmarket when I awaited on his Majesty who honoured me with an audience alone in his Bedchamber on ye 5th.

The King died on 11 June 1727. Within a week of the King's death, the Earl of Bristol had sought an audience with the succeeding monarch, His Majesty King George II. He pleaded with the King 'to provide' for his son, Lord Hervey.[53] It is clear that the Earl was aspiring to some court appointment for John, Lord Hervey of Ickworth, heir to the earldom and Member of the House of Lords. The Earl was suitably rewarded for his son was soon appointed the King's Vice-Chamberlain. In 1740, Lord Hervey was promoted to the high-ranking office of Keeper of the King's Privy Seal. The Lord Keeper's son, Frederick, the future Bishop and builder of the Rotunda, whose monument stands in Lownde Wood at Chevington, was then 10 years old.

The 1st Earl of Bristol lived in retirement at Ickworth until his death in 1751 at the age of 85. He maintained his reputation as a beneficent landlord, always alluding to his large estate and to his home at Ickworth Lodge with undisguised affection:

July 14th, 1728:[54] My wife ... and I sett out from London, lay at Newport, and arrived ye 15th at sweet Ickworth.

Many years before purchasing the manor of Chevington, the Earl of Bristol had attempted to consolidate his Ickworth estate. As early as 24 June 1697, he wrote in his diary:[55] 'I paid £650 being ye purchase money of Shaw's Farm at Chevington'. The acquisition of copyhold property continued throughout the 18th century. In 1782, the 2nd Earl's brother, the Honourable General William Hervey, wrote in his journal:

The 4th Earl, the Earl Bishop, was at Ickworth, 1781–1782, and I think a result of his visit was an extension of the parish beyond the Linnet into Chevington.[56]

18th-century buildings in Chevington

Although the back of Malting Farm House[57] (the home of the influential Kemp family in the early 19th century), is of the early 1600s, the rest of the house, with its elegant wrought iron railings and carriage entrance, is of the following century. A date — 1784 — appears on one of the chimney stacks. In the mid-1920s Limmer Bridge's orchard, which lay to the west of the house, was a favourite hunting ground on our way to school, especially during the early days of the apple season. There was a most convenient hole in the hedge. It is now an elegant garden of shrubs, flower-beds and well-trimmed lawns, beautifully maintained. Nearby is a fine old barn of the late 1700s, awaiting conversion.

Old Factory Farm House, now Stonehouse Farm, situated near the original Clothing Factory of 1852, is timber-framed and was previously thatched. It is mainly of the 1600s as is Braziers on Weathercock Hill with its attics and axial chimney of red brick. This is very possibly where Robert Somerton, a generous benefactor of the parish, had his house in the 1500s. In the early 17th century, Robert Gooday lived at Seburgh's, on the site of the present Hollybush Stud. Thatched and with a three-cell lobby entrance and an interesting chimney of red brick, Mill House appears to be c. 1680.

It is here that William Rolfe, the miller of 1850 and, indeed, all the millers from 1780, held sway.

The house for years known as Chevington Grove, but now racily styled 'Tallyho Stud', was owned by the Whites for close on a century. The rear is a Queen Anne fragment of about 1710, but the front appears to be sixty, or seventy, years later. This very beautiful house has a 19th-century service wing running at right angles on the back. Many of the trees mentioned in the long and informative sale catalogue of 1898 are still in existence.

The walker misses the delightful footpath in front of the Grove, flanked by Scotch pines, which led to Joe Mortlock's cottage and then on to College Green and Farrow's. It is to be hoped that the thatched cottages which date from the early 1700s and which, for many years, were the homes of my great-grandparents and, much later, of the Murkins and Pettingales, will receive some consideration, for few old cottages typical of Suffolk vernacular architecture now remain in Chevington. It is essential, therefore, to take care of what there is.

An excellent cottage stands on Church Road, inhabited throughout my lifetime by the Arbon family. Still thatched and attractively so (1984), the steep roof does not possess dormers (there are end windows) and there is a single prominent central chimney. The lean-to building on the west side was one of the village's three Victorian shops which, in the 1890s, was a popular haunt for children on their way to school. The building is certainly 18th century. The garden, I recall, was always well stocked with row after row of vegetables and today, with its lawn, multi-coloured flowers and dark *cupressus*, is still a joy to behold.

Also of the 18th century is the timber-framed Shoemeadow Cottage which has kept its name for more than two hundred years. Presenting a fine picture, and overlooked by sloping fields and the woods of Ickworth, Shoemeadow hides in the valley through which Chevington Way made its course from Ickworth, across Queen Hill, and so to Chedburgh. It was the scene of slow-moving, horse-drawn carts, travellers on horseback and on foot, and pedlars with their wares from the great St Matthew Fair at Bury, moving laboriously up the hill on their long and wearisome journey to Wickhambrook, to Clare, and even to more distant places. Dignitaries from the Abbey at Bury passed down Chevington Way and, having called at the Hall, resumed their journeys to monastic houses further to the south.

Another Grade II house of this period is Raie Wilman's house on Weathercock Hill. At one time the house was certainly divided into four, or five, cottages. Still thatched, the main timber-framed building has two storeys with a distinguished newel staircase leading from the ground floor. On a brick panel on one of the diagonal detached chimneys, the date 1605 appears, but it is likely that a house stood on the site during the previous century, although architectural evidence is absent. The right-hand block is of the late 1600s. The floor joists are scorched there which suggests a previous open fireplace on the floor immediately below. The Census Returns of the 19th century indicate that Weathercock Green, which probably lay between the house and the present Hill Farm, was once a more populous area than has been the case since 1900. There can be little doubt that in the 1600s the house on Weathercock Hill was one of considerable reputation in the parish, although distant from the centre of manorial activity along Chevington Way.

The thatched house in Depden Lane known as Batley's was the main house on an estate previously owned by Dr. John Battely, Archdeacon of Canterbury and the author of antiquarian books.[58] He was the son of a well-to-do apothecary in Bury and was educated at the Edward VI Grammar School and at Trinity College, Cambridge, as were his two brothers, Nicholas and Thomas. After serving as chaplain to the Archbishop of Canterbury, he became Archdeacon of Suffolk and, in 1688, Archdeacon of Canterbury. He died in 1708 and, in Canterbury Cathedral, there is a monument in his memory. In his will[59] dated 1708 Battely wrote:

> I bequeath to the said Charles Battely and to his heirs all that my estate lying and being in the parish of Chevington in the County of Suffolk or elsewhere which is all the estate my god-father left me with full power and authority and strictly willing and commanding him that forthwith after the decease of my dear wife, Mary Battely, he nominate trustees for the same estate who shall for ever employ the rents of it to the benefit of such of the poor of St Edmundsbury as are of good life and honest frame conformable to the Church of England as now by law established, the more particular ordering of this charity I leave wholly to the care and discretion of my said brother, Charles Battely.

Mary Battely died in 1741. A hundred years later, at the time of the 1841 Census, the Batteley estate consisted of a house, presumably the present house, out-buildings and about forty-six acres of land, then let for £26 a year. The Enclosure Award Map of 1815 refers to fields off the present Chedburgh Road as of the Poor Estate, but it seems virtually certain that part of Dr. Battely's original estate had been sold by that time, possibly to Lord Bristol, or to another landowner such as the Reverend John White I. After allowing for various expenses, the rent was divided between two poor men of Bury, Batteley's birthplace. Throughout the 19th century, the farm was known as Hole Farm when it was occupied by members of the large Simkin family. Certainly before the First World War and during the 1920s, 'Nimbly' Nunn, the carrier and smallholder, lived at Hole Farm which, a little later, was granted the more dignified style of Batley's. The house, secluded and pretty, has been privately owned for many years.

Sir Edward Gage, Lord of the Manor of Chevington, had served as a general in the King's army during the Civil War and was severely wounded during an engagement near Oxford.[60] Although he wielded authority in Chevington for nearly sixty years, there is no evidence that Sir Edward lived at Chevington Hall, or at the Lodge, for a sustained period. Chevington Hall was certainly let to tenants in the early 17th century; for example, in his *Hundred of Thingoe* Thomas Gage[61] stated that the Hall at Chevington was let to a James Baldwin in 1602 for a period of 20 years. It is indeed likely that Sir Edward maintained the tradition set by his predecessors of hunting in Chevington Park and only staying from time to time at Chevington Lodge, or at the Hall itself. As the present Chevington Hall farmhouse was re-roofed and altered certainly by the late 17th century, it is reasonable to conclude that Sir Edward Gage exerted a strong influence on the re-building at that time. He died in 1707 in his 91st year, having been married five times. It was his eldest son, Sir William Gage, and his grandson Thomas who, in 1716, sold Chevington to John, 1st Earl of Bristol,[62] and the advowson to the Reverend Edward Grove.

The rectory and the village

Edward Grove, son of a Bury St Edmunds 'gentleman' was educated at Queens' College, Cambridge and one of his sermons had been published. He had married Anne, the daughter of John Risby, Esq., a large landowner of Thorpe Morieux. His son, Edward, who had died at the age of 24, was a graduate of his father's college.[63]

The rectory, originally moated and the old home of the three Underwood parsons, was built in the 1500s, but was reconstructed in the early 1700s, probably by Grove himself. The back of the house is the earliest part of the building. A later glebe terrier of 1780,[64] signed by John Biddell, churchwarden, and by Charles Kemp, Simon Last and other principal inhabitants, referred to the rectory house as 'lately rebuilt'. At the same time, it appears that the interior was restructured. There is frequent mention in the terriers of a barn of five bays, which was probably the tithe barn, and of the stables 'for five horses'.[65] Even before the house became the rectory, 'a capital mansion house', it was clearly a house of architectural distinction. It was a very likely house for a branch of the Paman family who, before the 1600s, were already rising in the social scale to the status of lesser gentry.

Within four years of his institution as rector in 1694, Edward Grove had shortened the length and lowered the roof of the chancel of the Church of All Saints. Beautifully simple, the roof was built in the late 1690s with the name of Edward Grove deeply embedded into one of its beams. It is clear that the rector had persuaded some parishioners to sign the petition for permission to carry out his drastic alterations.[66] The Bishop of Norwich replied most generously:

> John, by divine permission Bishop of Norwich, to our well beloved Edward Grove, Clerk, Rector of the parish Church of Chevington, in the county of Suffolk and Diocese of Norfolk, Greeting. Whereas by the certificate of the Churchwardens and principal inhabitants of the parish Church of Chevington aforesaid at the Foot of your petition to us . . .

In 1716, Dr. Grove purchased the advowsons of Chevington and Hargrave from Sir William Gage[67] of Hengrave who had been Lord of the Manor of both parishes and who, in the same year, had sold the manors to the 1st Earl of Bristol of Ickworth. The Reverend Doctor, of considerable wealth, probably owned land and property in both parishes in addition to his glebe.* It is conceivable that, sometime in the early 1700s, he had given his name to two outstanding houses, Chevington Grove and Hargrave Grove.

Eighteenth-century clergymen, especially in rural parishes such as Chevington, were figures of an almost monolithic authority. The social status which they enjoyed, based on affluence and, in Grove's case, learning, was not directly related to their work as spiritual leaders. It is, however, clear that church attendance and church activity exerted some influence on the lives of the rural population. The parson was indeed a reckonable force in the social structure, but his eminence was mainly based on territorial power and a consequent prestige to which emergent nonconformity was unable to offer an effective alternative.

A study of the glebe terriers of the late 17th and early 18th centuries throws interesting light on the social history of the parish at that time. There is mention in 1686 of Sir Edward Gage's lands in Chevington[68] when the rectory was described as 'a capital mansion house'. College Green, presumably to contrast it to Broad Green and, maybe, to imply that the college no longer existed, was referred to as Little Green. In the terrier of 1699,[69] the rector, the Reverend Edward Grove, stated that the '15th May was Rogation Monday, the customary day of the annual perambulation and procession for ye preservation of ancient rights of our township'. On a fly-leaf in one of the parish registers appears this statement, probably in Dr. Grove's handwriting:

'The parish is 11 miles and a half, in circumference, or near that'.[70] That conclusion, no doubt, had been reached as a result of years of experience of 'beating the bounds' and demonstrating parochial and territorial rights. In the 1699 terrier[71] it is of interest to note that a Robert Underwood was mentioned as landowner. The name Anthony Mayhew also appears and two members of another prominent Chevington family, Robert and John Kemp, signed the terrier.

The five bells of the Church of All Saints, the biggest weighing 12 hundredweight, were mentioned in a terrier as early as 1706.[72] The town house — i.e. the workhouse near the church — was rented yearly at £2, and the town lands at £3. Dr Henry Paman's gift of £50 was held 'upon personal security' and there is mention of Lady Kytson's gift which was distributed annually.

There is a hint that there had been some disagreement in the parish about Dr. Henry Paman's bequest of 1695 for, in 1709, the Reverend Doctor wrote:[73]

> The sum of £50 left by Paman having been put out upon personal security was, upon ye discontent of some parishioners, called in in Dec. 1707 and lieth now dead in ye hands of Edward Grove, clerk, till some purchase and, or land, security can be met with, acceptable to yᵉ ministers and churchwardens for the time being.

However, in 1716,[74] the rector, as the new patron of the living, helpfully added that 50s. 0d. had been given to the poor 'since it (i.e. Paman's bequest) has been in hand'.

The 1723[75] terrier describes the rectory as containing 'in one contiguous dwelling' five main rooms. Among the outhouses and stabling there was 'a cowhouse for four cows'. There is mention of Farrow's and, again, of 'College Green called Little Green'.

The Reverend Edward Grove, Doctor of Divinity, 'a staunch lover of truth and right', died in 1726. He left two young orphan daughters, the elder, Mary, and the younger, Anne, who was only thirteen. It was Anne who later married John Underwood, a relation of the parsons of the previous century. The Underwoods became Dr. Grove's successors as patrons of the living at the Church of All Saints. As late as 1730, four years after Dr. Grove's death, a Commission of the Consistory Court of the Bishop of Norwich met at Chevington Rectory in order to establish:

> the appraisement of such goods, chattels, and personal estate of the said deceased as were exhibited and shown to us by the said John Turner, Esq. and the Reverend Mr. John Giles Gipps of the late dwelling house of the said deceased in Chevington.[76]

John Turner was an executor of the late doctor's will and John Giles Gipps, who was rector of Brockley at the time of Grove's death, had become rector of Chevington in 1727. The inventory compiled by the Commissioners reveals much of value and interest concerning the style of life of a country parson in the early 18th century. The main contents of the rooms, apartments, attics and outbuildings with their estimated value are listed in Appendix I. There are indications that some items of furniture had already been removed from Chevington Rectory to the homes of relatives and friends but, as Doctor Grove had died four years previously, such irregularities were to be expected. Furniture of the 'best chamber' was certainly at Mrs. Mary Risby's (possibly the late doctor's mother-in-law) in Bury.

> A chest of drawers [was] produced and showed to us at the dwelling house of Mr. Isaac Woods in Bury aforesaid, October 20th 1730, which Miss Grove calls her own.

The chest was valued at 15s. 0d. (75p.).

The silver included a tankard, soup spoon, a pair of salts, a salver, candlesticks and tea tongs, the total weight being 67 ounces and a half, valued at 5s. 0d. an ounce, giving a total value of £16 15s. 0d. (£16.75p.). A gold watch and case was valued at £11 10s. 0d. (£11.50p.). There were a silver watch, 3 gold rings and various gold coins ('*moi dores*' and '*jacobus's*') totalling £15. 18s. 0d. (£15.90p.) and silver coins which had been listed as 'Cash in ye House'. The doctor's 'wearing apparel' had been sold for £6 14s. 6d. (£6.72½p.) by Miss Mary Grove, 'for her subsistence'. All the house-hold linen is listed, the servants' items such as towels and table cloths receiving separate mention in the inventory. There were no less than thirty damask and diaper table napkins and, presumably for the servants, one 'huckaback', a rough linen towel. Two parcels of books were also left: one of these had been sent from Chevington Rectory by the Reverend John Giles Gipps. Their total value was £10. A large number of bonds, i.e. guarantees of payments, were found in the rectory, including two from John Sparrow amounting to a debt of nearly £100. There was a note for £10 from John Giles Gipps dated 10 November 1724. One list gives a total of no less than 16 bonds and notes stating the amounts owing to the Reverend Doctor, but no light is thrown on the nature of the debt. It is difficult to suggest the grounds of indebtedness, unless the money was owing from tenants. It is noted that among the notes listed occur two from Richard Gipps, almost certainly Sir Richard Gipps, the next rector's father, of Great Whelnetham Hall.

There is little doubt that Dr. Grove had been a 'squarson' of wealth and consider-able prestige. He had married the daughter of a Suffolk landowner and, on his memorial in the Church of All Saints, are shown his heraldic arms — 'the arms of Grove . . . are impaled with Risby'.[77] He was typical of the new type of clergyman that had emerged by the end of the 17th century, one who combined scholarship with the status of landed gentry. The descriptions given to the rectory by the Commis-sioners certainly indicate that it had been the house of a country gentleman although there are signs that, at the time of the valuation, the remaining contents in the house had deteriorated. Others had been removed. The last few years of the doctor's life had indeed been tragic for him for his eldest son, Edward, had died and his remaining few months were darkened by the death of his wife, Anne.

The evidence of inventories

A sample of the probate inventories* of the late 17th and early 18th centuries, at the time of Sir Edward and Sir William Gage's lordships of the manor, throws much light on the economic variations of the social classes although, in some cases, social status does not appear to be based on declared possession of wealth. The compilers of the inventories were apparently people living in the parish: the local gentry, the yeoman farmers and, occasionally the Solomon Milks. Ambrose Harrison, a local dissenter, was a compiler of the estate of 'Marcy' Bangs and E. Bell, and Thomas Underwood, 'gentleman', assessed the property of the collarmaker, John Wymarke. Farm equipment and reserves of hay and corn in the barn and outbuildings were also assessed. Examples of valuations of personal property together with typical possessions are given in Appendix II.

The shoemaker John Langley, with £37 in his purse, was certainly more affluent than another craftsman, John Wymarke, the 'collarmaker' (presumably a maker of leather collars for horses). William Paman and George Sparrow, yeomen, had possessions greater in value than those of George Frost, gentleman. Another yeoman, John Gooday, left estate which exceeded the value of those of the two gentlemen listed, George Frost and a relative of the rector, Thomas Underwood. Apparently Underwood, almost certainly a landowner, enjoyed the status of 'gentleman' on account of his family's long standing in the parish, while John Gooday, in spite of the association that his family had had with Chevington and of his residence at Seburgh's (on the site of the present Hollybush Green Stud) is listed as a yeoman. It is possible, of course, that Seburgh's, although a relatively large farm, was an estate farm of Sir Edward Gage's, and that Thomas Underwood lived the life of an independent country gentleman in a house similar in prestige to Chevington Grove.

Poverty and the 'town house'

In the glebe terrier of 1706[78] there is mention of the 'town house', i.e. the workhouse, which was rented, presumably from the churchwardens, at £2 a year. A search through the terriers before that date has not elicited any reference to the workhouse. As has already been shown, the terrier of 1729[79] refers to:

> a house called the Gildhall situated on a little green near the Churchyard now made into 4 tenements and at present inhabited by Widdow Copsey, Widdow Manning, Roger Adams and Thomas Frost, poor husbandmen.

In 1601 the churchwardens and elected landholders were appointed overseers of the poor by the vestry,* a type of parish council, mainly ecclesiastical in origin, whose appointments had to be approved by the Justices of the Peace. The main task of the overseers was to levy a poor rate on the owners of land and 'oversee' the distribution of the revenue to the necessitous poor. Therefore, paupers had to be provided for and, if necessary, set to work. Houses of Correction were set up but, so far, no evidence has come to light of such an establishment existing in Chevington. It is impossible to say when the gildhall was first used as the workhouse, but the two glebe terriers mentioned indicate that it was used in some such capacity in the early 18th century.

As early as 1662 a stranger who had stayed in a place for 40 days could claim that he was settled and, consequently, that he was eligible for poor relief if that became necessary. Thirty years later an Act decreed that a register be kept of all parishioners who were receiving poor relief and in 1697 parish paupers and their families, who were in receipt of relief, were compelled to wear the letter P prominently on their uniform, a degradation which from 1782 was repealed if the paupers could prove themselves to be of good character.

As is shown in the next chapter the workhouse or town house near Church Green received help from the levies imposed on the owners and tenants of land in the parish. It is very likely that occupants of the workhouse were set to work on neighbouring land, tidying up the churchyard, or working at individual tasks in the workhouse yard, which is clearly indicated on the Enclosure Award Map of Chevington and Chedburgh (1815).

In addition to parochial relief and the provision of a workhouse, the revenue of the 'poor estate' gave financial assistance to those considered by the trustees to be in need. In 1669 the earliest benefactions enabled property just past *The Oaks* on the

Chedburgh Road, formerly in possession of the Paman family, to be purchased. The cottages, with their yards and generous gardens, were let and the rent paid by the tenants was invested in the Poor's Estate Fund. After some disagreement, Dr. Henry Paman's £50 bequest was invested and held accountable by the rector and church-wardens. Dividends were allocated to poor relief. In 1816, at the time of the enclosures, a piece of land of nearly six and a half acres, lying alongside Chevington Way, now known as Queen Lane, was allotted for poor relief. Dr. Henry Paman's bequest was used to defray the expenses of enclosing the land later known as the 'town land'. The allotment was let for £10 a year and, again, the rent obtained was allocated to the parish's Poor Estate. In 1662, Lady Kytson, on inheriting the estates of her late husband, Sir Thomas Kytson II, charged her neighbouring manor of Lackford to provide a coat, or gown, to the oldest poor person in a number of parishes comprising her estate, including Chevington. In addition, a total payment of £2 was made, again chargeable to the Lackford manor, for the relief of the eight eldest poor of the parish.

In 1778[80] the Accounts for the trustees of the Charity Estates for the poor in Chevington show that the interest on Dr. Paman's bequest and the total rent received from land and property was £11 0s. 6d. (£11.2½p.). Eight received 5s. 0d. (25p.) each from Lady Kytson's charity and one, James Harris, the oldest 'town-born' poor person, received a coat. Payments from the charity account were made to 35 parishioners.

The Churchwarden's Account Book[81] shows that the vestry continued 'to make assessments upon the several inhabitants of the said parish for the repairs of the Church and other purposes'. At a vestry meeting held on Easter Monday, 19 April 1802, a rate of 2½d. in the £1 was resolved. As John Kemp (probably of the Lodge) paid a rent of £180, his contribution to the vestry was £1 17s. 6d. (£1.87½p.). Thomas Canham, a small tenant who paid a rent of £10, was assessed at 2s. 1d. Contributions continued, therefore, to support the poor housed in the town house, a responsibility expected of all parishioners who, because of their economic standing, were considered to be in a position to do so. In the Churchwarden's Account Book there is an entry that, on 5 November 1799,[82] 1s. 0d. (5p.) was spent on locks for the village stocks. It is interesting to speculate just where the stocks were placed. In order to give maximum publicity it is likely that the unfortunate malefactor was paraded on Church Green down Chevington Way, so that all travellers passing to and fro could chide and taunt as they thought fit.

No reference has been found in recent research to the brick coalhouse on Old Post Office Road. Tradition has it that, during the early 19th century, before coal was delivered to individual houses, the building was used as a distributing centre for the village when, presumably, an overseer would be in attendance to supervise the allocation to those receiving poor relief. The coal, probably transported by road from Bury, was unloaded from a horse-drawn wagon through an opening on the front of the building. The outline is still visible.

The Poor Law Act of 1834 abolished the parish administration, the poor law unions and the elected Guardians of the Poor taking the place of the overseers and parish workhouse. In the year 1835–6 the Union Workhouse was built in Hospital Road, Bury St Edmunds, by the 46 parishes which had elected to join the Union, including the 18 constituting the Thingoe Hundred. The accommodation was for no less than 'three-hundred paupers'. A study of the registers of baptisms and burials at the Church of

All Saints in the 18th, and the census returns of the 19th century, indicates that there were paupers in Chevington, some of whom were very elderly. From 1834, when the Union was built in Hospital Road, the pauper who had managed to eke out his life, either in the parish workhouse, or in his own poverty-stricken home, was confronted with the more serious choice of either straining his family's limited resources, or entering the Union and being separated from the comfort of his friends and neighbours. 'They've taken poor old Bill to the Union' was the customary way of referring to admissions of Chevington parishioners.

Education (I)

The quickened social conscience of the late 18th century, as evidenced in the attitude towards the poor, resulted in a deeper concern for education in general and for literacy in particular. Schools were set up in the main by craftsmen in the village, or by soldiers returning from military service but certainly by the 1750s at least, no-one was permitted to teach without a licence from the bishop of the diocese. In the early 1800s Jonathan Cooper (who according to family tradition was formerly in the army) was teaching the 'poor children of Chedburgh',[83] a service which led later to the building of Chedburgh School in 1814 by the Marquess of Bristol. Years later his daughter Sophia wrote from America to her nephew, another Jonathan and my grandfather, with undisguised affection about her early days at Chedburgh School where she was almost certainly taught by her father.

There is evidence that early in the 19th century, William Parker of Chevington, parish clerk and shoemaker, also performed the extra function of schoolmastering. At the same time Susan Fenton was teaching in the parish, in the stone-built house opposite College Farm. It is not known, however, what educational facilities, if any, were available in Chevington in the late 1700s, but it is reasonable to assume that the Reverend John Giles Gipps, M.A., son of Sir Richard Gipps of Great Whelnetham Hall, who was Rector of Chevington, 1727-34 and apparently a young and vigorous man, initiated some educational enterprise. Interest may also have been shown by his successor as rector, the Reverend Edward Burch, M.A., who was rector for 42 years, a kindly, benevolent man, who left £10 in his will to the poor of Chevington.[84]

However, the earliest known reference to any organised scholastic activity in Chevington, was in 1819 when there was one day school and one Sunday school. Both schools were supported by the rector, the Reverend John White II, 'and his family'.[85] It is likely that the idea of establishing the schools was first mooted in 1818 by John White I and his wife, Elizabeth. Both rectors had been Masters of the Perse School, Cambridge, and had had brilliant university careers. It is understandable that the Whites would wish to ensure that Solomon Milk and his family received the rudiments of education so that illiteracy was no longer a factor in failing to understand the church's teaching. A little later, from the Returns of an Education Enquiry, it was declared that 29 boys and girls were attending Sunday school, held presumably in the Church of All Saints, and 21 the day school.[86]

It is probable that the day school was held in the building opposite College Farm which consisted then of only two large rooms, one on each floor.

Clearly most parents at the turn of the 18th century and at the beginning of the 19th were unable to send their children to day school. They were needed to supplement the family income and, although at a later date funds were raised by subscription, some payment for schooling would be expected from the parents. Just before the National School was built on Church Green in 1847, £10 8s. 0d. (£10.40p.) was paid annually to the master and the mistress for teaching in the Sunday school and the day school mistress received an annual salary of £12 16s. 0d. (£12.80p.).[87] As has already been mentioned when referring to the growth of nonconformity in Chevington during the 18th century, the Sunday school was an effective agency in the teaching of reading and in laying the foundations of a general education. Later in life Solomon Milk and the rural craftsmen looked back on their Sunday school, not only with gratitude but, perhaps, with a genuine feeling of indebtedness combined with some affection. It was different, of course, for the gentry. The Reverend John White I had been educated at Wakefield and at a school in Ditchingham, in Norfolk, and later, at Caius College, Cambridge. He accepted the task of educating his only son, John, at home in Chevington. The Reverend John White II sent his three sons John, Edmund and Cyril to King Edward VI's Grammar School, Bury St Edmunds, then housed in Northgate Street, before they were admitted to Cambridge University. This was the school attended by the Underwoods and by John Giles Gipps, rector, in the 17th century and by the Pamans from the 16th. John, the first Earl of Bristol, had also been a pupil there. Founded in 1551, King Edward VI's Grammar School was of considerable reputation and prestige, drawing boys not only from the local gentry, but from a wider East Anglian field.

Bury, in the 18th century, during the time that the Reverend John Giles Gipps and the Reverend Edward Burch were rectors of Chevington, was a fashionable resort for the landed gentry and for the *cognoscenti*. Daniel Defoe[88] wrote of it:

> The beauty of this town consists in the number of gentry who dwell in and near it, the polite conversation among them; the affluence and plenty they live in: the sweet air they breathe in, and the pleasant country they have to go abroad in.

The character of Bury remained fundamentally the same for the next 100 years. Edmund Gillingwater[89] wrote in 1811:

> Beyond there venerable relics of antiquity, appear, uprising on the western ridge, the houses and public edifices of the town, ancient and modern, and the picture at length terminates in a rich horizon of hill and dale of wood and corn fields, just admitting of an indistinct sight of the superb, but unfinished, seat of the Earl of Bristol, at Ickworth . . . there is not a place in England round which can be found a greater number of seats of gentlemen of rank and fortune, than in the vicinity of this town: so that a traveller or stranger, visiting Bury, may pass a day or two very agreeably, by taking the circuit of its neighbourhood, to the extent of about six or seven miles.

In contrast, many years after those words were written, 45 parishioners of Chevington were receiving poor law awards varying from 3s. 0d. (15p.) to 1s. 0d. (5p.).[90]

The French Wars

The country was still at war against the French. On 5 August 1782 at a meeting of representatives of the entire country in Stowmarket it was resolved:

That the County of Suffolk, sensitive to the inferiority of the naval force of Great Britain compared with that of the other European powers with whom we are at war, do undertake by voluntary subscription to build a man of war of 74 guns for the service of the public.[91]

Chevington, with help from the Reverend John White I (he gave £10 10s. 0d. (£10.50p.)), the Kemps, Fentons and others, raised £37 6s. 0d. (£37.30p.), a relatively high total from the local villages. During the year ending 24 December 1809, 383 men and boys had been recruited for the French Wars from the Bury district.[92] It is not known what effect the Napoleonic War had on Solomon Milk and his contemporaries in Chevington, but the 10-year-old boy who, according to the 1841 census return,[93] had been encumbered by the name Napoleon Nunn, would, perhaps, be expected to know something of it.

Dog Rose. *Rosa canina agg.*

CHAPTER THREE

LIFE IN CHEVINGTON 1776-1926

'Another Spring! his heart exulting cries,
Another year! with promis'd blessings rise! —
Eternal Power! from whom those blessings flow,
Teach me still more to wonder, more to know.'

— Robert Bloomfield, Suffolk poet, 1776-1823.

The Reverend John White I

IN 1770, THOMAS UNDERWOOD, a descendant of the Underwoods who had been prominent in Chevington during the previous century, sold the advowson of the Church of All Saints to the Reverend John White, son of a publican of North Walsham, Norfolk and a former scholar of Caius College, Cambridge.[1] Although Whites were living in North Walsham between 1736-47 no reference can be found in the Overseers' Book to William White who, according to the matriculation lists of Caius College, was John's father. There is no mention of a John White in the baptism register of 1739-51, so it is likely that he was baptised in a neighbouring parish. Later he was sent to a boarding school in Wakefield, Yorkshire, possibly the Green Coat School, where he stayed for four years before returning to his homeland, this time to the village of Ditchingham, in order to receive private tuition from a Mr. Frost.

It was in 1776 that John White, the former Norfolk boy, began his long reign of 42 years as Rector and Patron of Chevington, Suffolk. From the memorial stones in the Chancel of the Church of All Saints, we learn that he was married to Elizabeth Keable (or Keeble), daughter of Ralph Keable, of Beccles, Suffolk. The Keables of Beccles, Westhall and Kelsale, were prominent landowners and it was evident that John White, soon to acquire the advowson and incumbency of Chevington's neighbour, Hargrave, was establishing himself as a member of the emerging class of rural gentry. In the course of time, he inherited part of the estate of Ralph Keable,[2] an inheritance which, together with the 33 acres of glebe and other lands in his parish, entitled him to be regarded as a local squire.[3] As Anthony Russell writes in *The Clerical Profession*:

> By the late eighteenth century, a marked change was taking place in the social status of the clergy, for both individually and as an occupational group they were experiencing a steady upward mobility. The new wealth provided for the clergy by the commutation of tithes* (in the form of rent from land similar to that of the gentry) allowed them to build parsonages which more closely resembled the Hall than the farmhouse.

So the Reverend John White became the progenitor of a long tradition of paternalism and squirarchy in Chevington, a benevolent leadership that was to serve that parish for 150 years.

43

White

Ioannes filius Gulielmi White de North Walsham in Agro Norfolc. Publicani natus ibidem, educatus per quadriennium apud Wakefield in Com. Eborac. sub Mag. Clarke deinde per biennium in Ædibus privatis Mr Frost apud Ditchingham in Com. Norfolc. Admissus est Mai. 21. Pensionarius Minor Annos natus 17 sub tutelâ Mr Smith et solvit pro Ingressu —

5. *The matriculation entry for John White of North Walsham at his admission to Caius College, Cambridge, in 1761.*

Elizabeth and John raised a large family. Their eldest son, John, destined to follow his father as rector, was born in 1786. Other children are buried in the chancel of the Church of All Saints and, outside in the churchyard to the immediate west of the tower, are the table tombs, grey, lichen-covered and obscured by saplings, of his three single daughters, Sarah, Elizabeth and Frances, who lived in the rector's impressive Queen Anne house, until recently known as Chevington Grove.

John Keble, probably the most distinguished church leader of the century, and co-founder of the Oxford Movement,* was born in 1792. He was a member of the Suffolk Kebles into whose family John White had married. In 1870 Keble College, Oxford, was founded in his memory. There can be little doubt that many later members of the family of Whites were given the name Keble in honour of their distant kinsman.

The closure of Chevington Way

Until 1814 Chevington Way remained the main approach to the village from Bury St Edmunds, with a connecting road to the south at Palace Green just past the Ickworth Park entrance. This ancient road, now barely traceable for much of its length, was the main thoroughfare to Wickhambrook before what is now the A 143 was completed. A trackway known as Lodge Road which began at the centre of the village between College Green and Broad Green, led into the area of the old Chevington

Park, the Kytsons' shooting lodge and, much later, to the Lodge Farm which replaced it. Chevington was a parish of wide-spreading greens. Lodge Road, on becoming Chedburgh Road, cut through Meeting Place Green[4] on the left and Tan Office Green on the right. Flanking Moor's and Batley's farms, Depden Road was a narrow and winding lane; a track on the right led to yet another green, Great Knowles Green in Hargrave, the main way heading for Depden over Depden Green. Near the Church of All Saints was Church Green. Opposite Hollybush Green Stud, formerly Seburgh's, there was a high, open expanse with small woods and a cottage or two at the edges: nothing is left.

In 1814 the Earl of Bristol constructed the so-called New Road, which led past the Lodge[5] to Great Saxham, in order to compensate for his closure of the ancient Chevington Way which wound through his park at Ickworth in the valley of the Linnet along Westley Bottom to Bury St Edmunds. In 1823, in order to stop all travelling on the Way, the Earl constructed a dam across the Linnet just where the ancient road approached the White House on the Chevington border. The cost was £500. As a consequence a lake of 15 acres was constructed, but it was short lived for, in 1842, the dam burst its banks, causing widespread flooding in the vicinity of the *Spread Eagle* in Westgate Street in Bury. The dam was never rebuilt.

So after a history of nearly eight hundred years Chevington Way became a memory. Gradually travellers from Bury made greater use of the road through Horringer, or of the route from the Saxhams along the New Road to the Lodge and on to Broad Green in the centre of the village. In order to obstruct all travel to Chedburgh, the Earl of Bristol built two cottages across the Way on Palace, or Iron Gates, Green so that the road over the fields to Queen Hill and Queen Lane, and then to Chedburgh and the world beyond, fell into disuse. It is now impossible to trace the track completely: small trees and undergrowth block the Way, the plough has taken its toll, and gates appear in unlikely places. When I last fought through the entanglement, birds were singing defiantly in the woods and bees droned along the headlands. Other than such intrusions, a great quiet hung over the hedgerows.

In 1813-14, the agent of the Bristol Estate, John Shillito, paid the firm of Robert Isaac and Son the sum of £31 10s. 0d. (£31.50p.) for surveying part of the old carriage roads, and for the construction of new roads with which they replaced them in the parishes of Chedburgh, Chevington, Rede and Little Saxham. Because of the considerable wage increases and expenses due to bad weather in December 1813, a further sum of £35 14s. 0d. (£35.70p.) was paid making a total payment to the contractors of £67 4s. 0d. (£67.20p.). It is reasonable to assume that their contract included the construction of the New Road to Great Saxham. Extensive surveying of the roads took place in the early years of the 19th century and in 1817 the altered boundaries of Ickworth Park, some of which were within the parish of Chevington, were surveyed for £241 16s. 0d. (£241.80p.).[6]

The 4th Earl of Bristol

In 1795, Frederick, 4th Earl of Bristol and Bishop of Derry (1730-1803), began the building of the present vast house at Ickworth[7] whose rotunda remains clearly visible and accessible from many parts of the village but, because of the bishop's sudden death in Italy in 1803, the building activity at Ickworth was seriously delayed. During the year 1816-17 on the edge of Lownde Wood, Messrs. John de Carle of

Bury, a firm of considerable repute, erected a monument to the memory of the Earl Bishop. About 100 feet in height, it was built of Ketton stone at an inclusive cost of £1,500 16s. 0d. (£1,500.80p.). On one side there is a lengthy description in metal letters, part of which reads:

> Sacred to the memory of Frederick, Earl of Bristol and Bishop of Derry, who during XXV years that he presided over that See, endeared himself to all denominations of all Christian residents in that extensive diocese. He was the friend and protector of them all. His great patronage was uniformly administered upon the purest and most disinterested principles.

A mile away, towering above Lownde Wood, the monument was clearly visible from our garden and from many other viewpoints in the village. On a summer's evening, it was seen to stand sentinel among the elms until dusk fell and bats swooped over the fields. In the same year the 5th Earl of Bristol raised the tower of the Church of All Saints so that it was visible from Ickworth. The work was carried out by de Carle's, at a cost of £120.

The Bishop's son, the 5th Earl (who in 1826 became the 1st Marquess of Bristol) decided, after some procrastination, to continue his father's massive building activities, so that in 1829 he left Ickworth Lodge in order to take up residence, not in the oval rotunda as originally planned, but in the east wing which is still the family home.

The social structure

The massive building operation obviously had repercussions on the social and economic life of the surrounding villages comprising the estate, including Chevington. Certainly until the 1940s the Bristol estate continued to impose powerful social impact on local life. Many Chevington men worked on the estate, most farms in the village were farmed by tenant farmers, and the village community was subjected to a benevolent, but firm, paternalism. The Bristols of Ickworth and the Whites of the Rectory gave a social cohesion to village life, an essential framework in which all aspects of rural thought and activity were not only interlaced, but co-ordinated. There was a recognisable stability in the affairs of men.

The Solomon Milks, the men of the fields, were to witness far-reaching changes in the style of farming which proliferated as the century advanced. The first momentous change was that of the enclosure of the remaining open and common fields by freeing them from shared ownership and appropriating them to a specified person as sole owner. Enclosures had taken place sporadically in Chevington from the early 15th century. Later they were imposed by the Kytsons and the Gages and sometimes by agreement among the tenants, but enclosure of the remaining common fields, commons and waste was by parliamentary enactment[8] as shown on the 1815 Enclosure Award map of Chevington. There can be little doubt that at this time additional ditches were dug round a holder's lands, the soil heaped up to form a bank on which hawthorn and some blackthorn were planted, as well as some trees such as oak, elm and hazel to supply the landowner with fuel and timber. Samuel Brewster of College Farm held many acres; Samuel Brooks, the Kemps (they appear to be living at the Hall and Malting at the time) and Mrs. Susan Prior are all prominent names. Fields which I remember well from boyhood days such as the Glebe, Ragman's (near the Old Rectory), Old Nick's and Farrow's (still so-called today) are clearly marked. The cost of the Chevington enclosures, excluding roads, but including solicitors' and surveyors' fees, was £3,969 9s. 0d. (£3,969.45p.),[9] a considerable sum in the early 19th century and indicative of the complexity of the operation.

At the time the White family, the 'squarsons' of Chevington, were actively consolidating their ownership of the Grove Estate which remained in their possession until it was acquired by the 3rd Marquess of Bristol in 1898. Exchange of lands occurred frequently, e.g. in 1844 there was a deed of exchange between the Bristol estate and 'John Worledge, Esq.', a banker, who was the owner of the impressive and newly built Ruffin's House at Brooks's Corner. White's *Directory of Suffolk* (1844) (no relation of the Chevington Whites) gives the 'principal owners of the soil' as the Marquess of Bristol, the Rev. J. & Misses E. & F. White, a Dr. Colville, J. Worledge, Esq. and Mr. J. Kemp. Another Kemp was a maltster at the Malting. James Simkin kept the beerhouse, William Rolfe was the corn miller; James Mayhew, the blacksmith; John Simkin, the thatcher, and John Webb, of Moat Farm, was a cattle dealer. William Parker fulfilled the double function of shoemaker and schoolmaster; William Edwards was the wheelwright and there was a bricklayer, a carpenter and two shopkeepers. Chevington had its own veterinary surgeon, Robert J. Simkin, and a Robert Rolfe whom the *Directory* lists, unusually, as 'gentleman'. The village was a well balanced rural community, with an interdependent and almost self-sufficient way of life, satisfying the main social needs of its 624 'souls'.

The Reverend John White II

The Rector, mathematician, scholar and preacher, died on 4 December 1818, in his 74th year. On 9 December 1818, the *Bury and Norwich Post* reported:

> He was an ornament not only to his College, but to the University, having been no less respected as the first scholar of his time, than for his exemplary conduct in every instance. In the continuance of life to its conclusion he was a most estimable character.

When probate was granted to his widow Elizabeth, the estate was valued at £60,000,[10] a considerable sum of money in the early 19th century. Elizabeth, from whose family, the Kebles, the fortune was inherited, received £20,000 and the future Reverend John White II and his four sisters were each granted £8,000. At the time of Elizabeth's death in 1834, £9,000 of her share remained unadministered, so the residue was shared by the Reverend John White II and his two remaining sisters, Frances and Elizabeth, of Chevington Grove.

The Second John White became Rector and Patron of Chevington in 1819 on the death of his father. If ever a son followed his father's footsteps, it was certainly the Reverend John White II.[11] He became an undergraduate of Caius, his father's college, where he was fourth Wrangler* and, having won classical and mathematics prizes, he became Fellow and Dean of his college. Ordained in 1808, he continued to follow his father's example by becoming Master of the Perse School, Cambridge. Seven years after his appointment as rector of Chevington (together with Hargrave) he married Mary Image, daughter of the Reverend Thomas Image, patron and incumbent of Whepstead, a neighbouring village. This marriage, as did many similar local alliances, strenthened the influence of the minor gentry in rural Suffolk: an important strand in the recognised social order, an order which impinged more intimately on the lives of the Solomon Milks than did the more remote aristocracy of the Bristols at Ickworth.

Tithe, the payment due by the parish inhabitants for the support of the church, which was usually payable to the incumbent, had been paid by the people of Chevington since time immemorial.[12] Originally such payment was in kind and consisted of the tenth part of all annual profits. Later, however, rent-charge, part of a national reorganisation after the 1836 Act and originally varying with the price of corn, replaced payment in kind. Such a rent-charge of £587 10s. 0d. (£587.50p.), known as 'modus',* was payable by the parishioners of Chevington in 1838 in place of tithes.[13]

Windmills

The medieval windmill in Chevington was almost certainly in Great Days. It is not known when it fell into disuse, but it is likely that it was active until the end of the 17th century with access from Chevington Way at Church Green and from the crest of Queen Hill. Windmills were replacing watermills by the late 12th century and there is a reference by Jocelin of Brakelond to a windmill being built on Abbot Samson's lands at Haberdon, near Bury St Edmunds, as early as 1191.

The earliest known reference to the post mill which stood near the *Greyhound* on Hargrave Road, formerly known as Mill Road, was in 1783[14] but it is reasonable to suggest that it was built at the beginning of the 18th century, or even earlier. Other than a few Court Roll references to changes in ownership, or tenancy, information on the building itself appears non-existent. On 20 December 1907, however, at a possible change of tenancy, there is mention of:

> that post windmill . . . with the round house, flour mill stones, sail's going gear, fixture appendages, and machinery and windmill paddock, 1 acre, 2r and 5p.

As the names of millers and millwrights are given in census returns and directories only until about 1900, it can be assumed that the mill fell into disuse about that time. Only the round house remained. Formerly used as an abbatoir by Fred Bridge, the butcher, it became a store, but was finally demolished in 1983. The timber body of the mill, constructed of weatherboard and referred to in Suffolk as the 'buck', contained the machinery and held the sails. This structure was mounted on a strong, vertical, oak post about 20 feet long, around which it revolved to face the wind. The movement was regulated by a vaned fantail which caught the wind and, by means of the internal mechanism, turned the 'buck' on its track. The base of the oak post was protected by the round-house that served no operative purpose other than providing additional storage space for grain, or flour. This was a brick, slated building with a cornice of protruding bricks under the slates.

At the beginning of the 19th century William Rolfe, the village miller, lived at the neighbouring thatched house on Mill Meadow. Later in the 1860s and 70s, John Steel, James Denton and James Steadman were millers. In 1865 one William Baldwin was a millwright and, as late as 1896, George Newman appeared as a flour dealer, but there is no mention of a miller. In 1892, however, Samuel Buxton of Hargrave, Ephraim Pledger of Depden and Peter Mansfield of Whepstead were named as 'millers (wind)', so it may be assumed that windmills were still operating in local villages in the late 19th century, even if the mill at Chevington was by that time inactive.

Village nonconformity in the early 19th century

During the early years of the 19th century, the influence of the Independent chapel on Tan Office Green grew steadily. By 1840 the chapel had been leased to the Primitive Methodists of the Wickhambrook and Newmarket Circuit, who paid a small rent to the Congregationalists in Bury. Twenty years later, an effort was made to buy the chapel. However, on 8 April 1863, it was resolved that the building be taken on lease for a further 10 years, an arrangement which continued throughout the century.[15]

Baptism of infants normally took place at the Church of All Saints even if the parents were merely nominal members of the Anglican tradition, or even if they were active supporters of Primitive Methodism. From 1856–72, records show that there were only 15 baptisms at the chapel: five from Chevington itself and 10 from the supporting villages.[16] Chevington was regarded as the local nonconformist centre. All the parents named in the baptism registers were classified as 'labourers' with the exception of Joseph Bolingbroke who was listed as 'charcoal-burner'. Throughout those years the primacy afforded to the place of the Scriptures both at the Sunday school and during Sunday and weekday worship was clearly evident. The Bible was a source of literacy in the village for, in the main, Sunday school scholars remained on the attendance roll until the age of 13, or 14, some years after they had left the village school. The consequence was that their reading ability was considerably enhanced. Many ageing local preachers as late as the 1930s attributed their level of education to the influences of devoted Sunday school teachers. Biblical names prevailed throughout the 19th century such as 'Eli Obadiah Daniel', given to the son of James and Emily Howe, who was baptised at the chapel on 21 April 1870. In the early 1880s there were living in the village Hannah Wallace, Jeremiah Byatt, Daniel Last, Elias Nunn, Eli Simkin, Jonah Mortlock, and Shadrack Clarke.

The evangelical response from 'Camp', or open-air meetings, which had been introduced by 1857[17] and which were convened on summer Sunday afternoons in a meadow on Tan Office Green, was such that chapel membership fluctuated considerably.[18] Such occasions were well attended, not only by the chapel fraternity, but by others who came to listen or, no doubt, to demonstrate their cynical disregard for what the chapel folk held dear. The number of adherents increased from 27 in March 1863 to 90 in the following June. During the quarter ending 8 September 1884, the 42 members contributed £5 1s. 3d. (£5.06½p.),[19] a sum which exceeded that of all other chapels including such acknowledged doyens as Newmarket and Wickhambrook.

Throughout the century, local preachers were subjected to a quite rigid discipline. Failure to arrive at a service was carefully scrutinised in spite of the long and lonely distances which the preachers had to travel. The journey from Chedburgh to Barnardiston walked by the redoubtable Jonathan Harris, a local preacher since 1863, was about twelve miles. After presiding at three services, he walked the same journey home. At the time that Poslingford, near Clare, was on the Plan – a programme for Circuit Services – Mr Carrick, the circuit minister, was asked to speak to Brothers Prewer and Seeley, both of Chevington, about neglecting appointments there, a village eight miles over the fields and footpaths. On a winter's Sunday the walk demanded not only zeal, but a strength of constitution already overtaxed by heavy physical labour during the week. Mrs. Ruby Edgeley of Depden reports that her grandafther, Robert, took a supply of bread, cheese and onions when setting forth on his missions to

Ousden in case he was not invited to a meal between the morning and afternoon services, an arrangement actually preferred by some preachers for it afforded an opportunity for meditating in private before the rigours of the afternoon.

During a Quarterly Meeting at Wickhambrook on 11 September 1871,[20] it was decided:

> that we consider Brother Cooper's reason for neglecting Saxon Street camp meeting insuffi-
> cient and urge him to take his appointments at camp meetings in the future whether the
> weather is favourable or not.

The chapel members themselves were subjected to the authority of the Circuit Quarterly Meeting. In 1875[21] it was declared 'that the Chevington people have not the liberty to put a new slate roof upon their chapel, but they have the privilege of thatching it with new reeds'.

Discounting temporary increases in attendance resulting from camp meeting evangelical ardour, membership grew until the late 1890s when, according to circuit records, there were 180 'adherents'. Riley Smith, a preacher of long, rambling discourses only relieved by his walks from one side of the pulpit to the other, was still proclaiming the Kingdom of God in the late 1920s. His welcome announcement, 'I shall now bring these rambling remarks to a close', encouraged his congregation to remain patient. As early as 1899 Riley had been the Secretary of the Chapel's Temperance Society[22] which elicited the modest membership of four adult and two 'juvenile' abstainers. Other stalwarts were Thomas Ashman, who played the harmonium — insured for £25 — Mr. and Mrs. Kimmens, Mrs. Starling Smith and Jonathan Harris. Jonathan walked from his home in Chedburgh, usually for the three Sunday services at 11 a.m., 2.30 p.m. and 6.30 p.m. and at 8 p.m. on Tuesdays. The Plan listed the preachers for the 12 chapels: formidable characters such as F. W. ('Willy') Pask, Jonas Leach, Benjamin Morley, and Frederick Newton, the Newmarket fishmonger, who grasped the opportunity of advertising his speciality of 'home-cured bloaters' in the pages of the circuit Plan.

The rural nonconformist did not share the radicalism which characterised urban dissent at the beginning of the century. There was a tacit acceptance of the natural order, and he proclaimed the Word of God and His Promise of Salvation which beckoned all who knew tribulation and sorrow in this world to the reign of God's harmony and peace in the next. The simplicity of the exhortation in no way indicated a superficiality of knowledge, or of thought. Two preachers in particular, Jonas Leach and F. W. ('Willy') Pask, were well-read, adept at abstract reasoning and acutely sensitive to the social, political, and religious problems of the day. Jonas was a farm horsekeeper from Kirtling, 'Willy' was the shopkeeper and sub-postmaster of Hargrave.

By 1909, however, Brothers Leach and Pask were introducing in their sermons an intellectual and progressive emphasis which conflicted with the more traditional thought of the circuit hierarchy. At a Quarterly Meeting held at Ousden in January 1909, they were asked to consider seriously their position as local preachers. They were then "relieved of the responsibility of their preaching appointments on the present Plan until March 4th next'.[23] Both, apparently, had been in communication with the League of Progressive Thought, the origins of which are unknown.

On 4 March 1909, Brother Leach accepted the findings of the Minister of the Circuit. Brother Pask, characteristically, declared that he was prepared to be loyal to connexional standards of doctrine and when he could no longer be so, he should resign, but he hoped his brethren could allow him to interpret those doctrines from his own standpoint and in harmony with his own mind.

Throughout this time, although there was a clear division between 'church' and 'chapel', my two grandfathers, Joseph Bradfield, a Primitive Methodist local preacher and a Liberal and Jonathan Cooper, a traditional Anglican and a Conservative, evidently maintained very friendly mutual contacts and, moreover, the Reverend John White III was known to be a good friend to 'the chapel pastor'.[24] However, prejudice continued. In October 1912 when my parents married in the Church of All Saints, grandparents Joseph and Lucy, in spite of harvest being 'safely gathered in', could not find time to attend the service; consequently, my mother's sisters could not see their way clear to serve as bridesmaids. After the service, held in the church because the chapel was not registered for marriages, a photograph was taken of the wedding feast held at the Hall Farm which was provided and attended by Joseph and Lucy. There were many Primitive Methodists present including Benjamin Morley and his wife, Martha, as well as representatives of the congregation of the Church of All Saints.

Walter Blake, aged 85 (1983), writes:

> I remember going to the Chapel. I was in the Sunday School until I was called up for the Forces. I can remember Sunday evening; the seats were all full. It used to be lovely: services with the Preacher and the Lord's people. It used to be lovely to be there.

The chapel remained throughout the years the centre of a closely-knit social life. Good Friday teas, followed by a Service of Song in the evening, were warmly acclaimed: the assortment of fresh vegetables, flowers and fruit, brought in abundance for the Harvest Festival, was sold in the chapel on the following Monday: Sunday School Anniversaries, when recitations and special hymns were 'rendered', elicited from a very scattered area crowded congregations splendid in their 'Sunday best'. Many Chevington people, not in any way associated with Primitive Methodism, regarded the Anniversary as a very special summer event. Sunday school scholars, choir members and recruited auxiliaries were seated on forms on a long platform faced with red curtains and edged with freshly-cut, white ox-eye daisies. The gallery was crowded with young men and boys from surrounding villages who, on one occasion, were rebuked by the preacher, Brother Ludkin, of Newmarket, for creating an unwarranted disturbance.

The Anniversary was followed by the Annual Treat. Mrs. Ruby Edgeley, of Depden, a former Sunday school supporter, writes:

> I expect our main event was the Anniversary treat, with the harmonium in one of the two wagons. We would sing our way to Chevington Lodge where the owners threw pennies on the lawn for us to scramble after, then on to Hargrave Hall. I forget what we got there; pennies, too, I think, and on to Depden Hall for an apple and orange, then back for tea at the chapel.

As early as 1902,[25] however, social and economic difficulties were recognised by the Circuit leaders. At a Quarterly Meeting in that year it was stated 'Owing to poverty and gradual depopulation of the villages, and the general depression in trade, we are unable to raise the minimum salaries of two ministers'. According to the Circuit Quarterly Accounts the chapel membership of Chevington fell from 47 at the beginning of the century to 30 in 1912. On 23 June 1927 a report was issued to the Quarterly Meeting that between 1909 and 1927 the Circuit's members had decreased by 40 per cent and the number of Sunday school teachers had fallen by almost a half.[26]

The preachers of experience and tested character were now old and some had died. Hewson Wray, a Hargrave preacher, had died in 1919. 'Especially at Camp Meetings was he a notable figure. His fellowship with God was real which made him a man of power in prayer'. My grandfather, Joseph Bradfield, died in January 1926. 'We rejoice in the fine work he did at Chevington and since his retirement in Hargrave'. At a Quarterly Meeting at Wickhambrook on 7 March 1925[27] Chevington's contributions occupied second place in the list but, in the main, the dearth of leadership in the Circuit and the reluctance of the younger generation to volunteer their services, resulted in a disastrous decline of rural nonconformity from which some individual chapels, including Chevington's, made no permanent recovery.

Education (II)

According to White's *Directory* (1844) William Parker was combining the craft of shoemaking with the art of schoolmastering but, in 1855, only one occupation is given for him: shoemaking. The reason for this curtailed activity could have been that a school had been built in 1847 by the National Society for the Education of the Poor. in the Principles of the Established Church, appropriately near to the Church of All Saints. The site on Moat, or Church, Green was given by the first Marquess of Bristol, a gift which received the active support of his son, Earl Jermyn. The cost of the building was approximately £600 towards which £40 per annum was paid from General Hervey's Charity for the 'general support' of the school.[28] In 1855, the education of the poor in Chevington was in the hands of Henry Needham Rising and his wife, Sophia.[29]

The building of the school exemplified the patronage of the Lord of the Manor, not only in Chevington, but in all the surrounding villages which formed part of the Bristol estate. In 1884 an additional room for infants was built on to the original school by the village builder, Jonathan Cooper, who had taken over the long-established firm from the Fenton family.

The large schoolroom, 38 feet long and 18 feet wide,[30] was stone-built with diamond-shaped window panes. It is apparent from the description that it was intended to house two separate 'schools' regardless of age, all the girls at one end of the room, all the boys at the other. The girls' yard was separate from that of the boys'. Two paths through the yards, divided by a high brick wall, led to the separate earth closets, euphemistically styled 'offices'. From the school's main passage, usually dark and bespattered with mud in the winter, a door led to the headteacher's sitting-room regarded by at least one unhappy pedagogue in the 1920s as a refuge from the hurly-burly of the schoolroom. The settlement of 3 May 1848 was explicit:[31]

> The said schools shall always be in unison with and conducted upon the principles and in furtherance of the ends . . . of the National Society for Promoting the Education of the Poor in the Principles of the Church of England and shall be open to Inspection under the manage-ment of the Rector of Chevington and Rector of Ickworth. The officiating Minister should be the chairman of the Committee. No person shall be appointed, or shall act as a master, or mistress, of the said school who shall not be a member of the Church of England.

It has been impossible to trace the school records for the mid-19th century but, when the accommodation of the National School at Chevington was reviewed, the managers were of the opinion that, if eight children were transferred to Horringer

National School,[32] Chevington would have no further accommodation problem. Moreover, the real remedy was two-fold: it was a matter of priorities: 'if the present Chevington National School is at once made efficient by improvement of the offices and the appointment of a certificated teacher, no further accommodation is required'.

In December 1875, however, the Reverend John White III, chairman of the managers, estimated that the school's income up to Michaelmas 1876 would be:[33]

	£	
Voluntary Subscriptions	70	
School Pence	11	
(31 boys, 33 girls and 18 infants would pay one penny a week)		
	£81	Total income

Expenditure	£	
Salary of Head Teacher	50	
Salary of Assistant	40	
Fuel and Lights	10	
Repairs	5	
Books and Apparatus	5	
Other Expenses	5	
	£115	Total expenditure

The Chairman and his fellow signatory, Joseph Simkin, did not indicate how the deficit of £34 was met. It was likely that either he, or the Marquess of Bristol, who was an *ex officio* member of the committee of managers, voluntarily balanced the accounts to avoid the slightest financial embarrassment.

At their meeting on 13 July 1903 the Foundation Managers agreed to accept the very satisfactory report from His Majesty's Inspectors and to appoint a school cleaner at £5 5s. 0d. (£5.25p.) a year.[34] On 1 August 1904 a letter was received from the Marquess nominating himself as a manager 'in accordance with the provisions of the order'. A teacher at the school, Miss Bridge, the daughter of Alfred Bridge, one of the Foundation Managers, was to have an increase in salary from £20 to £30 a year and Allan E. Kerridge, presumably another teacher, 'had to sign that he was a member of the Church of England'.[35] Furthermore, the signature had to be witnessed.

Brief and straightforward, the minutes refer to inspectors' reports, the occasional detail concerning the appointment of a teacher and frequent entries deploring blocked drains. Curricular matters and comments on individual pupils were very rare. There was an appropriate reference to the Chairman, the Reverend John White III, 'their first and only chairman and correspondent', who died in 1908. In an earlier year it was agreed to celebrate Empire Day on 24 May by having a lesson on the Empire in the morning and a half-day holiday in the afternoon. However, late in 1908, the Headmaster, Fred King, applied for permission to include gardening[36] in the curriculum. Mr. Fyson, a farmer of Ruffin's, expressed the opinion that

if boys could be persuaded to take an interest in such pursuits the knowledge ought to be useful to them when employed in agriculture. It was agreed that the correspondent apply to the Committee for necessary tools to cut three plots, four boys to a plot.

As a result of the zeal for gardening, the school playground was surrendered for plots. In future, Church Green, covered with mud and pools of dark water in the winter, was the official playground. It was there that boys played 'Mount-a-Kitty-mount-a-Kitty-one-two-three' at the stone wall surrounding the school and where occasional 'drill' lessons were inflicted on somewhat reluctant pupils. Boys followed a pattern of traditional games handed down by countless generations: in the spring, there were spinning tops, summer heralded the hoops and in the autumn conker fights, the contestants striking with conkers tied to string, had pride of place. A winning conker was the prized possession. Catapults, aimed at birds and prudently concealed from the village policeman, were the prerogative of the older boys. Girls, content with skipping games, would call in unison 'salt—mustard—vinegar—pepper' as the rope was turned with frenzied speed. Such seasonal folklore is now a mere memory down Chevington Way.

On 10 August 1910,[37] the 4th Marquess of Bristol inspected the school. Violet Coote was a pupil at the beginning of the century when the headmaster, Fred King, instructed the entire school on the importance of good manners and the correct etiquette of conducting themselves if. privileged to be spoken to by the Marquess. She says 'I remember what Mr. King told us but, after all that Lord Bristol didn't turn up when we were all expecting him'.

After the departure of Fred King and his family for Canada in 1910, the standard of the school declined noticeably. Shortly after the outbreak of the First World War, the school was inspected when the managers received an adverse report. However, ready to give praise where praise was due, the Inspectors declared: 'some creditable colour drawing has been done and the children sing nicely'.[38] However, it was clear that drastic improvement was necessary. 'Marked improvement in the general efficiency of the School will be expected on the occasion of His Majesty's Inspector's next visit if the payment of the grant in full is not to be endangered'. The improvement demanded by the inspectors was made by succeeding headteachers. Although standards fluctuated later, the level of attainment achieved at the school before the outbreak of the Second World War was noticeably high, and the managers congratulated those concerned.

Literacy and numeracy had rightly enjoyed pride of place in the school curriculum but it is, perhaps, unfortunate that, when the school covered the complete age range, i.e. up to 13 or 14 years, it was not possible to include in the school programme more practical and vocational issues. Such areas would have been relevant to those domestic and rural aspects of life to which virtually all pupils would be introduced on leaving school. Violet Coote (who as Violet Arbon left school in 1911) clearly states that needlework was her favourite subject. When Ol Pettit left school at the end of the First World War:

> Everything was difficult because we had not recovered from the War. On the farm I was sometimes horse keeper, sometimes milkman and any other job that came along.

Alec Norman, now living at Westley Bottom, who left Chevington school at 14 in 1933, would have relished something mechanical. However, 20 years previously, Fred R. Hughes, the Secretary for Education for West Suffolk, published a report, *The Work of Education 1902-1914*, in which he had referred to the cost of providing so-called manual training:

for gardening instruction, however, a plot of ground, a few sets of tools, and the necessary seeds, can be supplied at no great expense and, in addition, this subject has the special advantage of being congenial to country children.

In 1903 there were five school gardens in West Suffolk: in 1914 there were 45. It was clear that boys, on leaving school at 14, were well trained in an activity which was to play an important economic part in their lives at a later stage.

Changes at the Rectory

In 1864 Jonathan Cooper was appointed parish clerk by the rector. Jonathan married Hannah, daughter of the schoolmaster, William Parker, who died, apparently from tuberculosis, at a very early age. Three years later he married her sister, Elizabeth, after whose death, allegedly from the same prevalent affliction, he married at the age of 30 for the third time. This time his bride was Mary Rachel Avery, who was my grandmother. Tuberculosis, the scourge of the 19th century, although diminished in intensity, continued into the 1930s when I recall people in the locality dying from the disease. To arrest its spread by providing patients with maximum sunlight and air two wooden huts were erected in the village.

The Reverend John White II, who had ministered to the spiritual needs of Chevington for 33 years, had died on 9 July 1851 at the relatively early age of 65. His gravestone, to the west of the tower of the church, which includes the name of his wife, Mary, is slowly crumbling. The fading inscription reads: 'The Lord knoweth the days of the godly and their inheritance shall endure for ever'. In a separate grave lies Edmund Keble White, his second son, who was a victim of typhoid fever and died a few months before his father at the age of 20 while an undergraduate at Trinity College, Cambridge. Mary, 20 years younger than her husband, died in 1884. She had lost her husband, her infant children, two sons in their twenties and a daughter, Mary Catherine, aged 35, the wife of General Rawlins. The inscription on the gravestone is poignantly apt: 'In the multitude of the sorrows that I had in my heart Thy comforts have refreshed my soul'.

In his will[39] the Reverend John White II had provided for Mary and for all his children. He left the living of Chevington to his eldest son who became the Reverend John White III in 1853 and, on condition that he had qualified for priest's orders, the third son, Cyril, was presented with the living of Hargrave. At the time of his father's death Cyril was still at school in Bury. Therefore, in accordance with the terms of the very long will, the living of Hargrave was offered to the late rector's nephew, John White Westhorpe, his sister Mary's son, who was then living at Long Melford. The Reverend John White Westhorpe took up residence with his aunts at Chevington Grove and remained Rector of Hargrave until 1859.

John White III was the third John to have been at Caius College, Cambridge. He attended Edward VI Grammar School, Bury St Edmunds, as did his two brothers, Edmund Keble and Cyril, during the headmastership of Doctor Donaldson, the eminent Hebrew scholar. After reading Classics at Cambridge (he was a prizeman in 1848 and 1849), young John was ordained deacon in 1852,[40] but was unable to continue the tenure of the Whites as patron and rector of Chevington until he was ordained priest. The years 1853–55 were of lasting significance in his life. It was in 1854 that his younger brother Cyril, in his second year at Trinity College, Cambridge, decided to end his university studies. The Crimean War had begun and Cyril joined the 12th Lancers. Later, as Lieutenant Cyril White, he sailed for India and, in 1857, fought in the Mutiny. He died of fever in 1859 aged 23, at Nagoda, Central India.[41] A mural on the north wall of the chancel of the Church of All Saints, giving a full account of his short but, distinguished, career is an enduring tribute to a soldier who had known a simpler life among footpaths, trees and hedgerows. In 1855, at the age of 26, the Reverend John White III married Caroline Macdonell Rawlins of Handsworth, Staffordshire, who was a descendant of the Clan Macdonell of Glengarry. Later John's younger sister Mary Catherine married Caroline's brother, Major Alexander Macdonell Rawlins who, in course of time, attained the rank of general. The Macdonells were soldiers and, as such, had had brilliant military records. It is interesting to speculate how the Whites of Chevington in their Suffolk seclusion could ever come to know the Rawlins and Macdonell families whose style was markedly different from the academic and rural pursuits which characterised their own lives. John White and Caroline Macdonell were to control the social and hierarchical life of Chevington from 1853 to 1908, a reign of 55 years.

Agricultural change

Such a span witnessed great changes in farming and in rural life. A *Directory of Suffolk* (1855) emphasised a change in the accepted tradition:

> The old custom of letting the land lie idle one year in every three, for the advantages of what are called fallowing has here been long exploded, the necessity for it being superseded by a judicious course of cropping so that one crop may fertilize as another exhausts.[42]

Machinery, first experimentally, then more confidently, came into use in Chevington, and it is interesting to note that the *Directory* comments:[43]

> Both wheat and barley are either drilled (for which several kinds of ingeniously contrived barrow drills are used) or else planted with the hand by women and children, called dibbling.

In 1973 my aunt, Mary Jane Bradfield, then aged 92, wrote of her childhood in the early 1890s:

> I remember the men cutting the corn with scythes and their wives rolling and tying the sheaves by hand. I remember the sail machine cutting the corn and throwing the sheaves off to be tied by hand, and then the self-binder which tied the sheaves with binder twine. I have seen the engine coming to thresh the corn and now they have machines to cut and thresh at the same time. I have seen peas and beans threshed by hand with a flail on the barn floor. I remember the old iron plough, the harrows, roller chaff cutter, and the hand mangold and swede grinder. We made butter using a separator which strained and took the cream out of the milk straight away. There were no pans to be set and no skimming off of cream which had to be stirred twice a day. Churning day came on Monday. With a thermometer it was got to the right temperature and put into the churn which father usually turned by handle for anything from ½ to ¾ hour when we knew by the sound of it that cream had turned to butter and was ready for the buttermilk to be strained off.

By the end of the century the increased demand for agricultural machinery in the area prompted John Sangster of Moor's Farm to establish himself in Chevington as agricultural machinist. Traction engines were loaned to farmers and were a familiar sight until the 1920s when the tractor steadily gained precedence.

Juvenile labour on the farms was prominent throughout most of the century. In 1871 Samuel Talbot, aged 12, was employed at Ruffin's farm; George and Aaron Nunn, aged 11 and nine, worked at Hollybush. In 1861 a 12-year-old boy, John Fenton, is described as an assistant to his bricklayer father, and Alfred Osborne, aged 11, and John Nunn, 12, of Church Green, were listed as agricultural labourers. It was usual for children to start work at the age of 10. Women, too, worked on the fields. At 'haysal' and harvesting they would be particularly active, but they also helped at other times, particularly in 'clearing up' and with planting.

The clothing factory

1852 was a memorable year in the economic life of Chevington. According to White's *Directory* 1855 it was then that a factory was established in the village for the production of ready-made clothes mainly for the London and overseas market. Employing by 1861 about 600 women as in-workers, part-time or full time, or as out-workers, the factory was destined to play a crucial part, not only in the economy of the parish then with a population of 621, but in a large, scattered rural area, and to offer invaluable opportunities for supplementing the meagre pay of farm workers. It was a far-reaching rural enterprise.

For some years after 1855 William Beales, who was living in Bury St Edmunds, was classified as a clothes manufacturer at Chevington and at centres in Essex. From 1865, Samuel Beales, apparently William's son, was listed as manager to William Beales. An examination of the census return of 1871[44] reveals that Samuel, aged 36, who was then living in Malting Farm, Chevington, was born in Denston, Suffolk, but nothing is known of his father's early life.

Until quite recently, a farm situated along a lane off the Chedburgh Road, now occupied by Michael McCormack, was known as Factory Farm and the lane as Factory Lane. The enumerator of the 1871 Census, Jonathan Cooper, referred to the lane as Old Factory Lane which suggests that the original factory was at the farm at the bottom of the track. It is of interest and, perhaps, of importance to note that in the same year Alfred Smith, aged 33, a porter at the later clothing factory, is listed as living in part of Factory Farm, an entry which could be mere coincidence but, equally, suggestive of a continuing link between the Old Factory and the later wooden buildings on Hargrave Road. It is very probable, therefore, that the present granary at Factory Farm was the original factory of 1852 and that it remained operative until the new purpose-built manufactory was ready for production.

Constructed partly of brick and partly of timber, the slated granary, now used as a store, is a two-storey building. Part of the ground floor is open, presumably for the storage of wagons and, inside, a wooden staircase ascends to a long, low room which extends the full length of the building. It is lined with wood and has some small glazed windows, unusual features for a farm building intended mainly for the storage of grain. Through the large opening on the first floor, boxes, or baskets, containing completed garments could have been lowered into horse-wagons below. Before the railway station was opened in Saxham in 1854 it is likely that the goods were taken to the station in Bury. Albert Gooch, farmer, took over the so-called Factory Farm in 1904. His daughter, Lettie Ollett, still living in Chevington, is certain that the family was brought up to accept that their granary was the original clothing factory.

An examination of reference books and Post Office directories in the Guildhall Library[45] elicits the information that Messrs. Robert and Henry Parnall were wholesale clothiers, shirtmakers and outfitters of Bishopsgate, London. A Henry Parnall was trading there as early as 1838, but the first mention of Robert *and* Henry was in 1849. In 1861, a directory includes after the firm's address the information 'and manufactory, Chevington, Suffolk'. Among the assorted papers at Tan Office Farm, is a reference dated 1862 to 'a newly-built clothing factory'. Moreover, there appears to have been some exchange of conditions of sale of land between Messrs. Parnall and John Brewster, the village grocer, on 21 February 1862. As the village shop was less than 30 yards from the site of the factory, it is reasonable to suggest that John Brewster, owned land in the vicinity. The 1861 census return[46] clearly states that the manager of the 'Factory for wholesale manufactures of men's clothing especially for exportation' was William Beales of Cheveley and that the proprietors were Messrs. Robert and Henry Parnall & Co. of 187, Bishopsgate Street Without, E.C.2, wholesale clothiers, shirtmakers and outfitters. There were 30 sewing machines in the factory and there was a labour force, 'in and out of the factory, of six hundred persons in this and adjoining parishes'.

'Manufactory' was probably a more accurate name for what was a large workshop and not, in the strictest sense, a factory which could imply the application of power-driven machinery. As late as 1903, in a letter from a firm of Colchester solicitors to the then owners, there was a reference to the building's deficiency in steam, gas and motor power. It is virtually certain that in 1861–62, Messrs. Parnall built the large complex 'of brick & weatherboard', consisting of one large, high workshop and ancillary departments, on Hargrave Road, and appointed William Beales, the original owner-manager, to serve as manager of the new manufactory. The new wooden buildings were built on the west side of the road, about a hundred yards from the *Greyhound*. The 'Factory', known as such, not only by the people of Chevington but by the entire local community, existed for nearly 130 years, many years after the buildings had ceased to fulfil their original purpose. The reasons for a long-established East London firm to choose Chevington as a satellite site remain obscure unless Beales himself was in a favourable position to exert influence on the Parnalls. There was certainly spare labour not only in the village, but in Saxham and in Risby; Bury Railway Station was easily accessible from Liverpool Street Station and the London rail terminus was a short distance from Bishopsgate where Messrs. Robert and Henry Parnall & Co. were established. It is reasonable to think that the ready-made clothes from Chevington's clothing factory were transported to the neighbouring St Katharine's Dock and, finally, to markets overseas. There remained one further advantage of dealing direct with the Bury Branch of the East Union Railway in preference to Saxham and Risby: 'The Electric telegraph is in use here, and by it messages can be transmitted to London and other distant places, and answers received in a few minutes'.[47]

In 1861[48] 600 operatives, either in- or out-workers from Chevington and the neighbouring villages, were employed by Messrs. Parnall. Although there were only 30 sewing machines in use in the factory it is evident, mainly from later Census Returns, that women were employed in many associated operations such as coatmaking, dressmaking, tailoring, laundering and pressing. Employment at the clothing factory supplemented the family income and the following examples are typical: in 1861 Robert Argent,[49] a shoemaker, and Ann his wife, had a family of nine: three sons, aged 17, 13 and 10, were agricultural labourers; Joseph, aged 15, was a shoemaker, no doubt helping his father; two daughters, aged 14 and 11, worked in the clothing factory; two young children, aged 7 and 6, were scholars at the village school and the youngest, aged 5, was at home. In the same year William Smith aged 54, was an agricultural labourer, his wife, Amelia, aged 46, was an operative in the clothing factory, as were their two daughters Elizabeth and Mary: John, aged, 17, was an agricultural labourer, and his young sister, Jane, was at school. At Hargrave, 'Harriatt' Pryke was a tailoress, and her two daughters, Alice and 'Joannah', both worked in the 'machine factory'. In the early 1860s Fanny Cross, Susannah Clarke and Mary Pask, all aged 10, were listed as workers, but the 1867 Workshop Regulation Act prohibited the employment of children under eight years of age and those between the ages of eight and 13 were allowed to work only half a day.

The in-workers sat at treadle machines which were arranged in two long rows in the main workshop.[50] It was probably here that the coats, jackets and trousers were completed, the various parts of the garments such as sleeves and collars having been made up at home. On the large tables in the factory there was room to assemble and press the garments, to mark them according to size and, finally, to pack them securely ready for dispatch.

It is impossible to infer from the census returns of 1861–81 the number of women who were part-time, or full-time but, what is of greater relevance, there are no records of the very large number of women of Chevington and of the surrounding villages who must have worked entirely at home. Most operatives included in the 600 who, according to directories, were employed at the factory, were domestically-based workers who could have walked considerable distances to Chevington to receive instructions, to obtain material and then, on returning to the factory with their finished work, to collect their fresh assignments. Oral accounts contributed from parishioners support that generalisation. The total number of operatives obviously exceeded those listed in the census returns, but it is by no means certain that all the workers listed as 'dressmaker' or 'tailoress', were ever employed in the Chevington manufactory. However, the probability is strong. Allowing for those and similar imponderables the returns can be summarised as follows:

Village	Number of Workers in Factory		Number of Females according to Census	
	1861	1881	1861	1881
Chevington	46	42	327	268
Chedburgh	22	18	158	122
Depden	10	8	130	118
Hargrave	23	17	255	202
Great Saxham	5	4	126	122
Ickworth	1	1	38	51
Total	107	90	1,034	883

It is likely that other female workers were from the village of Barrow, before the manufactory was built there, from Whepstead and from Bury St Edmunds, but there were only 883 females in the six villages in 1881. It is clear from the above table that the annual total of workers for each year represents approximately one-sixth of the workforce of 600 employees. Therefore, about five hundred workers could well have been entirely home-based. The management necessary to distribute the material to those workers and to arrange for the finished work to be returned appears inordinate. Walter Blake, aged 85, reports that there was a reception centre for the factory in Denston, five miles distant. Home workers from the surrounding villages, Wickhambrook, Stansfield and Stradishall, having collected their material, returned their finished work to Denston.

Samuel Beales is listed as the manager in Harrod's *Directory* of 1864, but there is no indication that he lived in the village until 1871 when he and his wife Elizabeth appear to have acquired the Malting Farm from John Kemp. Samuel, aged 36, is described as 'Manager of Clothing Factory'. There were three children: the eldest daughter, Ann, having been born in Manchester where her father, then a young man of 22, may well have obtained some valuable experience of clothing manufacture. White's *Directory* of December 1874 lists Samuel Beales as manager, still living at the Malting, and William Beales, 'tailor, etc.' as living in Skinner Lane (Street), Bury St Edmunds and 'at Chevington' but, as no house in Chevington is shown to be occupied by William, it may be assumed that he maintained general oversight of the Chevington factory while living in Bury, detailed management of the 600 women being delegated to Samuel.

At the same time as William Beales was based in Skinner Street the enterprising family of William Henry Smith was also living in Bury.[51] William Henry himself, linen and woollen draper, conducted his business from 24, The Butter Market with his sons Cornelius, William Henry II and, later, the youngest son, Joseph. In addition to establishing William Henry Smith & Sons 'the wholesale and retail linen and woollen drapers, silk mercers, haberdashers, hosiers and general warehousemen and wholesale clothing manufacturers' operating from the Butter Market, he showed remarkable adaptability and business acumen in extending his enterprise to the nearby Cornhill where he traded with another son, Samuel Candler Smith, as W. H. Smith & Son: 'wholesale hardwaremen, general factors of foreign merchandise, importers of American clocks, earthenware, glass and china, trunk and blacking manufacturers, and lamp and oil merchants'. By 1875 this remarkable family had established a clothing manufactory in Barrow, a village about six miles west of Bury St Edmunds, and had acquired, no doubt from Messrs. Parnall, the clothing factories at Cowlinge and at Chevington.

William Henry Smith,[52] the son of Thomas Smith, a tenant farmer at what is now Blackhorse Farm, Wickhambrook, was born in 1799. His entire life exemplified not only the nonconformist tradition, but acumen founded on a capacity for hard work and commitment to service. His third marriage in 1857 was to a widow, Mary Ann Young who, according to the census returns of 1861-71, was born in Chevington, the daughter of Robert Adams, farmer. A study of the 1841 census returns reveals that a Robert Adams was then living at Hollybush Farm, but there is no known association between William Henry's marriage and his later acquisition of Chevington's factory. There is no evidence that he ever lived in the village, but his son, William Henry II, who inherited the Butter Market property after the death of his father in 1884, was living at Chevington Lodge in 1896.

In his will dated January 1884 William Henry Smith I,[53] having provided for a daughter and two sons, noted that 'my said son William Henry Smith [had] been already provided for by me'. The provision included the clothing factory at Chevington.

Samuel Beales is named as the manager of the clothing factory in the 1881 Census Return and in Kelly's *Directory* of 1885. William Beales was still living in Queen's Road, Bury, in 1902, apparently in extended retirement. The factory continued to flourish, the comment in Kelly's *Directory* of 1904 echoing that of the 1850s — 'in the village is a clothing factory employing a great number of females'. As no member of the W. H. Smith family can be traced as living in Chevington after the death of William Henry II in 1902, it may be concluded that the manufactory was sold at that time.

In his last will and testament, dated 9 May 1898[54] William Henry Smith II, of Chevington in the county of Suffolk, clothing manufacturer, having disposed of personal effects and of his shop and house in the Butter Market at Bury St Edmunds, decreed: 'All the rest of my real estate and all my personal estate & effects whatsoever and wheresoever, I direct my Trustees to convert into money by sale . . .'. His estate, including the clothing factory in Chevington, was valued at £4,300 18s. 7d. (£4,300.93p.). William Henry Smith II died four years later. The trustees arranged a sale: Chevington's factory was on the market.

A firm, Richmond and Lewis, of Colchester, were the owners in 1903[55] and a mantle manufacturer, Frank Wigley,[56] was prominent in the village seven years later. The last owners before the clothing factory closed in 1918 appear to have been J. Harvey & Co. of St John's Street, Bury, who remained in business in the town until 1937. Some parishioners still remember the factory at Chevington during the 1914–18 War, but the number of workers had declined seriously.

Violet Coote (*née* Arbon), aged 85 and now living in Bury St Edmunds, worked in the factory on leaving Chevington School in 1911 at the age of 13. In a conversation she recalls her days there:

> The factory was Harvey's in my time. The manager was Mr. Snell from Barrow. We lived on the Hargrave Road, near the factory. Others had to walk a long way, or come on bikes, and it was hard when it was dark. My mother, Sarah Arbon, already worked there; my father, Arthur George, worked for John Sangster on his threshing machines. I worked sometimes from 8 a.m.– 8 p.m. from Monday to Friday, but only four hours on Saturday. There were no holidays, only Saturday afternoons and on Sundays when we went to Church. We had cocoa at 11 a.m. and one hour off for dinner, so we sometimes worked for 59 hours a week. My mother had £1 a week: sometimes I worked the same hours for 10s. 0d. [50p.]. As far as I remember the pay would not have been more than 15s. 0d. [75p.] a week. Mother took work home very often. I worked the button-hole machine and helped to make ladies' coats. My mother was a sample hand and she made ladies' coats, capes and little boys' trousers, but some men's clothes were made. Sometimes she worked in velvet. Our machines were treadle machines, in rows. I think there was only one man working in the factory.
>
> Between thirty and fifty women worked in the factory. Some did the cutting out, others pressing. They worked on separate tables. There was a large stove, fed by coke, where the pressers heated their irons. Sometimes it was very hot in the factory and we took potatoes to bake on the stove. The toilet was bad. Luckily, we lived quite near.
>
> The factory was very large and high and we had hanging paraffin lamps with shades over each machine. Later, there were pressure lamps which went low so we couldn't see. We would have to call out, 'It's getting low, it's getting low, we can't see!'.
>
> Sometimes a Mr. Pearce came to look at our cutting. I think he came from London.
>
> The people who worked at home would bring back the things they made and give them in at a little window in the small room. They came from all over the place and walked a long way. We queued for our pay there.
>
> The finished clothes were packed in large wicker baskets. There were wicker baskets everywhere. There was a big pulley to load them on Nimbly Nunn's wagon which was pulled

by two horses. Nimbly took them to Saxham Station and he collected stuff from there. Sometimes my brother Fred took them. I left the factory in 1914 when I was 16.

Violet Coote remembers 15 fellow workers by name; six came from Hargrave, two from Saxham, one from Depden, one from Chedburgh and five from Chevington itself. Her sister, Lily Clarry (now aged 87 and still living in the parish) worked in the factory at a later date; she has said 'We had to work very hard and the wages were low'.

The main reasons for closure are unknown but, by 1920, the empty buildings were bought by the agricultural machinist John Sangster who, after an interval of some years, sold the premises to Alfred Cawston Rolfe, a haulage contractor, who used the old factory premises as a petrol station. Eric Rolfe, of Chevington, brother of Alfred, who worked at the garage, says 'I remember all the buttons, the crane in the roof and the old blackout curtains of the 1914–18 War'. Job Willis, of Chevington, who worked as a clerk in the garage for many years after the 1939–45 War, writes:

in the passage way on the left of the main doors was a small sliding panel 14 or 15 inches wide and about 2 feet high through which factory workers were paid their weekly wages. Mr. Rolfe told me of all the buttons, cottons and pins which were lying about when he first started.

In the 1920s, the growth of the sugar beet industry in West Suffolk necessitated the transport of the pulled beet to the Sugar Beet Factories in Lavenham and later in Bury St Edmunds, so the haulage business, together with the ancillary provision of the petrol, taxi and servicing stations, were in brisk demand. The business continued for 60 years, until 1981, when the former wooden factory was irrevocably gutted by fire. A Chevington landmark, reminiscent of a great enterprise, had passed into oblivion.

The Reverend John White III

Although changes were discernible, the main flow of social life in the village continued throughout the second half of the 19th century. The Reverend John White, his wife, Caroline, and their large family provided the fulcrum for the rural community of Chevington. The main focal point was clear to all: an event in the life of the Whites was a major event in the life of the parisioners. On the occasion of the impending marriage of John White's daughter, Sara Geraldine, to M. de Perrot of Neuchâtel, Switzerland, a large and handsome collection of wedding presents was shown to all the parishioners who chose to call at the rectory:

Every women received a new shilling and every child a penny.[57] Good wishes and congratulations were abundant and reciprocal. On Tuesday a deputation (Mr. Bridge, Mr. Ward, Mr. Cooper and Mr. Byford) attended to present a gift from the parish, subscribed for by every inhabitant. The present was a handsome spirit stand and biscuit box. The villagers had built three floral arches between the Rectory and the Church door, inscribed with mottoes, 'Farewell, Miss White', 'God bless the happy pair', 'Our best wishes attend you', 'Health and happiness' and, over the Church porch, 'A happy New Year to the Bride and Bridegroom'.

The damaged undated cutting from a local newspaper adds that among the bridesmaids were 'Miss Millais (daughter of Sir J. Millais, the great painter)'.

It is of interest to note that on 2 February 1882, John White's youngest daughter, Edith Macdonell White, who was deaf and dumb, married William Randall who was also a deaf mute: 'The breakfast and rooms were adorned with a profusion of the most recherché flowers, the gift of the Marchioness of Bristol'. Again the parishioners presented an impressive trophy, 'a handsome English skeleton time-piece' and, inevitably, the bells of the Church of All Saints rang throughout the day, and in the evening the handbell ringers attended at the rectory'.[58]

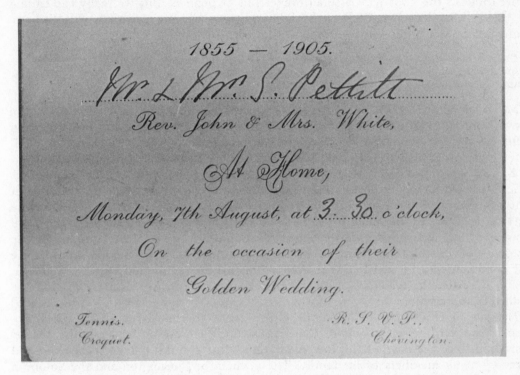

6. Invitation extended to parishioners by the Rector and Mrs. John White, 1905.

There appeared to be a continuing relationship, authoritarian, but benign, between the Whites and their parisioners. A newspaper cutting of February 1901 gives an account of the funeral of Mrs. Blackburn who, for many years, was in service at the rectory and who was the wife of Robert Blackburn, the Whites' coachman. She was evidently respected by all the family, some of whom attended the funeral such as Mrs. White, Major-General Alexander Rawlins, and the Reverend Arthur Keble White, the son of the rector. There were floral tributes from Madame Geraldine de Perrot, the rector's daughter, and other members of the family, indicative of their respect for their former employee 'who, for several years had suffered from a painful malady, but bore her sufferings with cheerfulness and fortitude, having a bright smile and hearty words for all'. The Reverend John White III conducted the funeral. The village schoolmaster, Mr. Fred King, played *O Rest in the Lord* and, as a concluding voluntary, the Dead March from *Saul*. The coachman's wife had been given an impressive valediction.

Another newspaper report, 1902, gives prominence to the importance of 'Valentining':

> The young inhabitants were kindly encouraged by the Rector and several gentlemen to observe the ancient custom.

The children visited the chosen residences at the appointed hour to say, 'Good morrow, Valentine', to the various patrons in return for which they received 'liberal gifts of money and fruit'. Irene Pettit, aged 86 (1983), remembers that 'Mrs. John White came to the door with a small basket full of pennies. But we really had to sing for them'. Miss Joscelyn, of Bury St Edmunds, another octogenarian, writes of her grandmother, Mrs. John White, a Macdonell of Glengarry:

> She was tall — and no nonsense! She was wonderful in the village, looking after the people and seeing what she could do for them when they were ill. She walked miles around the village until she was too old and had a pony and 'tub' cart.

Mr. John White, the rector's eldest son, apparently continued to live in Chevington Grove, part of the Whites' estate, until after the sale of that estate to Lord Bristol in 1898. He was the first John for three generations not to continue his family's ecclesiastical rule at Chevington, but he was described in 1902 as a principal landowner. In Kelly's *Court Directory* of that year John White, a landowner of Chevington, was officially listed as an 'esquire'. His father, the Reverend John White III, was at that time a member of the West Suffolk County Council, a Justice of the Peace for the Western Division of the County of Suffolk and Chairman of the Bench. The Lord Lieutenant and *Custos Rotulorum** for the County was the Most Honourable the Marquess of Bristol. The publican of North Walsham, William White, would have had good cause to be satisfied with the advance of his family and even the Herveys, who had settled in Ickworth 400 years previously as country squires, would have nodded in approbation.

The sale in 1898 of the Chevington Grove estate to the Marquess of Bristol profoundly shocked the parisioners of Chevington, for it had not only been in the Whites' possession since the days of the Reverend John White I, but it had been the cherished home of many members of his family. The yeoman of Chevington and the Solomon Milks had regarded it as an outward and visible sign of the Whites' beneficient authority in matters of church and parochial concern. Village gossip was rife and the occasion was still regarded as a mystery 40 years after the event.

In spite of the loss of his territorial power in the village, and of the enhanced influence of the Marquess of Bristol, the Reverend John White III maintained a high level of respect and esteem among the people of Chevington, a reputation which was only slightly dependent on squirarchical prestige. A map of the village in the Catalogue of Sale shows a Mr. Nutter as the owner of part of Farrow's Meadow, traditionally regarded as the glebe, and landscaped in order to present a park-like appearance from the windows of the rectory's panelled drawing room. The family of Nutter was to play a prominent part in the history of the Whites but, for another 10 years, the continuity of their leadership was assured, a stability to which the Solomon Milks later looked back with affection and pride.

Subsequent to the Local Government Act 1894 which had established parish councils, the first Parish Meeting was held in the school on 28 March 1895. The Reverend John White III was Chairman of the Council, Jonathan Cooper was Clerk, and one of the councillors was 'John White Esq.', the rector's eldest son. The 'Esq.' was usually appended after the name which appeared in the minutes of the Parish

7. *Plates from the catalogue of the sale of Chevington Grove Estate, 1898.*

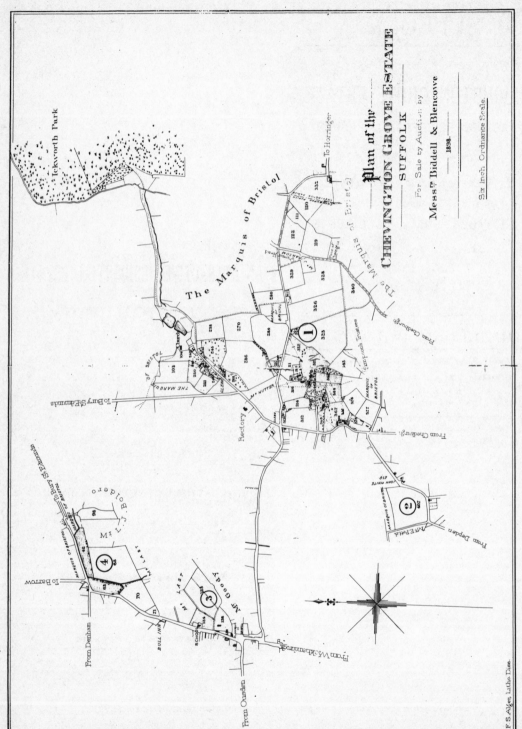

8. *Plan showing the extent of the Chevington Grove Estate, owned by the Reverend John White III at the time of its sale by auction, 1898. The estate was purchased by the 3rd Marquess of Bristol.*

Council until April 1912, the likely year of his departure from Chevington Grove on his appointment as agent for Sir George Agnew's estate at Rougham. Other parish councillors were John Evered of the Shop, Alfred Bridge of the Hall Farm, John Sangster, the agricultural machinist, Samuel Pettit, farmer, and later, Joseph Bradfield, my maternal grandfather, of the Hall Farm. The duties of clerk were retained by Jonathan Cooper until his death in 1904 when the village schoolmaster, Fred King, was appointed to succeed him.

The last time that the Reverend John White, J.P., M.A., signed the minutes of the Parish Meeting was 4 March 1907. The business transacted was never demanding, but on that occasion the minutes were mysteriously brief, almost prophetic:

> Parish Meeting held Tuesday 27th March 1906. The Rev. John White presided. The Chairman presented the accounts of the Lady Kytson's and Paman's Charity which were passed. No other business being forthcoming, the Chairman closed the meeting.

The Chairman, the Reverend John White III, died suddenly in 1908 after a long and momentous reign. On 21 February 1908 the *Bury Post* published the news that stunned West Suffolk:

> The mournful toll of the tenor bell on Monday evening at half-past nine conveyed the news to the sorrowing parish that their dear rector had passed away. Father of the parish . . . he was ready to aid by his sound practical advice or, where necessary, from his purse.

As a Justice of the Peace John White had presided over the Thingoe and Thedwastre Bench: 'He tempered justice with mercy. The name White spelt Chevington'. The full report alluded to the very close association between the Marquess of Bristol and Chevington Rectory and 'the loss of a beloved friend whose memory would be forever remembered and venerated by the people of Chevington'.

On the south wall of the chancel of the Church of All Saints there is a mural tablet in his memory. The heraldic arms include a white swan with the motto *Cantabit Moriens* (he will sing while dying). According to the College of Arms[59] the shield is that of Sir William White, draper, who was Lord Mayor of London in 1489 to which, no doubt, the late Reverend John had a right, although the descent has not yet been traced. This leading personality, warm, reassuring, and generous had passed from the homes of Chevington; my father, then a young man of 27, was deeply moved; the entire village mourned their loss and Solomon Milk doffed his cap as the cortège moved silently and slowly from the rectory towards the Church of All Saints.

Politics

Members of the landed families, the Herveys of Ickworth, the Jermyns of Rushbrooke and, later, the Fitzroys of Euston, usually represented Bury St Edmunds and Suffolk in Parliament. As early as 1614 Sir Thomas Hervey and Sir Thomas Jermyn, both ancestors of the Marquesses of Bristol, were M.P.s for Bury. In 1714 Lord Hervey received an earldom for supporting the Hanoverian cause and, throughout the 18th century, the family remained influential Whigs. In December 1806 the Right Honourable John Upton, Viscount Templetown, brother-in-law of the 5th Earl, later the 1st Marquess of Bristol, was elected for Bury.

In 1832, the county was divided into two. Chevington and the surrounding villages of the western division elected Col. Robert Rushbrooke, who had acquired his family's ancestral home at Rushbrooke Hall by arrangement with the Herveys. At that time two Privy Councillors who had served in no less than six Parliaments represented Bury: Lord Charles Fitzroy, son of the Duke of Grafton, and Earl Jermyn, eldest son of the 1st Marquess of Bristol who, in 1859, succeeded as 2nd Marquess having sat for the borough in seven Parliaments. Possession of land was the passport to power over people. Such authority was softened by the paternalism extended to Solomon Milk, but this ceased during the late 19th century because of the democracy engendered by the extended franchise and by the election of county and parish councils. In future Solomon Milk would be able to express his opinion on local and national affairs by secret ballot, free from the surveillance of his masters.

In 1884 Solomon Milk received the vote. The following year, Chevington was allocated to the Sudbury division when the future Sir William Cuthbert Quilter, Bt., J.P., a Liberal of Hintlesham Hall, was returned to Parliament. At a time of acute agricultural depression the farm workers had voted Liberal in defiance of the continuing Conservatism of the farmers and squires. The market towns were Conservative. In 1885 Bury returned Lord Francis Hervey, brother of the 3rd Marquess of Bristol. From 1900-06 Bury elected a different type of Conservative, Sir E. Walter Greene, Bt., a sporting country gentleman. He was a member of the Suffolk Foxhounds, and of the Carlton and Cavalry Clubs. In 1906 Sir Walter was succeeded as M.P. by Captain Frederick William Fane Hervey, nephew of the 3rd Marquess of Bristol, who served one year before succeeding to the peerage as 4th Marquess.

Chevington and its rural neighbours elected a Liberal M.P. in 1906, and again from 1918-22 and from 1923-4. However, in 1924 Col. H.W. Burton, O.B.E., was elected Conservative member, polling nearly 54% of the vote. As a young man he had fought in the South African and First World Wars. During 1939-45 he commanded the 1st Essex Battalion of the Home Guard. In the 1920s election posters were stuck on the coalhouse at Chevington and on the barrels of tar piled along the road verges. The Marquess of Bristol's tenant at Chevington Grove, Major Rawdon, and Rev. Arthur Keble White called at homes to offer parishioners lifts to the polling booth. The rector's car, referred to as 'Keble's Tin Lizzie', exhibited a large blue rosette on the bonnet. The senior boys chanted on their way to school: 'Vote, vote, vote for Colonel Burr . . . ten, Kick them others up the arrse . . .' Generally, farmers voted Conservative, Primitive Methodists Liberal and Solomon Milk was unpredictable. Colonel Burton held his seat until 1945 when, for the first time in the constituency, the electorate returned a Labour member with a majority of 247. The election exemplified the spirit of a new age. The old type of aristocratic conservatism and patronage had passed into history.

Agriculture and other occupations in the later 19th century

At the 1871 Census 15 farms were listed in Chevington: in 1881 there were 13, which suggests that non-farming tenants were living in at least two farmhouses, the land being cultivated by neighbouring farmers. The number of working farmers and farmers' sons remained more or less constant until the year 1871 when 29 are recorded. In 1881, there were 17. The following table indicates the size of seven representative farms in 1881 and the number of labourers employed by each tenant farmer.

A Selection of Chevington Farms 1881

Village area	Farm	Acreage	Farmer	Labour Force	
				Men	Boys
2,429 (approx.) acres	Lodge Farm	465 acres	Charles Dyer	12	3
(990 (approx.)	Ruffin's	300 ,,	William Paine	8	1
(hectares)	Hall Farm	250 ,,	Alfred Bridge	9	8
	Hollybush	200 ,,	James Finch	8	2
	Tan Office	92 ,,	John Steadman	2	1
	Horsepool	72 ,,	John Simkin	2	2
	Mill Farm	29 ,,	Albert Tredgett	1	—

The Marquess of Bristol was the principal landowner, and the second largest land-owner, the Reverend John White III, then owned 300 acres. Nine men and one boy were employed on the rector's three farms, which were cultivated by three tenants. In 1871, Thomas Gardener of the Lodge, a young man of 25 who farmed 450 acres, employed 27 men, 10 boys and five women together with an indoor staff of two servants and one groom. Gardener was evidently a man of some influence, for it was he a few years later who persuaded his landlord, the Marquess of Bristol, to build a new large house for the farm.[60] In 1871 William Paine of Ruffin's employed a total labour force of 17 (13 men and four boys) on his 300-acre farm;[61] ten years later, as is seen above, there were only nine. In 1871, James Finch of Hollybush employed 13 workers on his 200 acres; in 1881, there were 10.

The Lodge Farm[62]
1889–1890
Weekly Labour Account, ending Friday 10th October 1890

	Saturday	Monday	Tuesday	Wednesday	Thursday	Friday	Labour (i.e. wages)		
							£	s.	d.
Philip Clarke	Ploughing	Ploughing	Ploughing	Ploughing	Ploughing	Ploughing		13	0
William Clarke	Ploughing	Ploughing	Ploughing	Ploughing	Ploughing	Ploughing		13	0
John Smith	After Stock					⟶		11	6
Stanley Smith	Ploughing					⟶		11	0
Arthur Cross	Spreading Muck					⟶		11	0
James Sharpe	Filling Muck					⟶		11	0
Albert Clarke	Jobbing	Carting				⟶To Bury after sacks		4	6
Philip Smith	Ploughing		⟶	Absent	Ploughing	Ploughing		5	0
Fenton							1	1	0
							£5	1	0

Other costs for the week included thatching, horse-keeper's candles, 4 ft. broom, string
  for sacks.   Total = £2 12s. 10d.   2 12 10

                                                                           £7 13 10

NOTES: (i) Fenton's status is unknown.
            (ii) Some of the workers were undoubtedly boys.
            (iii) There were 15 labourers on the farm in 1881; there are 9 listed above.
            (iv) The farm was one of 465 acres at the time of the 1881 Census.

The reduction in the number of workers was due in the main to the acute depression in agriculture which started in the mid-1870s and lasted until the beginning of the following century. In the census return of 1881, 105 of a total population of 288 males of *all* ages were classified as farm labourers (i.e. 36.3 per cent.). Twenty years previously there had been 123 in a population of 293 males (i.e. 42 per cent.). It is clear, therefore, that, although the percentage of farm labourers decreased during the period 1861–81, approximately 40 per cent. of *all* males in the parish were still employed as such in the early 1880s. However, it is important to note that occupational mobility had markedly increased during the century. In the return under the Population Act of 1830, cited by Gage in his *Thingoe Hundred*, the population of Chevington is given as 573 and the number of families as 117, no less than 70 per cent. of whom were employed in agriculture, only 20 per cent. in 'trade, manufacture and handicraft' and 10 per cent in other pursuits.

Half Year's Rents: Marquess of Bristol's Estate, Chevington[63]

		Michaelmas 1878			Michaelmas 1888		
		£	s.	d.	£	s.	d.
Charles Dyer	Lodge Farm	300	0	0	175	0	0
Alfred Bridge	Hall Farm	150	0	0	100	0	0
John Simkin	Horsepool	54	0	0	43	5	0
Robert Rolfe	Hill House	70	0	0	52	0	0
Thomas Brown	—	7	10	0	7	10	0
James Finch	Hollybush	135	7	6	—		

From the Weekly Labour Account of the Lodge Farm 1889–90 (see page 69), it may be inferred that the number of men employed on Charles Dyer's 465 acre farm had decreased since 1881. His weekly expenses were £7 13s. 10d. (nearly £7.70p.) in 1890. The half-yearly rent was £175 in 1888 (see above). In 1878 the rent had been £300. Throughout the agricultural depressions of the 19th century the Marquesses of Bristol had shown consideration in rent assessment for which the tenant farmers and others had indicated their gratitude. In the dining room at Ickworth House there are two candelabra which were presented to the 1st Marquess by the tenants, one in 1826, the other in 1840, for not raising the rents during the recession — which was to recur with even deeper impact during the last quarter of the century.

In the Bristol Estate Book (Chevington) for Michaelmas 1887, Clare Sewell Read, M.P., wrote an introduction, presumably at the request of the printers of the provided book.[64] His summary presents a devastating commentary on the year under review:

> However dark and dreary for the British farmers' position at Michaelmas 1884 it is much worse than it was then. Four such years of a continued fall in the value of all farm produce has never been recorded in the days of modern agriculture. Not only did wheat come down to the unprecedented price of 32s. 0d. (£1.60p.) per quarter, but barley, wool, meat and dairy produce have all sunk in value until not one pays the cost of production.

There had been a series of disastrous harvests, particularly the harvest of 1879 which was not completed until late October. To aggravate conditions, the importation of relatively low-priced farm produce after 1860 by steam transport was a severe blow to the Suffolk farmer; consequently, the agricultural workers, most of whom were employed on a daily basis, found themselves without work or, at best, working severely reduced hours. During the 1890s the village farm workers were receiving about 12s. 0d. (60p.) a week. Jack Arbon of Chevington, a septuagenarian, and formerly a landworker, recalls the plight of his father's generation:

The hours of work were 6 a.m.–6 p.m., six days per week. No holidays. Xmas days only off. Plenty of poverty. A very modest existence and hard to make ends meet.

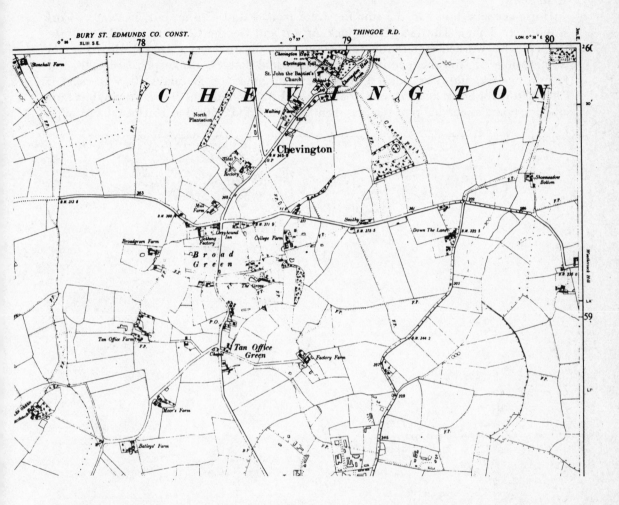

9. *The village centre, 1902, showing Chevington Way. Note the misnaming of the church following an error made by Gage in* History of Thingoe Hundred, *1838.*

A representative of the Royal Commission on Labour, probably Wilson Fox, visited Chevington on 15 June 1892 when John White Esq., landlord and farmer of Chevington Grove and eldest son of the rector, and 30 parish labourers were present to give evidence.[65] It was confirmed that the prevailing slump was responsible for the reduction of labour on farms, that a labourer was obliged to work from 'light to dark' in winter, and that he was allowed only half an hour for breakfast and an hour for dinner. In mitigation it was added that it was 'very unlikely that a man would always be sent back in wet weather'. Such treatment could reduce weekly pay by 2s. 0d. (10p.). It was agreed that the Solomon Milks preferred piece-work and Mr. White enthusiastically reminded the Commissioners that 'if piece-work is paid for at a fair price a man can earn 15s. 0d. a week' (75p.). There was the possibility of earning 3d. an hour overtime at 'haysal' and, although only at some farms, free beer was provided as an extra.

Horse-keepers' hours in the summer were from 4 a.m.–7 p.m. but, in winter, work stopped at 6 p.m. The fathers of Jack Arbon and George Copping were both horse-keepers who worked apparently for 'about 12s. 6d. (62½p.) a week)'. However, the Commissioners, after the meeting in 1892, reported that a horse-keeper earned 14s. 0d. (70p.) a week, but was obliged to work four hours on Sundays. It was usual in Chevington for horse-keepers and stockmen to be allocated rent-free cottages, but farm labourers paid an annual rent ranging from £3 10s. 0d (£3.50p.) to £5 10s. 0d. (£5.50p).

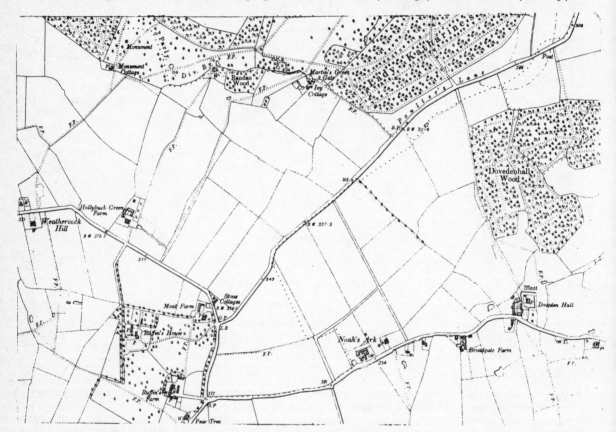

10.   *Moat Farm at Brooks's Corner and the road to Bury St Edmunds known as Poulter's Lane. Reproduced from the 1904 Ordnance Survey Map.*

There were many opportunities for girls to find work as domestic servants. Local girls were employed at the farms and at the large houses such as the rectory, the Grove and Ruffin's. In 1841, William Jennison of Chevington Lodge had two domestic servants, John Kemp at the Malting employed three and at the rectory there were no less than five. Twenty years later a housemaid, parlour maid, cook and a 20-year-old groom, Alfred Bridge, were considered necessary to staff Chevington Grove and to attend to the needs of Frances White, the rector's aunt, and her occasional visitors.

Jonathan and Mary Rachel Cooper employed one 'domestic' to assist them and their family of five young children, eventually to increase to twelve. Pay for domestic servants was pitifully low but, at the large houses, all meals were provided free in the servants' quarters and discarded clothes were often made available to the domestic staff who took them home for members of their family. It was a boon, too, for parents to know that their daughters – and sons – had the security of 'a place' and were no longer relying on the limited household resources of the typical agricultural worker's home.

In addition to the Solomon Milks there were the wheelwrights, carpenters, brick-layers, shoemakers, blacksmiths, millwrights, thatchers, butchers and shopkeepers. In 1855, there were three shoemakers and two shopkeepers: William Beales, the clothes manufacturer; William Rolfe, the corn miller; 'John Worledge Esq.', the banker, who lived at Ruffin's and whose son was a barrister, and Henry Rising, the schoolmaster. Samuel Fenton, on the Chedburgh Road, was the Chevington builder, specialising in repairs, decorations and alterations of houses and farm buildings, a business later taken over by Jonathan Cooper, who employed five men, five 'boys' (i.e. youths under the age of 21) and the occasional apprentice. In 1844, John Kemp, a member of a large family long resident in the village, was a maltster at the Malting farm and, in the same year, a member of the prominent Simkin family, Robert, who lived at Garrod's farm, was impressively styled 'veterinary surgeon'. It would be of interest to know how a Chelsea pensioner, William Howe, came to be living in Chevington in 1851;[66] the nature of the work of Joseph Bolingbroke, a charcoal burner; and the whereabouts of the *Royal Oak* where Sophia Reeves was a 'retailer of beer' in the early 1860s.[67]

The poor in the 19th century

Some overcrowding and poverty in the parish were evident. In the 1871 census return, the three terraced two-bedroomed stone cottages down Chevington Way at Almswater were listed as accommodating respectively families of eight, seven, and five, the last with one lodger. In the same year, Lucy Polly, aged 80, of Martin's Green, and Ann Newman, aged 99, living on the Chedburgh Road, were described as 'paupers'. Twenty years previously, in 1851, eight parishioners of a population of 615 appear as 'paupers', but only one, Isaac Elsdon, who lived near the Moat Farm, was entered as receiving parochial relief. In the same year Thomas Eley, 79, a blind gamekeeper, was living at Martin's Green as was a youth, aged 17, who was listed 'an idiot'. Others are included in the census who have 'weak intellects', or 'mental infirmities'.

In 1825, the overseers of the poor levied a rate on land holdings. The Earl of Bristol, William Jennison of the Lodge and John Kemp of the Hall were among the 45 contributors. From the proceeds, 'Suttle's child' and 'the Canham child' received allowances together with parishioners who were suffering from illnesses, e.g. 'the girl Prewer'. No less than 55 parishioners, including inmates of the Workhouse, received benefit.

In 1833 John Kemp and William Jennison were overseers. 'The Farrow widow' received £1 12s. 6d. (£1.62½p.) and the 'Harris child' £6 0s. 0d. £11 5s. 4d. (£11.27) was granted to the Workhouse, together with the cost of 13 weeks' 'fireing' at 2s. 0d. (10p.) a week. The overseers continued as assessors after 1884, but there was occasional disagreement with the Guardians of the Poor who had been appointed by the Poor Law Act of 1834 especially through the agency of the parish council which was established in 1894. At the fifth Annual Parish Meeting on 28 March 1899, the grocer, draper and overseer, John Evered, expressed his concern about:

> an unusually high call made by the Guardians of the Union and the Rural District Council necessitating a poor rate to be made at 2s. 0d. [10p.] in the £. The matter was discussed and it was ultimately decided that the overseers must make provision for the call by making a rate in accordance therewith, but an expression that such calls should be more equalized was desirable.

Occasionally very poor parishioners, especially those suffering from mental illnesses, were admitted to the Union Workhouse in Bury, or to the hospital at Melton, near Woodbridge, established by the Suffolk magistrates in 1827. White's *Directory* of 1855 describes Melton's inhabitants:[68]

> They are all Suffolk paupers for whom their respective parishes pay at the rate of 7s. 6d. a week [35p.] ... The government Commissioners inspect the asylum yearly, and in their report of 1852 they say about 200 of the patients are pretty constantly employed.

Population changes

In 1801 the population of Chevington was recorded as 446. In spite of a small decline from 1821–31, it rose markedly throughout the first half of the century. The census return of 1841 registered 323 males and 301 females in the parish. That total of 624 had risen to 636 by 1871. By the end of the century, however, the population had fallen to 545 and, in 1931, the population of the parish was 417.

At least six young man are known to have emigrated from the village during the years 1905–10, some of whom could have been those referred to by Miss Joscelyn of Bury St Edmunds when writing of her uncle Henry J. M. (Ted) White, the youngest son of the Reverend John White III, who, when a young man, emigrated to Canada:

> He took up a government grant, made it pay well, 'sold it' and bought a store. Some Chevington boys went out with him, but found the work too hard and came home.

Rene Pettit, aged 85, writes 'my father, Sam Pettit, emigrated to Australia sometime in 1891 with his older brothers, Robert and Herbert, who never returned. In the two years my father lived in Australia he worked on farms. He returned because he was homesick'. A local girl, my great-great aunt, Sophia Cooper, emigrated to America in the 1850s to work as a children's governess. On 24 November 1865, at the conclusion of the American Civil War, she wrote to her nephew, Jonathan, 'It is a great comfort to me to think the cruel war is over and that there is no bloodshed now'. Later, when looking back on former days, she recalled with affection the Whites and other friends in Chevington and the garden at Chedburgh school where her father had been headmaster. On the occasion of Queen Victoria's Golden Jubilee 1887, she expressed a wish to return to England but, as far as is known, that wish was never fulfilled.

In the 1880s and 1890s more children continued their education in the village school until the age of 14; consequently, on leaving school, more young people felt qualified to pit their wits in a different environment, free from recurring agricultural depression. The loss of 20 Chevington men during the 1914–18 War, most of whom would have undoubtedly returned to their native village and raised families, was

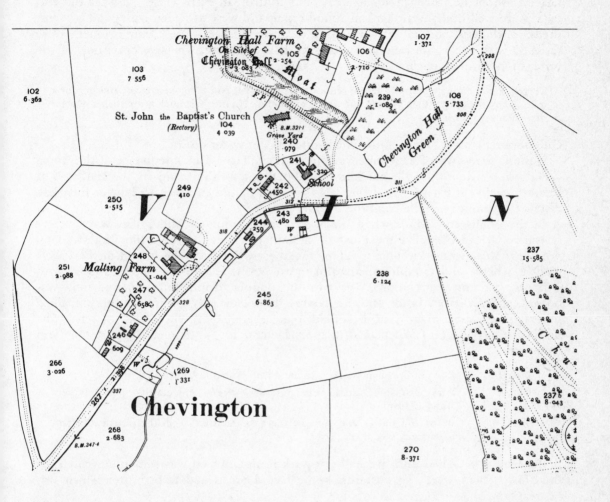

11. This map shows the site of Chevington Hall and the Church of All Saints, misnamed St John the Baptist's. Note the site of the original rectory. Reproduced from the 1904 Ordnance Survey Map.

another contributory factor in the fall of population. The decrease was accentuated in the late 1920s by acute agricultural decline and a resultant voluntary reduction in the size of the family by the agricultural worker.

Daily life in Chevington

Chevington was a 'close'* parish in the sense that, as the principal landowner was the Marquess of Bristol, movement into the village by indifferent property owners was restricted.[69] Although Suffolk had a relatively high proportion of freeholders, there were few in Chevington. Moreover, in 1898 the Marquess increased his territory in the parish by purchasing the Whites' estate of approximately 300 acres, including 25 cottages and the three farms which were cultivated subsequently by his own tenant farmers whom he, through his agent, could control. In such 'close' parishes the cottages were well built, were kept in sound repair and were provided with good gardens, sheds, outhouses and closets. In most of those respects the Commissioners were satisfied with the conditions prevailing at Chevington with the sole exception of the water supply which was inadequate:

> There are not enough wells. Near the school there are two, and then there is not another for a mile. Many people get their water from ponds or ditches. No one has much more than a quarter of a mile to go for it.

One labourer stated, 'I have only a little ditch to get water out of'.

Nothing is known of any improvement in the village as a consequence of the Royal Commission's Report 1893, but it is probable that a well was sunk by the Marquess of Bristol's agent on Palace — or Iron Gates — Green at the entrance to Ickworth Park, a distance of about one mile from the school.

In the 1880s and 1890s when times were bad, Solomon Milk's diet was severely restricted. Bread occupied the most prominent place in the daily diet, followed by potatoes. Meat was occasionally eaten, together with vegetables grown in the village gardens, cheese and dumplings. Mention must be made of suet puddings laced with currants, jam, or even onions. Tea was the popular drink, but skimmed milk was bought cheaply from farms and, at harvest time especially, beer was the prevailing beverage. My aunt, Mary Jane Bradfield, remembered that, when a girl of ten in the neighbouring village of Whepstead, a typical menu for a summer's day at the farm would be:

Breakfast	— Basin of bread and milk, bread and jam. Sometimes eggs, tea.
Dinner	— Pork, probably salted, with potatoes, greens and carrots. Jam rolypoly. Water to drink.
Tea	— Bread and butter and jam. Lettuces, or radishes, from the garden. Currant, or caraway seed, cake. Tea.

A pig would be killed and 'we had salt pork in pot' which was sometimes eaten for breakfast. There were egg custards, home baked bread and farm butter which was 'a great help'.

There is no doubt that poaching was common in the village. When a boy I was often told exciting stories of former skirmishes between gamekeepers on the Marquess of Bristol's estate and the skilled poachers of Chevington. One character was known by his particularly large pockets, his gun and 'long dog', and the experience of another adventurer, hiding for hours one autumn night in a culvert while he listened to a conversation between two gamekeepers intent on his capture, always aroused my excitement and secret admiration.

At Saxham Station, Fred ('Bonkers') Arbon collected his barrels of herrings from Brightlingsea in Essex. He smoked them in his little shed and sold them to Chevington homes where they were welcomed as a change from the usual fare. He was a rumbustious character, full of good cheer. When young he learnt to play the cornet at the Barracks in Bury and he formed a brass band in 1892. He, with his fellow musicians, walked miles to remote villages to give concerts at flower shows, Foresters' fetes and

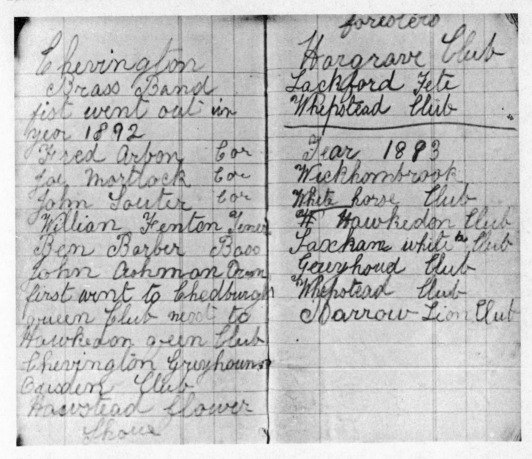

12. Pages from Fred Arbon's diary listing the engagements of the Chevington Brass Band, 1892-3.

celebrations in honour of the Queen's Diamond Jubilee of 1897. All engagements are carefully listed in his own bold hand in a small, black diary.

In addition to the brass band at the beginning of the century, there was the annual flower show, the culmination of the Cottage Garden or Horticultural Society, which met under the chairmanship of the rector. In 1907, the *Post* reported:

> On Friday last a series of lectures on 'Cottage Gardens and Allotment Cultivation' given by Mr. H. Coster, gardener to the Marquess of Bristol, under the auspices of the Technical Instruction Committee of the West Suffolk County Council . . . were brought to a successful conclusion. Great enthusiasm has been shown in regard to the lectures, the average attendance being 72 and it has been decided to hold an exhibition of vegetables etc. during the summer.

The Assistant Commissioner's report of the visit to Chevington in June 1892 mentioned that there was a cricket ground and formerly a reading room in the village. Bell ringing remained a popular activity during the early 1900s under the leadership of Fred King, the schoolmaster, and Arthur ('Pearly') Rolfe, the Insurance Agent. My father, and uncle Elijah Bradfield, were zealous bellringers and often rang in Bury and in neighbouring villages. At Christmas, the handbells, an acclaimed institution, were rung throughout the village, a difficult and demanding art which lingered on in a desultory way until the 1920s. Led by the very active schoolmaster, the church choir of about twelve members had been popular for many years. Referring to the period after 1908 Jack Arbon, still living in Chevington, writes 'I had to go to Church, Sunday School first, then Church service later. I was a member of the choir for several years'.

In July 1907, Louis N. Parker 'invented and arranged' the Bury St Edmunds Pageant in the Abbey Gardens. The production created a sensation in rural West Suffolk. Some Chevington parisioners, including my father and uncle, took part, travelling to frequent rehearsals in horse-drawn carts. Visits to the pageant in open wagonettes were organised by the rector and, for six glorious days and for many years to come, certainly until the mid-1920s, the Bury St Edmunds Pageant was regarded as one of Parker's outstanding creations.

Probably the most influential village activity was the Friendly Society, the Ancient Order of Shepherds. In June 1892, the representative of the Royal Commission on Labour reported that 'a good many men belong to the Lodge of Shepherds'. Since 1877 grandfather Jonathan had been secretary to the Suffolk Independent Order of Shepherds and had been active down Chevington Way in fostering local support. The procession to his funeral service at the Church of All Saints on a day in mid-May 1904 was preceded by the various members of the Friendly Societies, 'those of the Shepherds coming first, carrying crooks'. Alluding to his terminal illness, an undated newspaper report stated:

> But 'man proposes, God disposes' and the Angel of Death summoned Bro. Jonathan Cooper to join a larger wider brotherhood than any with which he had previously been connected.

Friendly Societies did much to encourage planning for times of illness and bereavement, especially among rural workers, but an added benefit was the 'brotherhood and concord' which existed between the members. No doubt they would meet to discuss their business in the *Greyhound* where they would comfort a brother member in times of stress. During an acute agricultural depression such as existed in the late 19th century, the social contribution of the Ancient Order of Shepherds to Chevington farmworkers was inestimable.

Farmers' horizons were extended in some measure by their visits to Bury and the Corn Exchange where they would meet fellow farmers from other villages on Wednesday market days and, from time to time, dealers and agents with a more sophisticated business acumen and vigour of approach. High horse-drawn carts, later pony traps, would convey the farmer and his wife to Bury Market, but Solomon Milk rarely had the chance of leaving Chevington Way for the bustle of Bury. In 1844 Robert Savage was the village carrier. His horse-driven wagon travelled to Bury on Wednesday and Saturday mornings, returning from the *Three Goats' Heads* with the passengers and goods in the afternoon. At the end of the century and certainly until 1911, 'Nimbly' Nunn of Hole Farm conveyed passengers to market on Wednesdays and Saturdays travelling via Saxham where, on other days, he would meet trains at the station and take travellers to their destinations. Later, 'Billy' Rawlings and George Nunn provided carrier facilities until competition from the Eastern Counties Omnibus Company proved prohibitive for small rural services.

The turnpike roads in the county were good. In the 1840s coaches left the *Angel* and the *Bell* in Bury daily for Piccadilly and Charing Cross, travelling via Saxham *White Horse* to Newmarket, but the Whites of Chevington and the Marquesses of

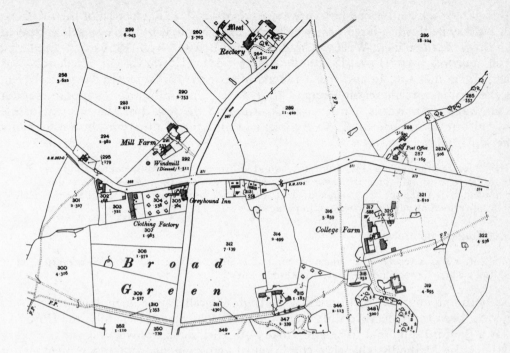

13. The Greyhound *Corner. Reproduced from the 1904 Ordnance Survey Map.*

Bristol would travel to London and elsewhere in their own horse-drawn carriages. The small stone house opposite College Farm, formerly Mrs. Fenton's school, later became the coachman's house where a Charles Parr, coachman, was living in 1871 and, in 1901, Robert Blackburn, who drove a 'four in hand' for the Reverend John White III with consummate control and elegance.

The Reverend Arthur Keble White and Mrs. Helen Maud Keble White

The third son of the Reverend John White III, Arthur Keble, was born at Chevington Rectory in 1862. Having been a pupil at Dedham Grammar School, in Essex, he entered Trinity College, Cambridge, where he appears to have taken an Ordinary Degree. After a theological course at Ely — he was the first rector of the parish to receive specialised training for the ministry — he served in Bedford and in Hampshire, before returning to Suffolk. Perhaps he had the Chevington living in mind when he became rector of neighbouring Great Saxham in 1894 and, 11 years later, rector of another near neighbour, Chedburgh. On the death of his father in 1908 Arthur Keble travelled a mere three miles to his birth place where he became the fourth generation of Whites to serve as parson of the parish. His tastes were simple and, in general style, he was unobtrusive, quiet and urbane. Seventeen years previously he had married Helen Maud, the eldest daughter of John Frederick Nutter J.P. of Caldwell Priory, Bedford. Mrs. Keble White, as she was known by all the people of Chevington, became a powerful personality in the ecclesiastical, domestic and social life of the village, a force to be reckoned with throughout her husband's tenure of the living.

John Frederick Nutter had been private secretary to J. & F. Howard of the Britannia Iron Works, Bedford, a large firm which had been inspired by the evangelical zeal of John Howard, an eminent Wesleyan, and Mayor of Bedford from 1858-61.[70] Frederick Nutter married John Howard's grand-daughter. John Howard's son, Frederick, was knighted; another son, James, was a Liberal Minister of Parliament; a daughter, Helen, was the mother of Colonel Sir George Farrar, Bart.[71] In addition to his appointment at the Howards' Iron Works, Nutter was Chairman of the Board of Management of the new Bedford County Hospital. A very long and adulatory obituary in the *Bedfordshire Times* on 11 May 1906 states:

> The finest testimony to his diligence, sound judgment, and conspicuous ability is the magnificent Hospital which the town and county now possess, the cost of which is not quite defrayed, it is true, but the balance of debt would have been much greater but for the indefatigable efforts of our late townsman to reduce it.

The obituary concludes:

> Mr. Nutter was a regular early morning communicant of St Leonard's Church and attended St Paul's where he took a deep interest in church work.

As both the churches mentioned were High Church Anglican, it is apparent that there had been some decisive shift from the dissent of his wife's family, the Howards. It was a Bedford quip that to be a foreman at the Britannia Ironworks it was necessary to attend the Methodist chapel, a condition of employment from which members of the secretarial staff such as John Frederick Nutter were, no doubt, excused. However, Nutter possessed two attributes which were of importance to the Whites' social and squirarchical leadership at Chevington: the first was his High Churchmanship, the second his financial and managerial standing. His name, printed on the map of the Chevington Grove Estate at the time of its sale in 1898, indicates ownership of part of Farrow's. As the patrons of the living at Chevington in 1906, the year of Nutter's death, are stated to be the executors of F. Nutter, it appears that Helen Maud's father had already purchased the living from the Reverend John White III. Since the sale of the Chevington Grove estate in 1898 it had been rumoured in the village — always a close and intimate ambience for gossip — that the Whites were not as financially sound as had been evident earlier in the century. Helen Maud had clearly obtained the living from her father's executors by 1908 for in that year, on the death of her father-in-law, the Reverend John White III, she, as patron in full right, presented her husband, Arthur Keble, to the rectory of Chevington. As there is neither mention of a transference of the advowson in the Reverend John's will nor reference to it in the diocesan register of advowsons, it may be assumed that there was no formal transaction, but merely a family arrangement resulting in Helen Maud's final acquisition of what had been held by the Whites for well over a century. Helen Maud Keble White, as she preferred to be styled, had certainly succeeded to the throne which she was to hold for 18 years. The school records reveal that a Chevington boy, evidently of some independence of character, was caned for not raising his cap to Mrs. White; about the same time another boy was reprimanded with a lesser punishment for indecent exposure.

The new rector and his very active consort began their tenure in Chevington with an extensive restoration of the Church of All Saints. A list of subscribers of February 1910 indicates a total revenue of over £793. Helen Maud's relatives, Sir George Farrar, her mother's cousin, and Sir Frederick Howard, her great-uncle, generously subscribed. The Nutters of Bedford made substantial contributions, a total of £418 16s. 0d. (£418.80p.). The Marquess of Bristol contributed £10, Lord Francis Hervey £5, the Reverend Lord Manners Hervey, £1 15s. 0d. (£1.75p.), and Prince Frederick Duleep Singh, £1 0s. 0d. Among the 100 subscribers, it is noteworthy that only one was a local farmer. Times were, of course, bad. However, Fred King, the village schoolmaster, arranged a concert, no doubt mainly for the parishioners, which resulted in a total of over £8. There was, in addition, the very encouraging collection of £15 11s. 0d. (£15.55p.) at the Dedication Service on 5 April 1909. The initiative officially taken by the rector and fostered by Mrs. Keble White and the Nutters and Howards of Bedford was commendable but, in the opinion of some, precipitate. It was conceded that, after his father's long reign Arthur Keble, prompted by his wife, had decided that there were new objectives to be gained and other worlds to conquer but, in a few years' time, Chevington and the entire country had their horizons extended even beyond the Restoration of the Church of All Saints. War with Germany came in 1914. Life in the village would never be the same again.

Chevington and the First World War

Twenty men of the village, including three brothers in each of two families, the Coppings and Quantrills, were slaughtered on the Western Front. Lieutenant John White, eldest son of John White, farmer and landowner, formerly of Chevington Grove and nephew of the rector, was killed at Gallipoli in 1915. He was the last of the Johns, the fifth since his great-great-grandfather became rector and patron in 1776. His commemorative tablet may be seen on the north wall of the chancel of the Church of All Saints with the appropriately chosen quotation from Horace which was applicable to all the Whites, Coppings, Smiths and Quantrills who fought and died in other lands: *Dulce est pro patria mori*. Ernie Wheal (aged 79) remembers his brother leaving their cottage near the forge in 1916:

> I was only 10. When he said goodbye, he said, 'You can have my bike because I shan't come back'. I saw him go.

Will Wheal was killed in action on the Western Front in the following year.

Some parishioners still recall that Chevington Grove became a prisoner of war camp. Prisoners were marched along the village lanes to work on farms; on Saturday afternoons they played football; on Sundays, the prisoners' choir sang lustily and, frequently on a summer's night, the strains of *Deutschland Über Alles* surged over the fields of Chevington. When I was a boy in the village my imagination was aroused by my parents telling me that, when all was quiet in the dead of night, they could hear the guns in France, very softly, but quite unmistakably, reminding them of the agony of war. On 26 February 1915 Alice Pettit's brother, Dick Clarry, wrote home from his prison camp in Munster requesting 'a box of good eatables and ten shillings as I have nothing with me' but assuring his old Chevington friends of his well-being. Ruby Edgeley still cherishes the memory of her brother, Robert, a victim of war wounds, returning to Chevington one grey November day. He died at his home in the following February. In 1916 Hezekiah Smith, a son of the local preacher, Riley, died in hospital in Ismalia at the age of twenty.

14. *A letter from Dick Clarry, a prisoner-of-war in Germany in 1915, to his sister Alice Pettit.*

When all was over, Chevington's War Memorial Cross, erected on the western side of the church path, was unveiled and blessed on Sunday, 12 June 1921, by Lieutenant-General Sir Charles Briggs. Chopin's *Funeral March* was played, the large assembly of county families, clergy, farmers and Solomon Milks processed silently from the Church of All Saints to the churchyard where, as they faced east, the Reveille was sounded by buglers of the Suffolk Regiment. Thoughtfully they listened to the words from the Book of Wisdom: 'In the sight of the unwise they seemed to die and their departure is taken for misery and their going from us to be utter destruction: but they are at peace'.

The Hall Farm Sale

The year 1918-19 was an important one for sales of farm stock and implements. Prices seem to have been high, for at Holly Bush Farm in 1919 a pedigree Suffolk mare, foaled in 1913, reached 180 guineas (£189). At Ruffin's in the previous year, at a sale by Mr. John Fyson, nine 'powerful and active young cart horses' were sold. On 7 October 1919 Salter, Simpson and Sons were instructed by my grandfather, Joseph Bradfield, who was retiring from farming, to sell by auction '17 cart horses, deserving the notice of horse buyers' and having such names as Snip, Smart, Brisk, Smiler, Blossom and Kitty. '10 fine young mares, 1 gelding, 1 2-year-old cart colt and 3 yearling colts and fillies, a cart foal and a Bay Cob'. There were 21 head of neatstock (cows) with names such as Polly, Pansy, Froster and Daisy and a white sow 'forward in pig'. The farm machinery included 'Deering's self-binder (6 ft. cut, nearly new)', a 'piano' self-binder, Samuelson's reaper, Smyth's corn mill and Martin's swathe turner and rake. There was also a 'cream separator'. An examination of the entire sale catalogue[72] gives valuable insight into the development of farming in Chevington during the first 20 years of the century.

Leisure and pleasure

In September 1920 some parishioners, probably led by Mrs. Keble White, became actively concerned about building a village hall to act as a meeting place for the men of the village and to offer accommodation for certain social and parochial occasions. Early in the following year when donations rose to nearly £120, the local committee led by the rector and consisting of John Sangster, Sam Pettit, and Mrs. Etherington of the Grove, resolved to purchase one of the army huts then redundant at Felixstowe and priced at £95. The site chosen for 'The Hut' was opposite Broad Green Farm at the junction of the Chedburgh Road and the lane leading to Chevington Grove, on land given by the Marquess of Bristol. At the official opening of the 'Hut' in January 1921 the Reverend A. Keble White, chairman, declared:

> Since the war especially has the need been felt for a place wherein men particularly could find a home, a place of rest and recreation, of warmth and light. . . . May I say how grateful we are to the Marchioness of Bristol for putting the coping stone upon all the kind interest and sympathy and held she has evinced, by gracing the occasion with her presence.[73]

The Marchioness then declared the 'Hut' officially opened. In recent years, 1979-81, the corrugated iron building, lined with wood, has been restored and partially rebuilt

HALL FARM,
CHEVINGTON
3½ miles from Saxham Station, and 6 from Bury St. Edmund's.

AGRICULTURAL SALE
OF
17 CART HORSES
AND COLTS, viz.:
10 Fine Young Mares, 1 Gelding, 2-year-old Cart Colt, 3 Yearling Colts and Fillies, Cart Foal, and Bay Cob;

21 Head of NEAT STOCK,
COMPRISING
7 Choice Young Dairy Cows, 5 Well-bred Shorthorn down-calving and in-calf Heifers, Roan Yearling Bull, 2 Steers, and 6 Calves;

WHITE SOW (forward in pig),

And POULTRY;
WHICH

SALTER, SIMPSON & SONS
Are instructed by Mr. JOSEPH BRADFIELD, who is retiring from Farming, to Sell by Auction, without reserve,

On TUESDAY, October 7th, 1919,
TOGETHER WITH THE
Agricultural Carriages, Implements, &c.,
INCLUDING
2 Road Wagons, 3 Tumbrils, "Plano" Self-Binder, *Samuelson's Reaper*, Grass Mower, *Smyth's* Corn Drill, *Martin's* Swathe Turner and Rake, Root Mincers, Horseshoes, Ploughs and Harrows, Cart Harness, Dairy Utensils, Cream Separator, about 12 cwt. Superphosphate, and Miscellaneous Effects,

Dog Cart by *Bridges*, and **Luggage Cart** on Springs.

Sale to commence at 1 o'clock punctually.

Auctioneers' Offices: Bury St. Edmund's and Attleborough.

Printed at the "Free Press" Works, Bury

---

6   SALE OF AGRICULTURAL EFFECTS.

HORSES.
The following Mares include several very smart and active young animals, with plenty of size, particularly deserving the notice of horse buyers.

LOT				AGE
1	SNIP ...	... Bay Mare ...	... ...	4
2	SMART	... Bay Mare ...	... ...	6
3	BRISK	... Bay Mare ...	... ...	6
4	DIAMOND	... Bay Mare ...	... ...	7
5	BLOSSOM	... Bay Mare ...	... ...	7
6	TINKER	... Black Gelding	...	... aged
7	SCOT ...	... Bay Mare ...	... rising 4 years	
8	VIOLET	... Bay Mare ...	... rising 4 years	
			(covered by Mr. Stanford's horse)	
9	SMILER	... Bay Mare	(ditto)	... 7
10	KITTY	... Black Mare ...	...	
11	POPPELL	... Bay Mare ...	... ...	6
12	Her Bay Colt Foal, by "Billingford Merry Monk" 32095			

COLTS.

13	Bay Cart Colt, 2 years old	⎫
14	Bay Yearling Cart Colt	⎬
15	Ditto	by "Billingford Merry Monk"
16	Bay Yearling Cart Filly	⎭ 32095)

| 17 | Bay Cob |

---

15. A list of horses for sale as indicated in the sale catalogue of Chevington Hall Farm, 1919.

BY SALTER, SIMPSON AND SONS. 3

LOT
45 Bean barrow
46 Ditto
47
48 .

PLOUGHS AND HARROWS.

49 *Cornish's* G.C.B. foot plough with horsetree and whippletrees
50 Ditto
51 Ditto
52 Ditto
53 *Cornish's* double furrow plough
54 Northumberland plough
55 Four iron plough slades and 1 wood ditto
56 Lot of new plough irons and 2 iron whippletrees
57 Gang of 4 heavy iron harrows
58 Gang of 4 iron harrows
59 Gang of 6 ditto
60 Gang of 6 ditto
61

IMPLEMENTS, DRILLS AND MACHINES.

62 Set of duck-foot harrows and horsetree
63 Horsehoe, by *Cornish*
64 Ditto
65 Shim horsehoe
66 Capital horsehoe, by *Murtin & Turner*
67 *Nicholson's* iron cultivator
68 Root mincer
69 Ditto, by *Woods*
70 Oil cake breaker

4 SALE OF AGRICULTURAL EFFECTS,

LOT
71 Hand-power chaff box
72 Capital *Martin's* side delivery rake and swathe turner
73 Excellent 10-coulter 7ft. " Nonpareil " steerage corn drill,
by *Smyth*, with extra barrel for seeds
74 *Garrett's* horsehoe for corn, to follow drill
75 Pair-horse Cambridge roll
76 One-horse flat roll
77 Corn and mangold drill
78 *Deering's* self-binder, 6ft. cut, nearly new
79 " Plano " self-binder
80 Two cwt. binder twine
81 Capital pair-horse reaper, by *Samuelson*
82 Pair-horse reaper
83 Grass mower, by *Frost & Wood*
84

HARNESS.

85 Set of cart harness with collar and bridle
86 Ditto
87 Ditto
88 Set of thil horse gears with collar and bridle
89 Ditto
90 Ditto
91 Ditto
92 Ditto
93 Two pairs plough trace and sales
94 Two ditto
95 Two ditto
96 Three ditto
97 Two collars and 2 bridles
98 Two ditto and 2 ditto
99 Two ditto and 3 headstalls

16. *The sale of the stock and implements of Chevington Hall Farm, 1919.*

by volunteers who have raised money by organising many village events. The Village Hall, as it has come to be known, is still the centre for the vigorous Women's Institute.

In April 1921, when the Women's Institute was formed, the subscription was two shillings (10p.) a year, but if a member was unable to afford the complete subscription (and some could not) arrangements were made for her to pay sixpence (2½p.) a quarter. As an association of country housewives, it gave ample opportunities for members to meet socially, to learn all kinds of handicrafts, to collect eggs, which were then given to the West Suffolk General Hospital, and to visit the coast, or even London where packed lunches were eaten on the steps of the Prince Albert Memorial. Cultural activity was fostered: the Chevington Women's Institute trained its own choir to sing at local Festivals and, from time to time, lectures were arranged on serious topics.

A Men's Club, led at one time by Augustus ('Gus') Randolph Dodson, the blacksmith's son, met in the small room at the 'Hut' where members played cards and darts and yarned about the rigours of the day. The 'Hut' became the village centre for Saturday night dances. For the less active, whist drives preferred more sedate entertainment. At Christmas there were parties for the children when the Prudential insurance agent, Arthur Rolfe, appearing in a different guise as Father Christmas, announced his arrival from an undeclared habitat by hammering on the corrugated iron exterior of the Hut.

In the late 1920s, zealous local musicians with skill and enterprise formed a modern dance band, the Roosters, two members of which, Rene and Ol Pettit, are still living in Chevington. In the quiet of a frosty Saturday night the strains of the Roosters could be heard, loud and clear, along the seclusion of Chevington Way. Much in demand, the band not only performed in the village, but invitations were received from many other quarters, for the reputation of the Roosters ranged far and wide. In the early '30s, Pal Copping, the Roosters' drummer, a very popular Chevington man, died suddenly but the Roosters dance band continued until the outbreak of the Second World War, having made music at no less than 1,000 dances.

From time to time there were variety shows, or 'concerts', in the Village Hall, featuring such artistes as Florrie Clarke of the Shop, Rene Pettit, of Broad Green and College Farms, Eva Sangster, of the *Greyhound*, Nelly Clarry, Jimmie Ashman, and Alf Last, the gardener at the Grove. On one occasion Mrs. Keble White presented a concert which included a riotous turn by no less a personage than Horace Barker, the curator of the Moyses Hall Museum, in Bury, who regaled a packed audience with a musical turn, 'See me dance the polka, see me cover the ground'.

In the 1920s Chevington fielded football and cricket teams. I remember local Derbys played on Great Days with such stalwarts as 'Postle', Sammy Avis, Ol and Hub. Pettit and George Pask. Later, football was played on College Green. My father, a bowler of some repute, played cricket with Ol Pettit, Charlie Bowers, the blacksmith, Arthur Turner, and Charlie Jackson of Hill Farm. Matches, played away against rivals, sometimes included journeys to Dalham Hall, or to Culford, near Bury, and often, when allowed to accompany my father, I spent long sunny Saturday afternoons lying in luxuriant grass encircled by trees in the shadow of the great house itself. There was a spirit of camaraderie, a seriousness of purpose bordering on dedication to a cause. Teas, with buns and the inevitable cucumber sandwiches, gave the contestants an opportunity for specialised discussion on the progress and tactics of the game, but otherwise the air was full of the sights and sounds of a summer's day.

The Friendly Society, the Ancient Order of Foresters, was formed in 1834. In 1924, after a sojourn in Hargrave, the Marquess of Bristol Court of the Ancient Order of Foresters transferred to Chevington where the Shepherds had been active at the beginning of the century. During the '20s and '30s, Sam Pettit and Charlie Quantrill were leading figures in the movement which held its main meetings at the *Greyhound* and which, as a result of its gala and church service, served as an important social institution exemplifying the fundamental principle of 'brother helping brother'. The quarterly subscriptions ranged from 2s. 6d. (12½p.) to 10s. 0d. (50p.) and the benefits in time of personal or family illness, when members were officially 'on the club', were paid accordingly. At that time there was a death 'benefit' of £20. Before the days of National Health and Security, such societies performed a most valuable social function by offering security in times of illness and bereavement. Later, in the 1930s, there was the annual Foresters' Gala with the excitement of motorcycle racing provided by such intrepid Chevington riders as Arthur Murkin. It was the most eagerly anticipated event of the year. At the more formal occasions, such as the services at the Church of All Saints, the regalia worn by Sam Pettit and others was colourful and impressive. Medals were surmounted by stags' heads, hunting horns and two arrows, and the trustees' ribbons included the motto which epitomised the spirit of the Ancient Order: 'Unity, Benevolence and Concord'. One such an occasion was particularly memorable: Lady Erskine, daughter of the 4th Marquess of Bristol, came over from Ickworth to be present.

Throughout the century, particularly up to 1860, the Simkin family was very influential in Chevington, members of the family living at Hole Farm (now Batley's), Garrod's Farm, Tan Office Farm and the present *Greyhound*. Robert was a farmer and veterinary surgeon at Garrod's, Joseph lived at the Hole Farm, John worked as a thatcher, and James gave good cheer at 'the beerhouse'.

The *Greyhound*, a brick-built early 19th-century building, now stands at the cross roads in the virtual centre of the village. It is likely that it replaced an earlier 'beer house' but, as the crossroads between the former College Green and Broad Green was not on an important route, the *Greyhound* did not assume the importance of the *Queen's Head*, now Mallaby's, the *Plumber's Arms* at Denston, or even the *Marquess of Cornwallis* at Chedburgh. In the 1860s there was a 'beer house' known as the *Royal Oak* somewhere in the Depden Lane. The Lane, certainly until the mid-19th century, was a relatively important route to Depden Green, connecting the former Chevington Way (now Queen Lane), through the present Stonehouse Farm to Depden.

In the 1860s James Ransom was at the *Greyhound*. The earliest deeds, dated 26 March 1872, include a conveyance from a Chevington farmer, James Finch, and others, to a John Henry Ransom who probably remained at the inn until the Sangsters arrived there in 1874. John Sangster, the father of the agricultural machinist, was the host in 1875. In 1891 Daniel, another son, who married Mary Cooper, my father's sister, succeeded his father as landlord of the *Greyhound*. In the winter of 1899, after a short illness, Daniel died at the age of thirty. The inscription on his grave is apt and concise. It is on the south side of the Church of All Saints: 'He brought down my strength in my journey and shortened my days'. As the Ransom family, the hosts of the *Queen's Head* in Queen Lane, brewed beer on their premises, it is probable that beer was also brewed at Chevington's *Greyhound* and that brewing continued until 1898 when the inn passed into the hands of Clarke Brothers, Brewers, of Bury St

Edmunds. It was not until 1917 that the *Greyhound* was taken over by Greene King, of the Westgate Brewery, Bury St Edmunds, when Clarke Brothers was absorbed into that company. After the death of Daniel, Aunt Mary commenced her rule of the village hostelry with a strong and resolute grip. She remained the Queen of the *Greyhound* for 30 years. Aunt Mary was succeeded by William Beavis whose son Bill was an artist of considerable talent. Not only was he commissioned by Greene King, the brewers, to paint the inn sign, depicting an alert and virile greyhound, but he painted Andrew Newman and the Hall Farm. The paintings were later exhibited in the *Greyhound* for all to see. After a year or so Bill, the village artist, proceeded to the Royal Academy Art School, helped on his way by the generosity of the Marchioness of Bristol. Until recently members of the Stutely family have kept the inn which became a centre for village social life, where farmers and the Solomon Milks drank their beer, spoke and grinned about the trials of the day and shared gossip.

In the late 1920s the West Suffolk Education Committee introduced an imaginative scheme of providing village 'libraries'. As Clerk of the Parish Council, my father received three large wooden boxes crammed with an assortment of novels, biographies, and technical manuals. The 'Hut' was the appointed centre for the distribution and return of books on Friday evenings. A local teacher, Hilda Argent, was an early librarian. Later Job Willis, a Welshman, officiated. The welcome opportunity for requesting books for inclusion in the next assignment enhanced the value of the service which enjoyed a long period of popularity in Chevington. Together with the wireless set, or 'loudspeaker', the availability of books in the village provided the community with the opportunity of extending their horizons beyond the confines of village life. For many years the local *Bury Free Press*, a Liberal publication established in 1855 and available at the village shop on Fridays, was the most popular newspaper but, at some farmhouses the *East Anglian Daily Times* and *The Daily Mail* presented the national view. On Sundays not only was *The News of the World* read for its sports coverage but also for its entertainment, gossip and salacious content. Isolation was slowly broken down. In 1925, a telephone exchange was installed at the Post Office when seven Chevington residents had telephones. Later, a public kiosk was built on Post Office Road. Nine residents owned 'motor-cars' in 1924. When tennis parties were held on summer afternoons at the rectory many guests arrived by car. Boys competed with one another in calling out the greatest number of 'motors' they had seen during the afternoon. In spite of such advances, carts, pony traps and wagons were still dominant and, occasionally on a slumberous summer evening, one or two members of the Marquess of Bristol's family at Ickworth would drive sedately in a horse-drawn phaeton, or gig, through the village to Little Saxham and then back to Ickworth at dusk.

Ecclesiastical change and strife

After a long and serious illness, the Reverend A. Keble White, M.A. died at Chevington Rectory on 24 February 1926. His grave on the north side of the Church of All Saints is inscribed 'Pray for the Soul of Arthur Keble White, Priest'. The influence of the Whites on the social order of the village had lasted for exactly 150 years. Other changes were already disrupting the traditional life of Victorian Chevington so that the Solomon Milks began to contemplate new pastures. They were wise men.

In spite of an apparent appearance of calm, Chevington, on the death of the fourth White to serve as rector, became the scene of a religious dispute which was not only widely published in Suffolk but which, at one stage, seemed likely to assume wider dimensions. The parish, customarily remote and unknown and free from the gaze of local historians and hearty visitors, became for a brief, but troubled, time a source of conversation in wider circles than its boundaries.

As we have seen, having acquired the advowson of the living of the Church of All Saints, Helen Maud White had presented her husband, the Reverend Arthur Keble White, to that living in 1908. On the death of the rector in 1926 his widow, known by the parishioners to hold unfamiliar views, granted the advowson to an Anglo-Catholic patron, the Guild of All Souls. On 8 May 1926, Reginald Harry Nottage, B.A., formerly rector of Kettlebaston, Suffolk, and sometime Senior Master at the West Suffolk County School, was presented by Helen Maud Keble White 'the true and undoubted patron thereof in full right of the Rectory and Parish Church of Chevington'.

Even today tradition dies hard in the country, but over 50 years ago conservatism was the way of life. Changes in the tradition of worship in particular parishes have occurred when advowsons have changed hands. Some would urge that such changes are best introduced gradually after patient and prolonged teaching of their significance. It was, perhaps, not in the new rector's style to proceed in that way, although this suggestion in no sense seeks to impugn his deep pastoral concern for his congregation. He was cultured, intelligent and of marked ability and initiative. The typical Chevingtonian in the mid-1920s was in no way a zealot, but the church was central and, as such, significant to what he silently acknowledged to be his evaluation of life. Changes were not accepted uncritically. Furthermore, the reign of the Whites, and its accompanying paternalism, were over: the parish was on the threshold of a new social and religious order.

By July 1926 the rector had made up his mind about alterations to the interior of the church and, little more than two months after his induction, he wrote to the Archdeacon informing him of innovations which he himself had already introduced — presumably without a Faculty* — but that he intended 'to apply for a Faculty covering a pretty extensive scheme, some points of which I have not yet decided'.[74] By June, or July, the services changed in character and became distinctly High Church: the name 'mass' was introduced as an alternative to communion and was said daily, more candles appeared on the altar, crucifixes were hung here and there, Hymns Ancient and Modern were excluded and, perhaps most contentiously of all, incense was introduced as an important accompaniment to worship.

Mr. Dyson, a Londoner known locally as 'Dicky', who was then living with his son-in-law, Ernie Bridge ('Limmer') at the Malting Farm, was the self-appointed leader of the opposition. He strongly supported the visits of the 'Wycliffe Preachers', a group of Low Church evangelicals who had descended on Chevington, and the protestations of a Mr. Vercoe Abbott, of Ipswich, and his endeavours to win acclaim from the parishioners. Meetings, held on the green between the churchyard and Chevington Way at which Mr. Vercoe Abbot once spoke for two hours, were attended by the members of the Primitive Methodist congregation, supporters from other villages, many parishioners who professed no denominational allegiance and, more significantly, by some members of the worshipping community of the Church of All Saints.

There is no doubt that, because of a scarcity of 'crystal' wireless sets and the small number of newspapers delivered to the village by the 'paper man' from Bury, the countrywide General Strike of May 1926 failed to make the same urgent impact on the local scene as the developing trouble at Chevington. Lively meetings were held during the week. The more important gatherings, however, were organised at the same time as the Sunday evening services. The rector wrote to the Bishop of St Edmundsbury and Ipswich, the Right Reverend Walter Godfrey Whittingham, asking him to intervene. 'I assure you', he wrote, 'the simple country people who are the majority of the church people of our diocese, are sorely puzzled'.[75]

In a letter to the people of Chevington, the Bishop, conciliatory and courteous in tone, stated that he did not question the motives of the Wycliffe preachers, but he regretted that they adopted the course they did.[76] Seven local village parsons including Lord Manners Hervey, Rector of Horringer and Ickworth and brother of the Marquess of Bristol, wrote to the rector expressing their sympathy and extending their goodwill.

Fortified by such assurance, the rector wrote a letter to 62 church members of Chevington thanking them for their support and reminding them that he had the goodwill of the Bishop and Rural Dean. It is reasonable to think that the majority of churchgoers held private opinions but, in general, they remained inarticulate about them. What was most unacceptable was the strife which was being engendered in the village for, at that time, confusion was a new experience; consequently, the effect on the village was disturbing. Today, such a dispute would probably pass without grave concern, not only in the locality, but in the village itself. In the 1920s, however, people regarded such issues seriously. In a communication to the parishioners, fastened on the south door of the Church of All Saints, the rector gave prominence to his future programme which included daily mass, private communion and confessions 'as arranged'. It is inferred from the available correspondence that the rector, in apparent deference to the parishioners' wishes, had agreed to experiment with Protestant services for a week or so but, for some inexplicable reason, these had not been enthusiastically received by the worshippers. One wonders if they had been enthusiastically led by the rector, for a Sung Eucharist had been retained during this period of conciliation. Job Willis of Chevington has kindly provided details of attendance at Communion Services at the time of the rector's induction in May 1926 and in the following September. Figures were not always recorded, but there would appear to be a decrease from 51 to 41. During the month of December, there were over a hundred communicants.

The Bishop, writing from Ipswich, assured the rector of his prayers and goodwill. On 15 October, again prudently, the Bishop wrote to the Rector of Chevington:

> What I feel is that I could so much more heartily and decisively express my disapproval of his actions (i.e. Mr. Vercoe Abbott's) if I could with equal decision and cordiality express my approval of all we do in the Churches whose teaching practices he comes into conflict with.

The Bishop's candour implied that Mr. Vercoe Abbott was not always misguided in his protestations. Later there was certainly open acrimony between the rector and Mr. Abbott but, in an early letter in August, the Protestant preacher wrote in a friendly way in answer to a characteristically courtly letter from the rector, but a later letter from Mr. Abbot on 16 October was in a different key:

> If you conducted services according to the law and the Prayer Book it would be better than making statements which are not correct. You have misled your Bishop whose authority you flout.

The Managers of the Voluntary School, chaired appropriately by the rector, refused an application from the 'Wycliffe Preachers' to hold a meeting on their premises. The preachers responded by organising a Protestant petition which was circulated to all parishioners when they were informed that, if they failed to sign it, Anglo-Catholicism and all that accompanied it would continue in the village. Furthermore, they and their families, when they departed this world, would be subjected to the same style of High Church funeral service as was held for the late Reverend Arthur Keble White in the previous March. The parishioners did not appear to be in any way unduly alarmed by that eventuality. About that time, although it was not established that the 'Wycliffe Preachers' were responsible, scurrilous messages were scribbled on the altar, candles and crucifixes.

In a report in the *East Anglian Daily Times* on 27 September 1926, Mr. Vercoe Abbott's specific objections, including prayers for the dead and the wearing of vestments, were listed. Early in October the same paper published a report stating that the clergy at the Harvest Festival Service received a hostile reception by a large audience outside the church, 'which proved that the people of Chevington were out of sympathy with the services in the Church where their fathers had worshipped'.

An article in the *Bury Free Press* dated 9 October 1926, however, presented a more optimistic story:

> Mass was sung by the Rector in presence of a good congregation. The service was bright and hearty and rendered with the customary adjuncts of vestments, lights and incense, and a short address was given, . . . Collections were for the Bury and West Suffolk General Hospital.

The *East Anglian Daily Times* on 9 October declared that 34 parishioners were in favour of leaving matters entirely with the rector; only two expressed a preference for the Protestant services. It is clear, however, that only a minority of parishioners had voted in the poll. Such an apparent lack of concern is again characteristic of the countryman of nearly sixty years ago; a reluctance based, perhaps, on lack of confidence to make a clear-cut commitment, and an understandable vagueness about the theological issues involved. Hearsay has it that the parishioners disliked the changes and, moreover, as the innovations were not intelligible to them, they remained unaware of the virtues, if any, of what the new rector was introducing. All they knew was that things were changing and that they were unable to state whether such changes were 'right'. Life in the country in 1926 was still hard and demanding. Villagers endured physical hardship as part of the natural order and, when emotional, or spiritual, conflict was thrust on them, they showed a courageous resignation.

The rhythm of life drummed on. The football team continued its fixtures on Saturday afternoons and, according to the *Bury Free Press* of Friday, 9 October 1926, at the weekly meeting of the Women's Institute, the 'best hat made in ten minutes from a newspaper and twelve pins was won by Mrs. H. Copping and, as the speaker failed to arrive, the rest of the evening was spent in games'.

In the confusion the rector continued to show a remarkable tenacity. Some members of the congregation left; many nominal supporters, who sat at the west end of the church and sang boisterously, disappeared, and the choir was no longer the hearty and extroverted accompaniment as formerly, but a dedicated few remained and it was they who formed the nucleus of a growing congregation in the ensuing years. Because of their inability to eliminate High Churchmanship, the 'Wycliffe Preachers' and Mr. Vercoe Abbott passed silently from the scene and 'Dicky' Dyson transferred his allegiance to Primitive Methodism.

In 1930, the rector published a book, *The Village Eucharist*[77] of which, in an introduction, a Reverend P. B. Bull, of the Community of the Resurrection, wrote:

> I hope this book will bring new courage and inspiration to many a village priest who has lost the spring of his first enthusiasm. Religion matures best in our villages where men see God in His Works and learn to be patient.

In his view, the author was 'not only a master of his subject, but also knew how to convey his convictions and conclusions to others with humility and sympathy'. The rector himself wrote on the first page of his book:

> Let me say at the outset that my experience . . . has been almost entirely that of a parish priest of two small and obscure Suffolk villages . . .

One of those villages was Chevington. The battle for High Churchmanship had been won.

On 8 December 1932 the *Church Times* announced the rector's appointment to the Church of All Souls, Clapton, in the Diocese of London. The report concludes:

> Chevington Church has now an excellent and united congregation. While regretting his departure his Suffolk friends rejoice that he is going to a sphere of work which should give him opportunities for a fuller employment of his abilities and enthusiasm.

The Reverend Reginald Harry Nottage died in 1964 while holding the rectory of an Essex parish, Rawreth. His grave is on the south side of the Church of St Nicholas overlooking the pylon-straddled dreariness of the Thames estuary. Helen Maud Keble White, widow, who had presented her living of the Church of All Saints to the Guild of All Souls, joined a Roman Catholic Order on leaving Chevington and died as a Sister of that Order in 1950 at the age of 82. The church remains today in the patronage of the Guild.

Village gardens

During the summer, a week or so before the 'harvest holidays', jam jars on the wide Victorian window sills at the school would be crammed with an array of wild beauty gathered by children on their long walks to school. In *The English Flower Garden*, first published in 1883, William Robinson wrote:

> Side by side with the adoption in most large and show places of the patterned garden, both in design and planting, disappeared almost everywhere the old English garden, that is, one with a variety of form of shrub and flower and even low trees.

This variety was undoubtedly true of cottage gardens and in Chevington, in spite of some variation, the 'old English garden' continued as the dominant pattern until the housing development after the Second World War. The earlier style satisfied the needs of those whose working lives were spent in the village, but it has now given way to other designs based on the sophisticated preferences of the new type of resident.

In former days, if the garden was in front of the house, the main door was approached either by cobble-stones (as at Ernie Nunn's, near the Malting) or by a grass path (as at the row of cottages which stood next door to the chapel, occupied by the Souters, Kemps, Newmans, Rolfes and Mrs. Starling Smith). The path bisecting the front plot was edged in summer with stocks, Mrs. Sinkin's pinks, pansies, sweet-williams, phlox, lavender and standard, or shrub, roses of the musk and traditional specie varieties. The hybrid teas did not arrive in the village gardens until the mid-1920s and even then were not widely adopted: the bush, climbing, or rambling rose, such as the Dorothy Perkins, and Paul's Scarlet, remained part of the traditional gardening scene.

Vegetables were grown in perfect rows behind the jumble of the flowers. In other gardens vegetables were in cultivation on the side of the cottage or, in a few cases, at the rear. In addition to a small shed for the custody of garden tools, sticks for beans, or peas, the wheelbarrow and time-worn odds and ends, there would be the earth closet which, at some cottages, would be one of a pair, or perhaps more. There were thus ample facilities for the effective fertilisation of the garden.

Potatoes, beans, peas, cabbages and onions were grown in abundance and, occasionally, there would be serried rows of cos lettuce. From March, or earlier if the season was mild, villagers would be active in their gardens, the men maintaining responsibility for vegetables, the women tending the flowers and making wine, for in rural areas the distinctive masculine and feminine roles were conservatively interpreted, not only in the cultivation of the garden, but in such domestic activities as dusting, preparing meals and washing up. There was, as always, some individuality. Bob Avis, a former thatcher, who lived opposite the school, maintained a flower garden beautiful to behold, Andrew Newman, a lame, retired horsekeeper, grew a fine assortment of flowers and, from time to time, he would present a single bloom to a child on her way to school.

Although the 1st Earl of Bristol's delightful 18th century summer house still exists, the walled gardens of Ickworth have fallen into disuse. Years ago they were well known by Chevington people who welcomed opportunities for seeing more exotic produce than their own gooseberries, rhubarb and potatoes: there were loganberries and figs and, hanging profusely, protected by nets in the special greenhouse, water-melons, almost ripe. Strawberry teas in high summer with Herbert Coster, Lord Bristol's chief gardener, were unforgettable occasions. Arthur Edwards ('Stumpy') of Weathercock Hill, Charlie Quantrill and Starling Clarke all worked 'in the gardens'; there were foresters such as George and Bill Wallace and Harry Smith, and Harry, or 'Terrible', Bridge who, in spite of his name, was a skilled hurdler on the estate which featured so prominently in the lives of Chevington people.

Many of the trees, hedges and cottage gardens of other years have disappeared. It is not evident that there has been any definite scheme in Chevington for the replacement of those trees[78] which formerly graced the fields, meadows and road-side, but a few small trees and shrubs have been planted here and there. In the main, neat lawns, drives leading to garages, and small, primly-edged flower beds and borders have taken the place of the traditional type of 'open' cottage garden. In spite of the continued cultivation of vegetables, the tradition is not allowed to monopolise the garden plots as formerly, for suburbia is certainly making its presence felt in the excessive housing development of post-war years. The majority of residents commute by car to their place of work in Bury, or beyond. Their approach to gardening lacks the urgency shown by the horse-keepers, cowmen, and Solomon Milks of the past for whom gardening was something more compelling than a refined hobby. It was, during the time of low agricultural wages, a stern necessity to provide a supply of cheap vegetables. There was not in those days down Chevington Way the choice of leisure pursuits now made possible during a shorter working week by the use of the car and television. Although he worked long and strenuous hours, Solomon Milk had the time and the will to cultivate his garden. It was, of course, another world.

Old Man's Beard. *Clematis vitalba*.

CHAPTER FOUR

THE PARISH CHURCH OF ALL SAINTS
AND THE PEOPLE

A thousand ages in Thy sight
Are like an evening gone,
Short as the watch that ends the night
Before the rising sun.
    Isaac Watts, 1674-1748

O enter then his gates with praise,
Approach with joy his courts unto;
Praise, laud and bless his name always,
For it is seemly so to do.
    W. Kethe, *Day's Psalter*, 1561

DOMESDAY BOOK (1086) reveals that there was at that time a church with 30 acres of free land in Chevington: *Ceuentuna ... ecclesia de 30 acres terræ liberæ*. It is almost certain that the pre-Conquest church was a wooden building which remained in existence for about a hundred years after Domesday when, during the years 1130–80, it was replaced by a larger stone church remnants of which are visible today.

The site of the church and the churchyard is considerably more ancient than the present building. To the north-east of the church the exceptionally strong camp, protected by bank and moat and enclosing the present Chevington Hall Farm, could date from the Romano–British period, i.e. from before the years A.D. 450,[1] or it could be of prehistoric origin although, in the absence of archaeological evidence, it is impossible to be certain. However, it is clear from inspections of the site that the stronghold is of great antiquity[2] and, as a consequence, its prior existence and prestige were likely factors, during the ninth or 10th centuries, in the choice of the site for the erection of a manor house actually within the stronghold and of the neighbouring site as a centre for Christian worship.[3] According to Gage it is probable that a drawbridge, presumably from the stronghold's western moat, connected the fortified enclosure with the Church of All Saints[4] but, again, there is no known evidence of such a construction.

The church is situated in relatively low-lying country at the geographical centre of the parish and is visible among the trees as the village is approached from Saxham, or from Hollybush Green Farm, towards Weathercock Hill. Although there has been much post-war housing development along the road leading to the Church of All Saints, its position in this 'large scattered village, on a picturesque acclivity'[5] is secluded. In the Middle Ages, however, it is clear that the church and adjoining hall lay at the centre of social activity: a windmill stood on Great Days, a little south-east of the church, the open fields lay to the north,[6] the Gildhall[7] was close to the churchyard and Chevington Way, from Broad Green to St Edmundsbury, passed a few yards from the church porch. It is virtually certain, therefore, that until the 17th century, people lived and worked very close to their church. Maps are in existence which show the original parsonage in Church Meadow to the immediate west. The date of the later acquisition of a rectory of considerable distinction is uncertain, but there is a reference in the glebe terrier of 1678, during the incumbency of Robert Underwood, to the rectory's being a 'mansion house'.[8]

The older part of the churchyard which, according to a terrier of 1728, was fenced in 'on the charge of the parish', lies to the south and east of the church. Graves of parishioners, who died after the beginning of the present century, are to the north and, in 1980, an area in Church Meadow was bought as a necessary extension. The village Women's Institute, led by Mrs. J. Mackay and Mrs. D. Stutely, and assisted by their husbands, have recently concluded an admirable survey of all graves in the churchyard. Some of the inscriptions on the gravestones, varying from the beautiful to the banal, are of considerable interest and a few headstones are of fine design, indicative of the stonemason's art. The three daughters of the Reverend John White I, Sarah, Elizabeth and Frances, rest in separate table tombs in the shadow of the tower; the Reverend John White II, his wife, Mary, and many of their children have their graves on the other side of the footpath; and the name of Edward Burch, rector 1734–76, can still be traced on a memorial stone at the east of the church, but it is now difficult to read the inscription which continues almost to ground level:

> Conscientious in the discharge of his pastoral office, steady in his friendships, benevolent in his disposition and in every relation of life.

The inscription on the grave of Samuel Brooks (d. 1830), a local farmer, and his wife Elizabeth (d. 1829) contributes a warning to posterity:

> This life hangs by a silver thread,
> Which soon is cut and we are dead;
> Then boast not reader of thy might,
> Alive at noon and dead at night.

But what can be revealed from the quotation 'A broken and contrite heart, O God, thou wilt not despise' which is incised on the grave of Elizabeth Jennison who died in 1846?

On the headstone of Emma Blackburn, the coachman's wife (d. 1901), in the north-west of the churchyard, is the simple imperative: 'Take ye heed, watch and pray for ye know not when the time is'. However, perhaps the most poignant of all are the words from the Requiem on the War Memorial which is passed on the left as one walks along the main footpath towards the south door:

> Grant them, O lord, eternal rest and let light perpetual
> shine upon them.

In a glebe terrier of 1699, the rector, the Reverend Dr. Edward Grove, and three 'substantial' parishioners, Robert Kemp, John Kemp and Robert Underwood, recorded that Monday 15 May of that year was Rogation Monday, the customary date for procession from the church and through the churchyard for the 'annual perambulation and procession for ye preservation of ancient bounds and rights of our township'.

Rogationtide was the annual blessing of the crops involving God's blessing in the promise of a good harvest.

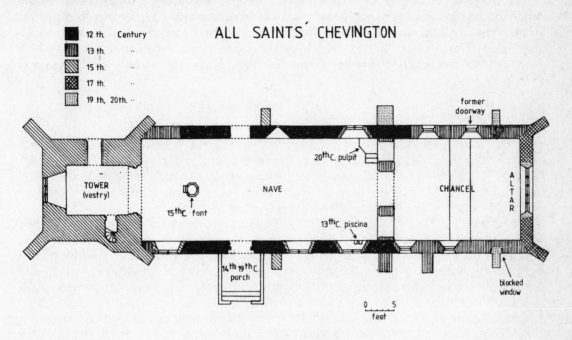

17. Plan of the church.

The Exterior

Of relatively small size, the church consists of battlemented nave, chancel, west tower and south porch. The main materials used are random stone, flint and clunch with a few modern brick insertions, particularly on the south side and across the top of one of the southern windows. High on one of the south wall buttresses is a medieval mass dial showing a set of radiating lines, similar to a sundial, to indicate the times of church services. The spike was set at the centre and one of the lines, which seems more prominent than the others, indicated the time of the Mass. To passers-by in the churchyard, which was the meeting place for many secular occasions, the dial would serve as a reminder of more serious obligations.

The original Norman church, parts of which still exist, extended approximately from the present altar steps to about seven feet east of the present tower. It was built in 1130-80,[9] a little later than the great Norman gate of the Abbey of St Edmundsbury. A Norman slit window* with a deep splay remains on the north wall and, during repairs in the early 19th century, traces of a similar window were found in the south wall of the present nave, a little west of the chancel.[10] It is reasonable to conclude, therefore, that the windows in the north and south walls of the Norman church were similar to the present slit window. The height of the Norman church is traceable (up to 12 feet) on the south wall, particularly above the porch. The roof was probably of the saddleback* type in order to give adequate height and it was almost certainly thatched. There was no south porch as seen today and there is no evidence of a Norman tower.

The Norman south doorway has engaged columns, one having a foliated capital, the other the dog-tooth ornament* which extends from the outer arch down to the outer jambs. The Norman north door, which appears to be earlier, is a plain and single-chamfered construction. It was probably the entrance for parishioners who lived on the north of the church towards Great Saxham, or in the vicinity of Chevington Park itself.

Later re-building: The chancel and the nave

In the latter part of the 13th century the building was transformed. The east end of the rectangular Norman church was extended approximately twenty feet in order to form a chancel and a wall was erected, with a central arch, to separate that chancel from the nave.[11] At the same time the Norman church was lengthened about seven feet westwards and it is possible that a tower was built at that time.[12]

An observer in 1828[13] reported that the eastern walls of the Norman church had been taken down to a height of four, or five, feet, and were still discernible at that level both on the north and south walls of the chancel. The 13th-century builders then built up the walls, provided a flat roof, and inserted lancet windows in the north and south walls of the chancel on a string course* of projecting hewn stone which still exists.

One window on the south side of the chancel is lower than the others, a custom which is by no means uncommon. Now glazed, the window was formerly fitted with a door, or shutter. Several theories have been advanced, but a writer at the beginning of the century held the view that a light was placed in such 'low side windows' to scare evil spirits from the churchyard.[14] It seems more likely that a bell was rung at the low open window during Mass so that the visitors from Bury Abbey resident at the Hall, the Solomon Milks working on Church Green, or on the open fields to the north, could hear and be reminded of the Celebration, or that passers-by could catch a glimpse of what was central to their faith.

Evidence of substantial alteration to the 13th-century chancel is visible. It was shortened by about twelve feet in 1697 during the incumbency of Dr. Edward Grove because of subsidence caused 'chiefly by the moat of standing water'[15] which was undermining the foundations of the east end. The present east wall is, therefore, late 17th century and has been plastered over. Two 17th century buttresses support the truncated east end. At the same time the roof of the chancel was lowered when it was confidently stated that the reduced building was more 'proportional to the body of the adjoining church'.[16]

When the Reverend Doctor shortened the chancel he inserted an 'unsightly wooden east window'.[17] This was replaced by a large three-light window in 1826, given by Mrs. Elizabeth White, widow of the Reverend John White I. In 1908, however, that 19th-century 'Early English' revival was removed — its existence is still marked on the exterior of the east wall — and was replaced by the present 'Gothic' straight-headed window with its five arched lights.

The nave has Norman walls up to a height of approximately 12 feet. The 13th-century builders heightened the nave, added the brick battlements and constructed a new roof. At the same time it was extended westwards approximately seven feet, in building material which can be compared with that of the chancel.[18] All Norman slit windows were filled in, with the exception of one on the north wall.

The Tower

On 12 December 1445 Robert Somerton left 40s. 0d. for the new 'campanile' bell tower.[19] In September 1475, Robert Paman, father of the then rector, another Robert, instructed his executors that his body should be buried in the chancel of All Saints. He made a number of bequests, including £20 towards the provision of three new bells, provided that the two old ones be sold *in expeditionem*, i.e. towards the new bells.[20] In the same year, Simon Goday[21] contributed 20s. 0d. (£1) to the new bells to be spent in equal portions in three years. The terms in which Robert Somerton and Robert Paman expressed their bequests confirm that a bell tower was already in existence, in which case credence is added to the possibility that it was built in the 13th century at the time of the lengthening of the west end of the church.

The present tower, a 15th-century construction, has its stair-turret on the south side. In 1817, it was heightened at the instigation of the 5th Earl of Bristol in order to make it clearly visible from Ickworth House: battlements were added to the additional stage of the tower, adorned with four crocketed* pinnacles. The work was carried out by John de Carle of Bury St Edmunds who presented a bill of £120 to the Earl for raising the tower and 'fixing 4 stone turrets'.[22] The upper stage is narrower than the walls below and the later stonework on the quoins and pinnacles is a softer stone than the medieval limestone. Relatively high, but somewhat out of proportion, the tower is impressive, especially since its recent restoration after years of preparation and fund-raising led by the rector and other dedicated workers.

In the bell loft, on the second stage with the arched and latticed openings on each wall, are five bells, now silent because of a dearth of trained ringers. In former years, they would have been rung: then, just before the service was timed to begin, the single and staccato toll: Come . . . Come . . . Come . . . , which acted as a reminder to worshippers, making their way to church, of the urgent need to quicken their step.

In the 15th century when the present tower was built, bells would ring at church festivals, baptisms and weddings, as well as at funerals. At times of rejoicing, or emergency, bells would toll.[23] According to Raven there were four bells at Chevington in the mid-16th century.[24] Tolling and the mere jangling of bells gave place in the late 17th century to change-ringing and tuning to a musical scale in mathematical order. Most bells in Suffolk are 17th-century in origin[25] and the oldest bell at Chevington, a tenor in F, is a small one founded by John Draper of Thetford in 1620. He was the third son of Thomas, famous bell-founder and Mayor of Thetford, 1588.[26] Another famous East Anglian bell-founder was Thomas Gardiner of Sudbury who was respon-sible for the large bell in Chevington dated 1737.[27] A second 18th-century bell is inscribed 'Thos. Osborn, Downham, Fecit, 1780'. Mears of London founded a bell in 1848 which was apparently provided by the Reverend John White II and his sisters, Elizabeth and Frances, of Chevington Grove, whose names are inscribed on it. In 1905, in order to mark the Reverend John White III's golden wedding, a fifth bell, dated 1760 by Lesto Pack, was recast by Mears and Stainbank of London. The commemoration including the re-hanging of all the bells and a restoration of their frames[28] which are now massive and squarely built structures.

A framed notice in the ringing gallery states:

> On Wednesday November 20th 1907 there was rung on these harmonious bells a peal of doubles consisting of 5,040 changes, being 6 score of Bob Doubles, 6 score of Morning Star and 46 score Grandsire. This is the first peal ever rung on the bells . . . Full time was 3 hours 3 minutes.[29]

Led by Arthur Rolfe, the insurance agent, the Chevington bellringers, a friendly and closely-knit fraternity, were well-known in all the surrounding villages.

18. South porch of All Saints' Church, from a 19th-century drawing.

The South Porch

It is unlikely that the Norman church had a porch although many ceremonies would have been enacted 'at the door' — *ad portas*. In his will on 10 May 1498 Edward Crispe gave 2s. 0d. (10p.) towards a new church 'porta'.[30] When the porch was erected at Chevington in the 14th century, part of the baptism service before the later ceremony at the font, and the solemnisation of marriages, took place there. The Pamans and Solomon Milks would foregather in the porch to discuss everyday affairs, and notices were officially nailed to the church door. According to Munro Cautley[31] penance was performed in the porch for all to see. There the penitent stood in a white sheet on three consecutive Sundays, pleading for the prayers of his fellow worshippers.

The timber craftsmanship of the porch of the Church of All Saints is of uncommon interest, particularly the two carved beams and the grooved entrance arch which is pinned visibly at its shoulders into two verticals. The beam nearer to the door is of billet decoration: a chequerboard *motif* of raised rectangles, a moulding used frequently in Norman architecture. It is conceivable, therefore, that this single beam was carved by a Chevington craftsman 200 years before its insertion into the porch. The arch consists of two weighty, carved timbers split from the same great piece of wood. The only method of ensuring such essential matching was to produce a 'split image'. The plaster above the arch, probably a 19th-century addition, is to be deplored but, in the main, the porch is a fine medieval timbered construction which warrants the closest attention. A heavy oak door, probably 18th-century and showing some signs of a fixture for a light, or lantern, is usually unlocked and invites entry down the steps, across the stone floor and into the nave of the church.

The interior

When viewed from the west the aisleless rectangularity of the church is immediately apparent. The noticeable features are the tall chancel arch and its side openings, the arch-braced, tie-beam roof and the 15th-century pews in the chancel and at the west end of the nave. The font, which formerly stood in the opening leading to the north door, is octagonal and of the early 15th century.[32] The shields are worn and it is interesting to speculate that the initials 'G.P.' inscribed on one side of the bowl might be those of a Giles Paman whose family lived in the parish for at least four centuries.

The treble arch effect, which separates the nave from the chancel, is impressive.[33] Seven feet in width, the chancel arch rests on heavy moulded corbels*; in medieval times the two plain side openings, each four feet in width, accommodated small altars.[34] The 1908–10 restoration included the erection of an oak screen with curvilinear tracery, which obscured the view of the chancel from the nave and which was headed by an organ loft and pipes, the central ones rising above the apex of the central arch. That entire superstructure, screen and organ, was removed in 1937,[35] so that the arches now present an uninterrupted view into the chancel.

The cambered roof with bold collar beams could be of 13th-century construction, but it was subsequently reinforced by three tie beams to take the thrust, carved with a riband pattern: the eastern is inscribed '1590 Thomas Frost', the central, 'S.P 1638' and the western 'CP 1638'. It was almost certain that the initials are of Simon Paman and Clement Paman who gave money for the repair of the roof in the 17th century.

A gallery for the use of musicians and choir, probably 17th-century, formerly extended from the tower arch into the nave, but it was removed during the restoration of 1908–10 when the choir was transferred to the chancel.

During the recent restoration, traces of red pigment, apparently of medieval origin, were revealed on the north wall and, further east, near the pulpit window, there were signs of a geometrical pattern resembling brickwork, also in red pigment. Such evidence reminds us that, probably until 1600, the people of Chevington worshipped in a church brilliantly coloured so that, with the many flickering candles and statues, it presented a dramatic spectacle to the Pamans, Goodays, Somertons and Solomon Milks.

According to the wills of the 15th century, it is clear that altars existed in the side openings of the chancel arch. If Tymms[36] is correct, the altar of the Virgin Mary was at the end of the south wall and an altar, probably dedicated to St John the Baptist, occupied a corresponding place in the north. In 1450 Roger Nycole[37] left 6s. 8d. (33p.) towards the repainting of the Annunciation at the altar of the Virgin. Twenty-five years later Robert Paman,[38] a most generous benefactor, bequeathed £5 for 'building a window and support in front of St John', and on 10 May 1498[39] Edward Crispe left one cow: 'profit from which to go yearly to the rector . . . maintaining light for him in front of the crucifix'.

Before the Reformation of the 16th century a wooden, or stone, screen which traversed on the west side the width of the chancel arch, supported the gallery for the cross, or rood, bearing the body of Christ in the centre and the life size figures of the Virgin Mary and St John the Evangelist on either side. As Munro Cautley[40] states, 'The rood became an object of veneration and devotion, vying even with the altar'. It was from the rood loft that the Gospel was sometimes either sung by a small choir, or read by a priest. The loft was undoubtedly protected by parapets, enriched by niches which enclosed statues of angels and saints. Access to the rood loft was by means of a staircase built near the present pulpit. It led to a door in the wall high above the present pulpit at the side of the loft.

It is impossible to say precisely when the rood and loft disappeared from the church after the Reformation, but it is reasonable to assume that they were taken down in the 1540s. The screen could have lasted until the time of the Reverend Robert Under-wood (1630–1690) who, in 1646, had signed a petition[41] of the Suffolk Ministers in favour of Presbyterianism. It could, of course, simply have been left to decay. However, as late as 1828[42] the final vestiges of the screen, parapet, and rood loft, all expressions of medieval craftsmanship, disappeared: the staircase leading to the loft was 'cut out' and the 'pointed doorway removed'. So the great glory was irredeemably lost.

In the Middle Ages it was in the nave of the church that the Chevington church ales, or feasts, would take place such as plough-ale, at the time of ploughing, and lamb-ale at lamb shearing.[43] The churchwardens provided the beer which had been brewed in the parish brew house and the parish revellers paid for their ale, the profits from which would accrue to the Church of All Saints. Noise, revelry, singing and dancing were the order of the day.

The chancel

For 400 years prior to 1697, the chancel had extended 12 feet beyond the present east wall.[44] It is probable that a piscina and sedilia were included in the demolition of the eastern end of the south wall. There are two slender lancet windows on the north wall and two on the south, all 13th-century Early English.*. The east window, in a sense appropriately 17th-century 'Gothic', was inserted in 1910. It replaced the 1828 'Early English' window of three grouped lancets. The position of the sill of that former window is visible on the east wall behind the altar. Lowered, as part of the

Reverend Dr. Grove's alterations in 1697, the roof is striking in its simplicity and crowns a beautiful chancel free from distracting clutter and confusion. On the beam over the altar the words *Soli Deo* (To God alone) are inscribed in gilt lettering and, on another, the name of Edward Grove is clearly incised.

Included in the chancel were many box pews, one of which was known as the parsonage pew. A nonagenarian parishioner, who worked at the rectory at the beginning of the century, can still remember having to sit in the chancel discreetly close to the rector's family. Certainly until the early 1900s the residents at the Grove and farmers such as the Pettits and the Everards of the shop would have their own box pew. As late as the 1920s the Solomon Milks would crowd at the west end of the church and sing without inhibition. At the end of the evening services during the long weeks of summer they would retire to the '*Greyhound* Corner', the central village meeting place for banter and general conversation or, of course, to the more convivial atmosphere of the hostelry itself.

It was in the chancel — or, more rightly, in the original larger one — that rectors and monks, appointed by the Abbot of St Edmundsbury, would conduct the ritual of worship. In the slow fall of darkness of a winter's afternoon, it is now difficult to believe that for centuries colourful statues, tabernacles, flickering lights, and paintings abounded here in the chancel of All Saints. In 1524 William Paman[45] gave 'to All Saints Church a cow for the common light of the sepulchre' (this was the Easter Sepulchre* on the north side of the High Altar) and his kinsman, Henry,[46] had previously bequeathed the princely sum of £9 to the church 'where that is most necessary'. Robert, in 1475[47] gave:

> my 2 biggest candlesticks and 2 cows to the upkeep of 3 lights in Chevington, one in front of the Trinity next to the High Altar, another in front of St Mary, and the other in front of St John and St Edmund.

Standing in the nave, Solomon Milk peered through the rood screen in reverential fear, realising the symbolism, but failing to understand the great mystery of it all. English, the language known to the people, was used only exceptionally when the priest preached a rare sermon and then probably from the remote eminence of the rood loft itself.

Furniture and Memorials

The former box pews and the 20th-century choir stalls have been cleared from the chancel, although one of the stalls is still serving as a seat in the south porch. There are some 15th-century benches, similar to those at the west end of the nave which will be discussed later.

On the High Altar there was formerly a crucifix which had been placed there in memory of a headmistress, Florence Ellen Postle, who taught the children of the village 1927-1949, and to whom many look back with gratitude and affection.

On the south wall are mural tablets commemorating the life of the Reverend John White III, Rector 1853-1908, and his wife, Caroline Macdonell, with the apt quotation from the prophet Micah:

> What shall the Lord require of theè, but to do justly
> and to love mercy and to walk humbly with thy God?

His grandfather, the Reverend John White I, Rector 1776–1818, and his grandmother, Elizabeth Keble, rest in the chancel:

> His whole life presented a noble example of integrity, temperance and humility.

Elizabeth, his grandmother, who died in 1834, was 'eminently adorned by every virtue of the daughter, the wife and mother'. His brother, Cyril, fought in the Indian Mutiny and has his memorial on the north wall near his sister's. His son, George Edmund, a captain in the Sikh infantry, killed at Amritsar 1902, is remembered on the opposite wall with 'I have finished the work which thou gavest me to do'. There remain two tablets to his grandsons: Cyril Miles, who died as a result of a shooting accident in New Zealand at the age of 12, and John, a lieutenant in the Royal Hampshire Regiment, who was killed at Gallipoli in 1916 at the age of 24: *Dulce est pro patria mori.*

The two wives of the Reverend Edward Burch, Rector 1734–1776, are remembered in the chancel: the memorial to Ann, his second wife, is an attractive rococo monument, bearing heraldic arms. She was the sister of Dr. Robert Butts, Bishop of Norwich and, later, of Ely. The Reverend Doctor Grove, Rector, 1693–1726, and his family, have their commemoration with arms in the chancel which he himself had shortened and lowered: the vault is just east of the chancel arch. His son, Edward, died in 1723; his wife, a few months later.

On the north side of the nave is a clearly demarcated area in the floor which indicates the grave of a young 13th-century monk whose skeleton was discovered in 1828. Gage[48] writes:

> It contained a very perfect skeleton of a young ecclesiastic. The hands were found raised on the breast, and the remains of a leaden chalice, which had fallen from them, lay near the right shoulder.

The pulpit and the reading desk were erected in 1908 by the parishioners, family and friends, in gratitude for the life of the Reverend John White III, replacing the Victorian pulpit and reading desk which previously stood on the south side in front of the small south arch.

19. 14th-century parish chest from a drawing made in 1864.

The 14th-century chest, possibly 1307–50, which at present stands near the north wall of the nave is one of the two outstanding artistic possessions of the church. The carvings on the front of the chest shows arches, tracery, leaves, birds, and animals and, on the extreme left, two monkeys which appear to be shaking hands, a pair of imperious birds, an unidentified long-tailed creature and, to complete the assortment, two bunches of grapes. The chest, which has been deprived of its right-hand panel and foot was, according to Thomas Gage,[49] painted red in the early part of the last century.

Chevington's chest was proudly shown in 1930 at an Exhibition of Medieval Art held at the Victoria and Albert Museum. The catalogue states:

> *Chest, oak.* The front carved with an arcade of Gothic tracery, and the stiles (of which one is missing) with chimeras and birds. Late XIVth century.

The carved musicians with their instruments, serving as poppyheads*, or finials, to 15th-century bench ends in the chancel and at the west of the church, are of much interest and significance. Until the beginning of the 14th century, there were no seats in the church, the nave being an uncluttered, empty space. Tradition has it that the 12 symmetrical benches with traceried sides were originally in use along the north and

20.   *Carved bench ends of musicians, 15th century. Left, the lute; Right, the double pipes.*

south walls of the nave, hence exemplifying the expression 'the weakest go to the wall'.[50] An early 19th-century sketch of the interior of the church indicates that the seats were certainly in use in the north of the nave. They probably remained there until the 17th century when box pews replaced them. Cautley[51] is of the opinion that the panelling at the back of the benches could be part of the original rood loft.

It is likely that the carvings were worked by a local, possibly a Chevington, craftsman who, although oblivious of the refinements of church music, took part in parish secular occasions held in the churchyard, or elsewhere in the parish bounds, when carolling, dancing, and revelry were popular musical pastimes. Maybe the benches were presented to the church by a leading Chevington family, such as the Pamans.

The 15th century poppyheads depict the shawm, lute, cymbals, bagpipes, double pipes and psaltery. The *shawm*, ancient and double-reeded, forerunner of the oboe, was played mainly as a strident outdoor instrument for ceremonial events, processions and dances but, on occasions, it was played during ceremonies in church, or to augment the voices of a choir. Having originated in the Far East, the *psaltery* was introduced in England at the time of the Crusades and was popular from the 12th century onwards. It was played, while standing in the player's lap flat against his chest, by the finger,[52] or by the use of a quill.

During the Middle Ages, a portable organ and one, or two, singers were possibly accommodated on the painted rood loft. It is of interest to recall that John Wilbye, 1574-1638, the greatest composer of madrigals, lived at Hengrave Hall from 1595 and remained there for 35 years as the Kytsons' official household musician. It is not entirely presumptuous to think that any continuing concern with music at Chevington from the late 15th century received vicarious encouragement during the time that the Kytson family held the manor and were patrons of the living there. However, it was not until the late 17th century, or even later, that a musicians' gallery for the parish musicians was constructed at the west end of the church. In 1983 a fine organ made in 1829 in St Aldate's, Oxford, by a William Chambers, was installed close to the position of the former gallery.

In the vestry, there is a small commemorative plaque inscribed:

> To the Greater Glory of God in memory of the Reverend A. K. Shrewsbury, Rector of Chevington, 1934-1953, Rural Dean of Horringer, 1950-1953, RIP.

His rectorship, during the troubled war years when the parish experienced great and permanent change, will be long remembered.

Acquired during the time of the Reverend Dr. Edward Grove — 'a staunch lover of truth and right' — the Royal Arms of George I, 1714-1727, inscribed G.R. 1726, are on the south wall. At the beginning of the 19th century the arms were fixed to the musicians' gallery; during the early 1900s they were exhibited in the more conventional position above the chancel arch facing west, so members of the congregation could be reminded of the sovereignty of the King.

The church plate, of great interest, includes two patens and a chalice dated 1595 with a London hallmark, kept in safe custody in Bury St Edmunds. In addition, there are two chalices and two patens at the church, the larger chalice bearing the inscription:

> The gift of the Confraternity of the Blessed Sacrament
> to the Church of All Saints, Chevington.

More remarkable is a silver pyx, or travelling cup, in two pieces, made and designed by the distinguished silversmith, Omar Ramsden (1873-1939). Given by a Frances

Napier, it bears a London hallmark of 1929 and the enigmatic citation '*sua matre donata*'.

The parish registers, a beautiful collection dating from 1559, are housed in the County Record Office at Bury St Edmunds. In 1912 the registers, up to the year 1812, were transcribed by William Briggs and privately printed by subscription. They reveal a wealth of information about the people of Chevington: the Underwoods, Simkins, Kemps, Pamans, Smiths, Nunns, Clarkes and Frosts.

1561   Thomas Halles (who was slayne with a cart falinge upon him) was buried the first day of August.

1596   March 6. John Rush of Bury was drowned on 3rd March by mysadventure, viz. by fallinge owt of a boate into ye moate belonging to Chevington Hall.

1607   A marriage: John Raye (sonne and heir apparaent of John Raye of Denston) and Elizabeth Paman (the daughter of Clement Paman — gent.)

1785   Samuel West, a pauper, aged 35, died February 22nd.

People built the Church of All Saints down Chevington Way, enlarged and altered it, restored it and made it what it is. For centuries the people have met in this place which has witnessed scenes of their revelry, prayer and praise: the church ales, the baptisms and deaths, the joy of Christmas and the hope of Easter. It was the people's church. At worship and at work they were aware of the power of the Unseen. Life moves on but, for some, that power remains.

Cow Parsley; *Anthriscus sylvestris*.

CHAPTER FIVE

AN AGE OF TRANSITION

Fled are those times when, in harmonious strains,
The rustic poet praised his native plains;
No shepherds, now, in smooth alternate verse
Their country's beauty or their nymphs rehearse.

— George Crabbe, Suffolk poet 1754-1832.

If it warn't for hope the heart 'ud die.

— A Suffolk Proverb.

THE GREAT WAR of 1914-18 shattered many illusions. Village rumour had it that the Reverend Arthur Keble White's elder son, Alistair, would eventually take Holy Orders and continue the long tradition of the Whites' custody of the living at Chevington. Village gossip was often credible but, at that time, it was certainly wide of the mark for, when the war was over, Alistair started a commercial career while Geoffrey, the younger son, remained in the Royal Navy in which he had served as a captain during the war. In the 1920s Captain Geoffrey Meredith Keble White changed his surname by deed poll to Keble-White, an adaptation which was soon followed by other members of the family.

In 1929 the late rector's daughter, Cynthia Keble White, married Major, later Brigadier, Jasper Gray Frere, M.C., D.S.O., of the Suffolk Regiment, a member of an ancient East Anglian family. Later it was reported that the Freres, together with a fellow officer, had been kidnapped by Achakjai raiders during a visit to the Indian frontier and that a release was not secured until Afghanistan had come to satisfactory terms with the British government. About the same time the airship R.100 was gliding serenely and silently over the fields of Chevington.

The village school

Since its foundation in 1847 the school, attended by all the Chevington children from five to 14 years of age, had given the village a sense of cohesion and unity. As the last White, the Reverend Arthur Keble, had been the Chairman of the Managers and the official correspondent of the school, it was considered appropriate as a sign of respect, to close the school on the day of his funeral on 1 March 1926.

Under the leadership of Miss A. Burnett-Hurst, the head teacher, the school had made noticeable academic progress during the mid-1920s. In May 1926 the Inspector of the Diocese visited the school and inspected the teaching:

> there have been strides made since my last visit and with time there is no doubt that the tone and knowledge, will be greatly improved.[1]

On 21 May 1926, the head teacher recorded in the Log Book:

Empire Day was celebrated this morning at 11.45 when all the children saluted the Union Jack and sang the National Anthem. The upper classes had a lesson on the British Empire.[2]

On 7 June of the same year, the head conscientiously reported that, as the Chapel Sunday School treat was taking place that afternoon, the attendance at school was very poor.[3] Reports from the Inspectorate indicate that there was notable improvement in the standards of the school which, in the past, had been less than satisfactory mainly, but not entirely, because of frequent changes of head teacher. Entries in the Log Book concern such detail as visits by the medical officer, Dr. Bygott, who brought malt extract for a certain pupil, punishment of a boy from a particularly difficult family, verminous heads, severe snow, the vast amount of mud brought into the school and, inevitably, the state of the school 'offices'.

On 22 October 1926 the inspectors reported:[4]

Two boys of twelve years of age, one who does little work and the other of feeble intellect, might with advantage be transferred to a School where they could come under the influence of men.

(*Of the head teacher*). She will doubtless receive the support of the Managers in her efforts to bring about a general improvement in the tone of the School.

On 3 March 1927 Miss Burnett-Hurst recorded that she had attended a lecture in Bury by Professor Percy Nunn on the subject of the curriculum.[5] Nunn was one of the leading educationalists of the day who, at that time, was working in London where he was engaged in research and in lecturing to graduate entrants to the teaching profession. It is of interest that Nunn's progressive influence extended to the remote National School at Chevington. I recall Miss Burnett-Hurst, Miss Goldsmith ('Kitty') and Miss Ellwood very vividly. Miss Burnett-Hurst, recently arrived from India, gave some fascinating geography lessons and her readings from *Lamb's Tales from Shakespeare* were memorable.

Miss Florence Postle was appointed head of the village school in September 1927, consequent on Miss Burnett-Hurst's promotion to the headship of Long Melford Girls' School. An inspector's report in November 1929 referred to the general improvement and good progress in English composition, but 'big boys and girls write in a slovenly style and omit the full stops and capital letters'.[6] Florence Postle's teaching of nature study, of special interest to country children, and basic arithmetic were so successful that former pupils of those years look back to her work with genuine gratitude and appreciation. On completion of Flo Postle's 10 years' service on 31 December 1937[7] the Chairman of Managers recorded:

It was resolved that an appreciation of her services be placed in the minutes and all present joined in congratulations.

During the summer holiday of 1949 Florence Ellen Postle died suddenly. She had been headmistress for 22 years having made a valuable contribution to the education of many children in the little school down Chevington Way.

Since it was built, although to a lesser extent after the 1939–45 War, the village school in Chevington had been responsible for all the education that the boys and girls received. Very few pupils left the village elementary school at the age of 11 to attend the then secondary, or grammar, schools in Bury. The school was a co-ordinating social force in the village and was regarded as such by the parishioners, but numbers fell drastically to 36 in 1936 when closure was threatened. In the 1950s, however, the school was truncated to a primary school, the senior pupils having to travel to Bury for their compulsory secondary education and, more recently, the school has become a First School only, taking pupils from the ages of five to nine. At nine they are transferred to a comprehensive middle school in Bury, from which, at the age of 13, they enter a comprehensive upper school likely to be, in the future, the County Upper School. At present (1983) in the 1847 school at Chevington, 42 pupils await that great adventure. Although area schools had been established by some rural education authorities by the mid-1930s the all-age village school had been a major force in fostering a sense of community and village loyalty. Its disappearance, as at Chevington, was a crucial cause of the decline of a traditional way of life which had characterised English rural society for at least a century.

The big estates in the post-war period

Suffolk country houses continued to exert some influence on rural life. Throughout the 19th century the country house was the fulcrum of the rural economy and social life. A more practical consideration was that the country house and, moreover, the country estate, offered opportunities for employment. The greater the degree of participation by the estate workers, the stronger was the feeling of collective responsibility, fellowship and pride. Such benevolent authority engendered a sense of security among rural workers which, in the main, continued even in periods of agricultural stagnation.

As Lord of the Manor the 3rd Marquess of Bristol owned most of Chevington from 1864 until 1907, a reign of 43 years. He was a Member of Parliament for West Suffolk, 1859–64, Hereditary High Steward of the Liberty of St Edmundsbury and, although a Conservative, 'was desirous of financial reform'.[8] He possessed some fine pictures of the Italian, Spanish and English schools, and a collection of silver 'almost unrivalled in England both for its quantity and quality'.[9] At the time of his death, he owned 32,000 acres. In 1907, he was succeeded by his nephew, Captain F. W. F. Hervey, Royal Navy, who, as 4th Marquess of Bristol, became the principal landowner and Lord of the Manor of Chevington. He died in 1951 and was succeeded by his brother, Lord Herbert Hervey.

The influence of the large Suffolk landowner, in addition to that of the local squires such as the Whites, declined noticeably from the 1920s. Great Barton Hall was burnt down in 1918, the Afflecks were no longer in Dalham and the Riley Smiths had disappeared from Great Saxham. Livermere Hall, rebuilt in the early 19th century, was demolished in 1923.[10] Hardwick, a Jacobean house, but enlarged by the Cullums in the 1840s, disappeared in 1926. For many years, on August Bank Holidays, the West Suffolk General Hospital's fete was held there, a popular local event patronised by hundreds of people, including parties from Chevington, who would travel long journeys in their pony traps to meet old friends, visit the displays and exhibitions and gasp at the fireworks at the end of the day. Culford Hall, built by the great soldier, the Marquess of Cornwallis, became Culford School in 1935 when the large rural estate was broken up into suburban development. Lilian Redstone writing in 1930 observes:

Save for the Tollemaches in the East and the Herveys in the West, it (i.e. Suffolk) has few of those old established families which in other counties have borne for generations local responsibilities, but its yeoman stock became the backbone of our earliest settlements in the New World.[11]

The demolition of the country houses continued. Fornham Hall, built by James Wyatt in 1782, and Ousden Hall, where nothing remains but the 18th-century dovecote and the clock tower, were both demolished in 1955. In 1952, Hengrave Hall, built by Sir Thomas Kytson in 1525-38 and afterwards the main home of the Gages, became the property of the Assumption nuns who established a girls' boarding school in the 16th-century mansion. Perhaps the most lamented loss was the final destruction by fire in 1961 of Rushbrooke Hall after years of inexcusable negligence. Built in the 1550s by Edmund Jermyn, Rushbrooke was altered in the 1740s. The Georgian hall of that period was superb. The family of Jermyn at Rushbrooke had, throughout their history, been closely allied with the Herveys of neighbouring Ickworth.

It was not until 1956, however, that at Ickworth:

Five years after the death of the 4th Marquess, the house and part of the estate amounting to 1,792 acres (including the park and many acres of woodland) together with the greater part of the splendid collection of furniture, pictures, and other works of art, were accepted by the Treasury in lieu of death duties and handed over to the National Trust. The Marchioness of Bristol gave a generous endowment to the Trust for the maintenance of the house and property.[12]

Agricultural change

At the same time as rural life was experiencing the disintegration of the large estate and the disappearance of the country house as a social force, the farming industry itself was subjected to economic and technological innovation which not only revolutionised the industry, but resulted in permanent changes in the social composition of the rural community.

The Golden Age of the Suffolk farmer, heralded by the enhanced demand for home-produced food during the Crimean War (1854-1856) was dimmed during 1870-1900. The year 1879 was a particularly bad one in a long sequence of poor harvests when the farmer was compelled to compete against very cheap imported foodstuffs. Some farmers on the 'heavy' lands of Suffolk economised on labour, only employing men on a daily, or hourly, basis so that farm workers could be 'laid-off' at any time. Solomon Milk had most to endure.

The trend towards mechanisation in farming increased in momentum during the next 50 years, resulting in marked changes in the rural landscape and in the social composition of villages such as Chevington. The demands from the home market resulted in a temporary revival of agriculture during the Great War 1914-18 and prices remained relatively high until the end of the war as indicated by the good prices reached at local sales in 1918-19. However, the slump returned at the time of the exceptional drought in 1921. J. M. Stratton in *Agricultural Records, A.D. 220-1977*,[13] states:

1921. Wheat 17s. 6d. [87½p.].

An abnormally dry year, with almost unparalleled drought. January, very mild but rainy . . . February, exceptionally dry — one of the driest Februaries on record. Relatively warm. March, mostly showery and mild. April, mostly sunny and dry, with cold spell in middle of month. May, fine and dry. Severe frost on the 5th June, absolute drought in most places, especially in south. The driest June since records were kept. July, drought continued unbroken in most places. August . . . though with rainfall below average. September, mostly fine and warm . . . October, hot and dry for most of month. November, still dry, but cooler. December, mild, with rain everywhere except the south-east.

From the early 1920s Chevington farmers experienced renewed hardships, including at least one bankruptcy. The Beet Sugar Subsidy Act of 1925 did much to stimulate the sugar beet industry, for growing beet at a guaranteed price was an encouraging proposition. Alf Rolfe, who had by that time converted the old clothing factory into a garage as the centre for his contracting business, was in great demand for carting the stacked beet to the sugar beet factory which had been established in Bury in 1925. In 1973 this factory was extended and is now the largest in Europe.

The multi-purpose tractor, introduced into Chevington at the end of the First World War, was eventually responsible for continuing the revolution in agriculture pioneered by the binder-reaper and other harvest machinery at the beginning of the century. The first tractor, an American Titan, was used at Chevington Lodge by a prominent Suffolk farmer, Josiah John Marsh. By the early 1920s, the Fordson was on the fields of Chevington Hall. Throughout the next 15 years, the tractor, gradually, but certainly, was replacing the horse. At the outbreak of the Second World War there were 26,308 horses in Suffolk: in 1975 there were only 2,113.[14] As Ronald Blythe sadly reflects:[15]

Nothing has contributed more to the swift destruction of the old pattern of life in Suffolk than the death of the horse.

The Second World War had slowed down the mechanisation of the farm. By the late 1950s, the farmhorse had virtually disappeared from Chevington Way when, significantly, the remaining blacksmith's forge — at the beginning of the century a second forge stood on Broad Green — had already passed into obscurity.

Gladys Theobald, formerly Bowers, of Bury, writes of her grandfather, Peter, and father, Charlie, who were blacksmiths at Chevington from 1900. Peter was a great village character of the type that had almost disappeared from the Suffolk countryside; Charlie played cricket regularly for the village team and together, father and son, they contributed much to the life of Chevington. Horses were brought not only from all the farms of Chevington, but from Hargrave, where there was no blacksmith and, in spite of Bob Challis having a forge on Chedburgh Green, from time to time horses were led to Peter Bowers' forge from Chedburgh, Depden, Whepstead and Hawkedon. Gladys Theobald remembers:

My grandfather and father came to Chevington in 1900. Grandfather was a blacksmith and farrier for sixty years. He died in 1942 just two months short of his 88th birthday. For health reasons my father moved to Whepstead, but he only lived about four years after moving there, although we all remained there for the next thirty years or so.

   As far as I can remember they started work at about 7 a.m. and continued until 5—5.30 p.m. As for the fee they charged for work . . . it was 6s. a set (30p.) for shoeing horses, about 10s. 0d. (50p.) for repairing such things as harrows and other agricultural tools. Of course, they shod the cart and wagon wheels which, I should think, was a little more and they did a lot of fencing of the fields around the farms.

On a Saturday afternoon in 1934, when the village football team were booked to play at home, the news spread through the village that the two thatched cottages at the blacksmith's were ablaze. Hoses were run from College Farm, fire engines rattled their way from Bury and crowds of Chevington friends watched the tragic scene. Furniture was lowered quickly from the bedroom windows. They brought from the houses all carpets, chairs and curtains and some left only minutes before the burning thatch fell to the floor of the bedrooms. Charlie Dodson, the blacksmith, and his neighbour, Ol Pettit, and their families, were re-housed at the Lodge and College Farms, but the long, thatched cottages, with the five dormer windows, probably the most attractive cottages in the village, were irretrievably lost. In the late 1930s Solomon Milk earned about £1 11s. 6d. (£1.75p.) a week out of which he would possibly pay £1. 3s. 0d. (£1.15p.) for food and clothing for his wife, himself and two children. Rent was between 2s. 0d. (10p.) and 3s. 0d. (15p.) a week.[16] There were harvest and overtime allowances which helped a little and most farm workers had large gardens which produced a useful supply of vegetables. But life was hard and it was accepted as such: it was the natural order of things, a life which the farm workers had come to know over the years and to accept. Maggie Pask (now Pettitt), of Ousden, spent her childhood in Chevington, where her parents brought up their family of nine. She speaks of her childhood and of the years before:

Mum's father, Robert Argent, was a shoemaker in Chevington. He died when Mum, Margaret Argent, was seven, so her mother worked very hard doing laundry work to bring up a large family of eight girls and one boy. She had no help at all. They never had a lot of food, often they had to go without. When they left school the girls went into service at the age of twelve, going to London etc., except Mum who was the youngest. She helped her Mum and went into the clothing factory. Her brother, George — the only son — was killed in the First World War, so she had no support at all, only what she could earn.

My mother married Herbert Pask and they had a family of eight boys and one girl. Dad earned 10s. 0d. a week (50p.), but wages rose over the years to 30s. 0d. (£1.50p.) for horsekeepers and 28s. 0d. (£1.40p.) for farm labourers. Mum never got into debt. She paid as she went and often had nothing to eat on Fridays, only vegetables grown in the garden.

My father was a horsekeeper. He was working from 5 a.m. until late at night. He left in the morning only having a glass of water, came home for breakfast which was often fried potatoes and swede, or potatoes and cabbage. They used to have puttees on their legs, as they used to be so wet; there were no Wellingtons then. They had to clean out the ditches, standing often up to their knees in water.

Dad worked for Mr. Bridge, the butcher. He used to walk the cattle and sheep to Bury market for sale and bring some back. They used to run over all the fields and Dad was fit to drop by the time he got home. I remember he brought a fish home one week, a very long one. Mum did not know what to do with it. She had never seen one like it before. Anyway, she managed to get it in the boiler. I don't think I had any. It was an eel.

We had soup made with bones (some with meat on them in those days), vegetables, and dumplings made in a big boiler over the open fire. We had suet puddings with sugar, or jam, and fruit puddings. For breakfast, we had toast, or bread, with butter, or jam, but never together. For tea there would be bread and butter and sliced onions, or bread and jam. On Sundays we had cake.

In 1929 at the time of the general recession, the large family of Ballantine arrived at the Lodge farm from Northumberland. Selby Ballantine, one of the younger sons, settled in Chevington. He looks back to those early years:

It was very different. Up North it was mainly sheep and cattle. Suffolk was arable. We couldn't understand the Suffolk people and they couldn't understand us. The biggest problem was getting the land clean. The land was foul, the hedgerows overgrown and six foot thick.

When I was a student in the late 1930s, collating information on land utilisation in Chevington, Sam Pettit, of the College Farm, provided me with the details set out below. The list, which gives an allocation of 70 acres to the main cereals, is important as being representative of land utilisation immediately prior to the Second World War:

> *Crops:* Pasture 48 acres; wheat 36; barley 20; oats 14; beans 12; sugar beet 12; swedes 4; mangolds 4; fallow 6 acres. Total acreage: 156 acres.

The slight recovery in farming, just before the outbreak of the War, accelerated during the years 1939–45 as a result of financial incentives to cultivate neglected land with the consequence that the movement from arable to pasture was arrested. Widespread extension to pasture, however, had not been conspicuous in Chevington, the pasture shown in the list of cultivation at College Farm being little more than 30 per cent. of the total farm acreage. The War Agricultural Committee, colloquially referred to as the 'War Ag.', was active in the locality and was instrumental in maintaining a high level of efficient and productive farming.

The combine-harvester, the most revolutionary machine to be introduced in farming, lay at the root of all agricultural, economic and social change in Chevington. In 1938 there were fewer than twelve such machines in Suffolk. One of the first combines to be used in Chevington was a German machine, power driven from a tractor, on Lodge Farm in 1948. In 1968 the number in Suffolk had risen to nearly three thousand[17] giving an average, maintained in Chevington, of six to each parish. Change in village life had been in evidence since earlier innovations such as the reaper-binder, the traction engine (which had decreased the necessity for horse-ploughing) and the tractor. The combine harvester, however, accelerated that evolution into a revolution. Of such a fundamental change, there were two far-reaching consequences. Firstly, the harvester demanded larger fields for economic operation, necessitating the removal of hedges and the filling in of ditches. Secondly, it needed only two men who could complete the harvest in far less time than the teams of hand reapers working at the beginning of the century. Ronald Blythe writes:

> A single youth is now the undoubted lord of the harvest as he steers his vast pterodactylic combine across the lonely acres.[18]

Although a few fields were twice as large, the average size of the arable field in Chevington in the 1930s was about eight acres: the typical field now nears forty acres. In some surrounding areas, the size could well approach ninety.

When my father was a young man in 1900 there were 16 separate farms in Chevington: there are now less than half that number. During the last 30 years there has been a widespread amalgamation of farms and a letting, or selling, of farm houses to residents neither associated with the farm, nor with the parish. The size of individual farms has, as a result of consolidation, markedly increased. When Joseph Bradfield retired from Chevington Hall in January 1920, the farm was one of 300 acres: John Roberts now farms a total of nearly seven hundred acres, in four different tenancies, or ownerships.

The 16 farms of 1900 and the 14 of the mid-1930s each had their own farmhouse occupied by the farmer and his family. Of the seven farmers who now farm Chevington land, only five live in the house of the farm, or in an adjoining house. The College farmhouse, now much altered and restored, the Lodge, Malting Farmhouse and the former Stonehouse are examples of completely independent houses. In some cases, the farm buildings, once impressive as at the Lodge, are falling into serious disrepair, as indeed are the many outbuildings of Westley Bottom Farm which Chevington Way skirts on its course from Bury St Edmunds to the rural outposts beyond.

With the addition of two students at Chevington Hall, the total number of 'agricultural workers' in Chevington, a parish with a population of 545 at the 1981 Census, does not exceed fourteen. In 1920, at Chevington Hall Farm, Joseph Bradfield employed 12 men and a 'backh'se' boy on his 300 acres. When the Ballantines took over the 487-acre Lodge Farm in 1929, 10 agricultural labourers were employed there. Today, at the Hall, which has more than doubled its acreage, John Roberts employs about six full-time men, or their equivalent. These comprise one driver/craftsman, one gamekeeper (his work covers half of Ickworth), one stockman/unit manager, two 18-year-old students, one tradesman/builder and one part-time pensioner. The classifications of employment, at variance with the traditional pattern, are of considerable significance. Chevington, indeed, is now a different place, fulfilling the needs of different people whose lives are not 'bound to the soil'. Not only has the historic dialect passed into the unknown, but the lilted drawl of Suffolk speech has given way to 'standard English', the outcome of social mobility and the pervasive influence of television. Chevington's country way of life has yielded to a restrained urbanisation.

A son of a former working farmer, the late Charlie Gooch, who lived in retirement in the village, commented on life in 1983:

> Up Weathercock Hill . . . they are filling all the ditches and putting all the trees down. I heard it's going to be a strip for a private plane, but I could be wrong. Chevington is not the same place now: a lot of strangers. It used to be a lovely old village. The farmers are now 'combining' corn and rape. They grow a lot of rape here now. I think it draws all goodness out of the soil. If they keep destroying hedges and filling ditches and pulling down trees, I think the soil will blow one day. I don't like to see it. They use a lot of sprays. A little is all right. One field near here has been sprayed seven times. It must come up in the corn and get in the water.

The Second World War

The outbreak of the Second World War on 3 September 1939, will be long remembered in Chevington. The great world outside the concerns of the village came to life accompanied by news of its agonies and suffering. At such a time, Adrian Bell, the Suffolk author, wrote in *At the Tumbledown Dick*:

> That day before the whole world went to war
> We stopped at the *Tumbledown Dick*, do you remember?
> And sat out on the bench beside the door
> And drank our ale and thought how that old timber
> Had rested waggoners, farmers, men of yore,
> When fellowship burned clear, whose dying ember
> Was being trampled out this sweet September . . .

As the wireless had found a place in virtually every home, war news was circulated easily, in contrast to the remoteness of the world during the First World War. Twelve of us from Chevington fought in the war and three did not return. Under Platoon Commander Arthur Deaves, the Home Guard was active, a gun emplacement, or 'pill-box', appeared at the *Greyhound* corner and stone road-barriers were available, if required, near the coalhouse. On Sunday mornings, Lieutenant Deaves and his men were On Parade, and, from time to time, training sessions and lectures were held in the Hut.

During those stirring and eventful years, Chevington became accustomed to the heavy drone of bombers as they flew over East Anglia to their targets. In 1941 a squadron of Stirling bombers, the 214 Squadrom, a satellite of No. 3 Bomber Group, was based at Chedburgh, a neighbouring village. Just off Chevington Way as it approached Chedburgh, a domestic complex, accommodating 1,000 Royal Air Force personnel, was erected so that particular section of the Way, along Queen Lane to the centre of Chevington, teemed with military vehicles. The buildings were to stay for, after the war, minor industries developed on the derelict airfield. For years the empty domestic quarters remained battered, broken and forgotten.

With the exception of a stick of bombs, dropped by a lone German raider which damaged a row of cottages and the chapel, Chevington remained free from wartime damage. However, the village was in the main path of the British and American bombers as they returned to their many East Anglian stations. Its neighbours, Chedburgh and Stradishall, were branches of the No. 3 Bomber H.Q. at Exning, near Newmarket. There were other airfields at Tuddenham, Feltwell, Honington, Mildenhall and Shepherd's Grove at Stanton. Wellingtons, Stirlings and Lancasters, all bombers, often flew over Chevington. Occasionally the American Liberators and Fortresses, from the great American base at Rougham, shattered the quiet as they crossed Suffolk to Germany on their daytime attacks. At such times there was a thunder of planes everywhere.

Walking or motoring from Chedburgh, hundreds of airmen including in later years the Poles, who were stationed there, swarmed on Chevington. My mother and her assistant at the Post Office, which served a wide area, worked unceasingly during the day. At weekends, the *Greyhound* thronged with servicemen. Driven from Hardwick Lane by truck, German prisoners of war laboured on the fields and, often in the depth of night, other army lorries hurtled through the village. War had come to Chevington. In his quieter moments, Solomon Milk would look back over the years and, with some dismay, reflect on the future.

In summer 1939 a bus load of 30 evacuated children from East London, together with two of their teachers, arrived in Chevington for allocation to Chevington homes. As I watched the women of Chevington disappearing from the 'Hut' with little bundles of possessions thrust under their arms, and the London children trailing somewhat forlornly behind them, I wondered, not what was in store for Chevington, but what future those strange, leggy, wide-eyed children, uprooted from Bethnal Green in East London, could possibly face in an ordinary village in Suffolk down Chevington Way.

But all was well. The young guests settled down, but some asked where the fish-and-chip shops were and, for the first night or so, one or two, who were unhappy in their adopted homes, came to us usually bringing their foster parents with them. A quick look at the lists and, in come cases, suggestions about other homes, normally resolved difficulties. On looking back on those days, it is conceded that never before had Chevington people been required to adapt themselves to such a socially demanding experience. To their new task they brought unexpected talents and deep, hidden resources of sympathy and service.

About two months after the arrival in Chevington of the London children, it was resolved that the teaching of those children be combined with the teaching of the pupils of the village school[19] with effect from the following term, a liberal and progressive

21.   Chevington Way, 1984: between Ickworth and Westley Bottom.

decision which did much to forge friendship between the two distinct groups of children. During the war, school meals were introduced for all the pupils. The first reference was on 27 January 1943[20] when it was reported in the minute book that meals at the school would be 5d. (2p.) a day, or 2s. 0d. (10p.) a week. The meal for that day was: roast meat (unspecified), baked potatoes, 'greens' and steamed sponge pudding.

Between 1942–45, another 30 evacuated children from Surrey and elsewhere, were housed at the old *Queen's Head*, now Mallaby's, by the edge of Chevington Way, between Shoemeadow Bottom and Chedburgh. Mrs. Griffith, the mother of Raie Wilman, was in charge of the home which was under the patronage of the Anglican Pacifist Fellowship.

Throughout those momentous years, the Women's Institute was actively employed in knitting garments for the serving forces and organising fund-raising activities in order to send 'a little extra' to the village servicemen at Christmas. Large fish nets were pegged in members' gardens and laboriously threaded with strips of khaki, green and brown cloth for camouflage, before shipment to serving units at home and overseas. Rene Pettit, aged 85 (1983), vividly recalls those days and was one of 12 from the country chosen to march in the Victory Parade when peace came in 1945. A popular 'Pig Club' for men was formed in 1943 to augment the supply of food. It permitted registered members to rear pigs destined for slaughter by Ol Crysell, the Chevington butcher. Half the pig was transferred to the Ministry of Food, the remaining half was the property of the member on surrender of meat ration coupons. Concealed in neat, beguiling cases, gas masks were carried as people went about their work.

Blackout fittings were fixed to all the windows of the scattered village which, in common with other rural areas during the years of war, became overgrown and neglected. Having escaped through the broken fences and gates of Ickworth, deer were often seen on Chevington Way, generally at night, their eyes glowing in the darkness.

Early in the war, it was announced that Henry Bradfield Cooper, Royal Air Force, who had already been Mentioned in Dispatches, was to be awarded the DFC. Later, at the age of 25, he also received the DSO for 'his great technical ability and leadership' while flying as an Observer in 192 Squadron. Five men of Chevington were prisoners of war. Stanley Brinkley of Ruffin's Cottages was imprisoned in Java; Alec Norman, the wheelwright's son, in Siam; Alec Pask of the Shop Cottages, who had been captured in Italy, was a prisoner for two years in the stone quarries of Czechoslovakia; Stanley Copping, who played football for the Chevington team, was a prisoner in Germany: John Ballantine, Royal Air Force, and formerly of Chevington Lodge Farm, was captured in Crete. They had all known the fields and woods of Chevington and were former boys of the village school as indeed were the three who did not return: Percy King of the Suffolk Regiment and Henry Dodson of the Royal Medical Corps died on active service and were buried on the same day in the churchyard of the Church of All Saints; George Last of the Welch Regiment, formerly of Weathercock Hill, fell in action in Italy in 1944. Their names were added later to the 1914–18 War Memorial on the south of the church.

When everything was over and life had settled into an accustomed rhythm, there was a Welcome Home Evening in the *Greyhound*, organised by Mine Host, Harry Stutely and, later, a family gathering in the 'Hut', assisted by Billy Avis. There was restrained rejoicing, silent sorrow when thoughts turned to those who had lost their lives and an inward, but unexpressed, certainly that we could not go back, however hard we tried, to the life that we had known.

Changes at the chapel

In the 1930s the members of the Methodist Chapel (then Methodist as the result of the union of the three separate Methodist Churches in 1932) continued their witness in Chevington. The main chapel events occurred in traditional sequence, but there was a shortage of leadership which resulted in many problems of organisation. In spite of the dedicated service of a small band of workers, inspired by faith and undisputed zeal, the single-minded allegiance, which characterised the Chevington cause at the beginning of the century, appeared to be at a low ebb. However, as late as 1936, the current Plan showed that Chevington held two services each Sunday and an occasional one on Tuesdays. In addition, there were special services for the chapel and Sunday School Anniversaries and Chevington's income for the previous quarter was £5 16s. 7½d. (£5.83½p.), a total exceeded only by two chapels of the nine then in Circuit membership. The future for the 'cause', founded by the Bury Independents in 1799, appeared relatively auspicious.

In 1949 the Circuit Committee met to consider repairs to the buildings. It was resolved that the chapel should be purchased from the Suffolk Congregational Union from which it had been leased, certainly since 1840. The agreed purchase price was £150, and a grant of £75 was gratefully accepted from the Methodist Chapel Department. The chapel, to be known as Chevington Methodist Church, was formally conveyed to the Methodists on 22 July 1949. The first trustees of the re-designated church included a local zealot, Hugh Jackson of Hollybush Farm, and the inveterate Tom Ashman, the organist of former years. On the day following the official conveyance a rededication service was conducted by the Superintendent Minister, the Reverend Hugh Stevens, and a former Chevington boy, the Reverend Charles Clarke.[21] Despite the many changes in the village, the appearance of the chapel remained unchanged: the thatched roof, the lean-to shed, the old, battered door, the gallery and the elegantly arched windows were there for all to see. The report adds the welcome news that 'the chapel was full to capacity for the occasion'. A new hope was abroad and the post-war era inspired optimism and enthusiasm for the new world that was to be. Tragically, that new world proved an illusion.

In 1959, the Superintendent Minister of the Newmarket Circuit, the Reverend Eric Barton, wrote to the Central Chapel Committee informing them that the chapel roof needed between £500–£1,000 to repair it and that membership had fallen to eight who met for worship once monthly; furthermore, the eight members had no families who could, perhaps, resuscitate the Methodist 'cause' in the future. He added that, as the Thingoe Rural District Council were interested in purchasing the chapel in order to facilitate the planning of a housing estate, the trustees would never have a better opportunity for sale. The Reverend Eric estimated a figure of £250.

At a Trustees Meeting held on 7 January 1960, it was reported that steps had been taken to sell the chapel to the Thingoe Rural District Council and 'the Trust were given permission to dispose of the furnishings': Tom Ashman's organ to Kirtling Methodist chapel, the cross to Hargrave, the Communion Table and Bibles (Revised Version) to Ousden, the Hymn Books, pulpit Bible, and cups and saucers — which had served well at many a Good Friday tea — to Dalham, and the coke and coal — ordered for the winter for the time-worn 'Tortoise' stove — to a long-standing member, Mrs. Miller Stanford. The final Trustees Meeting was held at Ousden — inexplicably, not at Chevington — on 1 September 1960. Five of the original 12 trustees were present. The Reverend Leslie Chapman reported that the Quarterly Meeting, the Connexional Chapel Committee, and the Home Mission Committee had each approved the sale of the chapel to the Thingoe Rural District Council for £150.[22] There is no mention of a single dissentient.

On 9 June 1961, the *Bury Free Press* in an obituary article announced that, in spite of an appeal for £230 to save it, the 'little chapel' at Chevington had been demolished. The planners of the future, the Thingoe Rural District Council, had finally won the day. They began to build.

Some village personalities

Alf Rolfe had started a contracting business in the old clothing factory at the end of the First World War, renting the premises from John Sangster, the farm machinist. Starting with a three-ton Bellsuze truck and a Model 'T' Ford which he bought for £17, Alf employed 12 men to work in the garage, drive and maintain his six lorries. The business declined in the early 1970s, but he retained his garage and taxi services until his death in 1977.[23]

At the beginning of the 19th century Samuel Fenton was the village bricklayer and builder in Chevington and William Edwards was the wheelwright.[24] According to family tradition, Jonathan Cooper had left his native Depden about the year 1852 to join a firm of builders in North London where he learned the trade including, somewhat strangely, the craft of thatching. On settling in Chevington about three years later (Hannah Parker, the daughter of the parish clerk and schoolmaster, could have been the attraction), he eventually acquired the Fentons' building business together, apparently, with William Edwards' wheelwright shop which was in the meadow opposite Chevington Grove.

Although Jonathan built some houses on Depden Green, he worked mainly on farm buildings, farmhouses and cottages of the Bristol Estate in Chevington and the surrounding villages and, from time to time, extensions and renovations were carried out at private houses such as Plumpton Hall in Whepstead, at the large, local rectories and at the village schools. The building tackle, ladders, scaffolding, tools, wood and bricks were transported to the scattered sites by horse-drawn carts and wagons. A study of Jonathan's banking account with Birkbeck, Barclay and Buxton in 1892[25] indicates that bricks were obtained from the Woolpit Tile Company and that building material was purchased from Ridley's, the building merchants, in Bury. Jonathan was also the local undertaker and, since 1871, manager of the village post office. According to the census return of 1881, he employed 10 staff in the building business, five men and five 'boys', i.e. young men under the age of twenty-one. In addition, he was assisted by three of his five sons, Arthur, George[26] and William Henry.

Jonathan died in 1904. At the age of 23 his youngest son, William Henry, was presented with the demanding task of reviving the family business. Now over 80, Fred Pettingale was his apprentice at the end of the 1914–18 War. A study of the account books, estimates, timesheets, and correspondence throws much light on the organisation of a rural building business during the agricultural depression of the 1920s and '30s. In Wickhambrook, Barrow and Horringer there were similar small building firms and the business at Chevington was typical of the structure of the building industry in rural areas at that time. Fifty years ago, my father obtained essential supplies from Marlowe's, the builders' merchants in Bury and from Ridley's. There was frequent communication with the ironmongers, Andrews and Plumpton, who still trade in Guildhall Street.

The work continued until 1942 when William Henry was compelled to restrict activities because of his serious illness. He continued the undertaking side of the business with the help of Arthur Deaves and, in particular, W. F. (Billy) Avis, who gave invaluable help during those strenuous war years. My father died in 1947. In that year, Billy Avis started on his own account as village builder and undertaker, with a new builder's yard on the Chedburgh Road. For 20 years he contributed much, both professionally and socially, to the welfare of Chevington. The post-war boom had started which heralded a new period of almost frenzied building activity. In 1968, the firm was awarded a Diploma by the West Suffolk County Council in collaboration with the Royal Institute of British Architects for their building of Ark House at Whepstead. At Billy's death in 1967, his son, Harold, continued with the firm of W. F. Avis and Co. and, as his son is likely to enter the business in due course, the future of the rural enterprise, fostered by Samuel Fenton in the 1840s, is assured.

Chevington today

The Hut is now referred to as the Village Hall. It serves as the community centre for the village and, outside on a notice board, there are leaflets advertising meetings and events in Chevington and in the immediate locality, including concerts in Bury. For a long time the village was represented in the Bury and District Football League, but there has been no team for about ten years and no cricket activity for over twenty.

In 1871, before the great slump in agriculture, the population of the parish was 636. In 1931 it had fallen to 417 and, 20 years later, to 358. Numbers were more or less constant during the next 20 years, but then rose so that at the time of the 1981 Census there was a population of 545, the highest recorded population of Chevington for nearly a century. It is probable that the population will continue to rise during the next 10 years.

There had been some house building in the village during the first half of the 19th century such as the former brick, semi-detached houses on Old Post Office Road and the stone-built cottages originally known as Seburgh's Cottages at Brooks's Corner but, from the last quarter of the century, when the farmhouse at the Lodge and the brick houses opposite the school were built, the extent of re-building in Chevington remained minimal until the extensive and, in some areas, dense and indiscriminate development, subsequent to the Second World War. In 25 years of activity, more houses were built in the parish than had been thought possible, or desirable, throughout its entire history. The building continues. At the time of writing, after the demolition of the remaining round house, it is planned to erect houses on the site of the post mill off the Hargrave Road.

A new type of parishioner lives in Chevington. His work is elsewhere. In most respects the village is a dormitory for families who prefer to live in the country and to commute to their place of work, to Bury, or Newmarket, or even farther afield. As George Ewart Evans states about another Suffolk village in *Ask the Fellows who Cut the Hay*,[27] Chevington,

> having lost its self-sufficiency has necessarily also lost a good deal of its independence.

In the 1930s there was already evidence that 'outsiders' were choosing Chevington as their place of residence. W. S. Godfrey, the father of the eminent architect, Walter H. Godfrey, was the Marquess of Bristol's tenant at Chevington Grove. After the war, that distinguished house, in common with many others on the Bristol estate, was sold into private ownership when it became the property and home of the Marquess and Marchioness of Tavistock prior to their departure for Woburn Abbey. At that time the Grove was re-named Chevington Russell to commemorate the family name of the Tavistocks.

Electricity was installed in Chevington in 1947-48 when some householders complained of the loss of heat previously generated by the paraffin lamps. Lamps were sold for a pound or two, only to be re-discovered 25 years later in East Anglian antique shops at prices ranging from £40–£60. In the early 1950s water mains were dug and kitchen taps installed resulting in the many pumps and wells, which had served the village for centuries, becoming redundant and, later, derelict.

Certainly from the 18th century, the number of people leaving the village to accept employment on farms, or in domestic service, was an important factor. If young, they married and settled in their place of work. Consequently, the families remaining in Chevington for more than two generations were fewer than is often assumed. Of the 64 names in the Church Registers in the period 1730-43 only 15 occur during the years 1800-12, and only three of those names, Last, Nunn and Smith, remain until 1940. A survey reveals that of the 108 families living in Chevington in 1940, 34 had forbears in the village in 1880. Although movement from the village exceeds customary expectation, the immigrants coming into Chevington were, in the main, farm workers so that the common concern and shared experience continued, resulting in a fundamental bond of community and parochial allegiance. A common mode of employment no longer exists. Although the few long-established families, now ageing, can exert some influence on the course of affairs in the parish, it will be the developing responsibility of the newcomers, with some deference to the past, to ensure that the village as a social entity is re-shaped and maintained.

The concept of community is based, to some extent, on a place's social history and on a justifiable pride in that history. This social chronicle of Chevington, an ordinary Suffolk village, presents something of the people whose lives have been spent there, an account which is informative and, perhaps, from time to time, revealing. As Patrick Geddes, the social biologist, wrote: 'Every village, town and city, is not merely a place in space, but a drama in time'. It is essential, therefore, that the people living in Chevington today take care of what remains. Already, old cottages have been demolished and it appears likely that others will follow. It is the shared responsibility of all to know the buildings of special architectural and historic importance. In the recently compiled list, there are 31 such buildings in Chevington.[28] These are buildings which justify every attempt to preserve them:

> The fact that a building is listed as of special architectural or historic interest does not mean that it will be preserved intact in all circumstances, but it does mean that demolition must

not be allowed unless the case for it has been fully examined, and that alternatives must preserve the character of the building as far as possible.[29]

The Church of All Saints is listed as a Grade I building. Only about two in 100 of all the listed buildings in the country are classified as Grade I and, as long as the parish church is devoted to ecclesiastical purposes, it is not included in the scope of the general provisions. Moat Farm house is particularly important and is, accordingly, classified Grade II*.

As the initial procedure for establishing conservation areas is relatively straightforward, i.e., the district planning authority's consultations with the county authority,[30] it is fitting for residents and for visitors to a village to ask the question: if this village is not a conservation area, why isn't it? It is, of course, always easy for an outsider, who is uninvolved in the minutiæ of parochial pressures and administration, to make precipitate judgments. It is evident that the countryside has changed socially and economically and it is realistic to assume that change will continue. Already there is speculation concerning the establishment of minor industries in certain rural areas. However, it is the corporate responsibility of all the people of Chevington to ensure that the remaining beauty and character of their village are not lost in the materialistic evaluations of the day. A rigorous amenity society, or vigilante committee, could be a potent force in the conservation of this Suffolk village.

Whether the necessary initiative is taken by the Village Hall Committee, or by an imaginative Parish Council reaching beyond its purely legal responsibilities, is a matter of choice. For hundreds of people down the ages Chevington has been a home and the origin of their livelihood. That source has now disappeared for virtually all parishioners, but its Church of All Saints and many of the houses, footpaths, fields, hedgerows and woods remain. Moreover, the spirit of the past hovers here and there. Chevington remains a heritage which warrants our deepest care so that it may be conserved as a place of beauty for the future.

Honeysuckle. *Lonicera periclymenum.*

NOTES

Chapter One

1. *East Anglian Miscellany*, 1948 p. 31, SRO BSE.
2. Mawer, Allen: *Place Names of Northumberland and Durham*, CUP, 1920 p. XXVI.
3. *The Place Names of Worcestershire:* English Place Name Society, Vol. 4, 1927 p. 219.
4. Ekwall, Eilert: *The Concise Oxford Dictionary of English Place-names*, 4th ed., Oxford, 1960 p. 102.
   Skeat, W. W.: *The Place Names of Suffolk*, Cambridge, 1913 p. 96.
5. In the Curia Regis Rolls, 1201, and the Valuation of Norwich, 1254.
6. *East Anglian Miscellany, op. cit.* Skeat also agrees with this last insertion.
7. E.g. Robert Somerton's will, 1445. Baldwyn 64, SRO BSE.
8. E.g. *Valor Ecclesiasticus Temp. Henr. VIII* Vol. III. Printed 1827, SRO BSE.
9. *The Suffolk Traveller*, first published by Mr. John Kirby of Wickham Market who took an actual survey of the whole county in the years 1732-34. 2nd edition, London, 1764 p. 211.
10. *A Concise Description of Bury Saint Edmund's and its Environs*, Longman, 1827 p. 74.
11. Blatchly, John (ed.): David Elisha Davy, *A Journal of Excursions through the County of Suffolk, 1823-1844*, Boydell Press, 1982 p. 189.
12. Hengrave Records Vol. II. 2/613 p. 283, 2/593 p. 276, SRO BSE.
13. During the sinking of a well in the village in January 1936 about fifty feet of clay were dug through before any chalk was discovered. Water was found to be at a depth of 80 feet. Some wells in the locality are entirely in clay, and water has been found at a depth of 25 feet.
14. Rackham, Oliver: *Trees and Woodland in the British Landscape*, J. M. Dent & Sons Ltd., 1976 pp. 27 and 172. Rackham mentions an oak in Ickworth Park which could be seven hundred years old.
15. Gage, John: *The History and Antiquities of Suffolk, Thingoe Hundred*, John Deck, Bury St Edmunds, 1838 p. 323 *et seq.*
16. Pearsall, Derek: *John Lydgate*, Routledge and Kegan Paul, 1970 p. 23.
17. Gage, *op. cit.* p. 323.
18. *Ibid.*, p. 323.
19. Gottfried, R. S.: *Bury St Edmunds and the Urban Crisis, 1290-1539*, Princetown University Press, 1982 p. 229.
20. *Ibid.*, p. 229.
21. *Victoria History of the Counties of England: Suffolk:* Vol. 1, University of London Institute of Historical Research, 1911 pp. 588-89.
22. Scarfe, Norman: *The Suffolk Landscape*, Hodder and Stoughton, 1972 p. 153.
23. Gage, *op. cit.*, p. 323, quoting from Liber Domesday, 356 b.
24. Lane, L. C. (ed.): *The Chronicle of Jocelin of Brakelond*, Chatto and Windus, 1907 p. 71.
25. *Ibid.*, p. 44.
26. Gage, *op. cit.*, p. 323 (referring to Reg. Pyncebek, fol. 275).
27. *The Pinchbeck Register:* compiled by Walter Pinchbeck of Pinchbeck in Lincolnshire, a monk of Bury St Edmunds, began A.D. 1330, p. 155, SRO BSE.
28. Gage, *op. cit.*, p. 324.
29. Hail-Roll 021, BL.
30. Egerton MS 2371, BL.
31. Gage, *op. cit.*, p. 325.
32. Rackham, *op. cit.*, p. 200.

33. Copinger, W. A.: *The Manors of Suffolk*, Taylor, Garnett, Evans & Co., 1911 p. 6.
34. Gage, *op. cit.*, p. 325, citing Bristol evid.
35. This would be the so-called King's Highway, Chevington Way, or Abbot's Way.
36. Hallam, H. E.: *Rural England 1066–1348*, Fontana, 1981 p. 58.
    Titow, J. Z.: *English Rural Society*, George Allen and Unwin Ltd., second impression, 1972 p. 23.
37. Postan, M. M.: *The Medieval Economy & Society*, Penguin Books, 1975 pp. 101, 116, 197.
38. *Valor Ecclesiasticus, Temp. Henry VIII*, printed by command of George III, 1817, SRO BSE.
39. *Ibid.*, p. 400.
40. *Chronicle of Jocelin of Brakelond, op. cit.*, p. 71.
41. *Valor Ecclesiasticus* (Vol. 3), *op. cit.* p. 467.
42. Gransden, Antonia (ed.): *The Letter-Book of William of Hoo, Sacrist of Bury St Edmunds 1280–1294*, Suffolk Records Society, Volume V, 1963 p. 71.
43. Gage, *op. cit.*, p. 324.
44. E3/15.3/1.41, SRO BSE.
45. E3/15.3/1.34 (b) (1414), SRO BSE.
46. E3/15.3/1.34 (b) (1420), SRO BSE.
47. E3/15.3/1.34 (b) (1416), SRO BSE.
48. E3/15.3/1.41 (1540), SRO BSE.
49. Longe f309, SRO BSE.
50. Bell f1, SRO BSE.
51. See Note 46.
52. Baldwyn 61 (1445), SRO BSE.
53. See Note 50.
54. Hengrave MSS Thingoe Vol. I Chevington (the 'Churchreeve's Book'), CUL (pages unnumbered). I am grateful to Mr. Peter Northeast of the Suffolk Local History Council for providing me with supplementary information.
55. Redstone, V. B.: *Chapels, Chantries and Guilds in Suffolk*, PS1A, 1905 pp. 1–29.
56. See Note 54.
57. FL 550/3/1–16 (1729) SRO BSE.
58. Thornton, Gladys A.: *A History of Clare, Suffolk*, W. Heffer & Sons Ltd., Cambridge, 1930 p. 96 and Redstone, V. B., *op. cit.*
59. Redstone, V. B., *op. cit.*   60. See Note 54.   61. See Note 54.
62. See Note 54.   63. See Note 54.
64. Chevington Church Registers. Burials. SRO BSE.
65. FL 550/13/1 SRO BSE.
66. *List of Buildings of Special Architectural and Historical Interest*, Borough of Bury St Edmunds, Department of the Environment: St Edmundsbury House, Lower Baxter Street, Bury St Edmunds, 1983.
67. Hervey, Manners W.: *Annals of a Suffolk Village*, CUP, 1930 p. 110.
68. *Victoria History of the Counties of England: Suffolk*, Univ. Lond. Institute of Historical Research, Vol. II p. 152. (See Wingfield College Official Booklet obtainable from the College).
69. Clifton-Taylor, A.: *The Pattern of English Building*, Faber and Faber Ltd. 1972 p. 315.
70. Gage, J.: *The History and Antiquities of Suffolk, Thingoe Hundred*, John Deck, Bury St Edmunds, 1838 p. 326. See also Note 66.
71. Gillingwater, E.: *An Historical and Descriptive Account of St Edmunds Bury (Misrule of Bury Abbey)* 2nd Edition, J. Rackham, 1811 p. 152.
72. *Ibid.*, p. 154.
73. Knowles, David & Hadcock, Neville: *Medieval Religious Houses in England and Wales*, Longmans Green & Co., 1953 p. 61.
74. Briggs, Asa: *A Social History of England*, Weidenfeld and Nicholson, 1983 p. 120.
75. Gage, J.: *op. cit.* p. 103.
76. *Ibid.* p. 389.
77. *Ibid.* p. 505.
78. *Ibid.* p. 338.   79. *Ibid.* p. 325.
80. Trevelyan, G. M.: *English Social History*, Longmans, Green and Co. Ltd., 1944 p. 107.

Chapter Two

1. Gage, John: *The History and Antiquities of Suffolk, Thingoe Hundred,* John Deck, Bury St Edmunds, 1838 p. 325.
2. *Ibid.*, p. 185.   3. *Ibid.*, p. 186.
4. Ammunition of war, stated in the will, may refer to the weapons and 'accroutrements' of war which were probably stored in the Hall from that time for any emergency that could arise.
5. Gage, J., *op. cit.*, p. 187.
6. Gage, J., *op. cit.*, pp. 326–27.
7. This Mr. Long could have been the eldest son, Henry, of Margaret Kytson by her second husband, Sir Richard Long. He was two years younger than the young Thomas.
8. Gage, J., *op. cit.*, p. 325.
9. *Ibid.*, p. 131.
10. Thrower 14, PRO.
11. Gage, J., *op. cit.*, p. 188; quoting Churchyard's, A Discourse of the Queen's Majesties Entertainment in Suffolk and Norfolke.
12. Boynton, Lindsay: The Elizabethan Militia 1558–1638, Routledge and Kegan Paul, 1967 p. 171.
13. Gage, J., *op. cit.*, p. 199.
14. The original parsonage, now completely disappeared, was in the meadow to the west of the Church of All Saints which flanks Malting Farm. The 18th- and 19th-century moated house, now known as the Old Rectory (a Grade II Listed Building) was the rectory certainly from the early 18th century to 1978. The foundations are 16th century.
15. Ward, John: *Lives of Professors of Gresham College*, Lond., 1740 p. 279, and D.N.B. (Ed. S. Lee) Vol. XLIII, Lond., 1895.
16. Some of the Pamans attended the Grammar School in Bury St Edmunds, see Hervey, S. H. A. (Green Book: Bury St Edmunds Grammar School). Hervey feels that Henry could have walked along the 'Chevertun Way' to the school at Eastgate Bury St Edmunds – and back. A long walk. Sancroft was also a pupil at Bury (but not during Henry's time). In the admissions to St John's College Paman's father, Robert, is described as 'gent.'.
17. Or, perhaps, 'Starve a Fever'.
18. Torry, A. F.: *Founders and benefactors of St John's College, Cambridge*, Camb., 1888.
19. Mullinger, J. B.: *University of Cambridge* Vol. III, 1911 p. 383.
    Cooper, C. H.: *Annals of Cambridge* Vol. V, 1908 p. 383.
20. An entry in the history of the Royal Society states:
    June 24th 1680: 'Dr. Paman showed a stone of great bulk taken out of a horse's bladder, concreted of many stones, weighing four pounds and a quarter, one side rugged, the other smooth like pebbles. He was desired to take a particular account of the horse, stone, etc.' (1679–80), p. 512.
21. Venn, J. & J. A.: *Alumni Cantabrigiensis* Part I, Vol. 3, 1924 p. 302.
22. Ward, J., *op. cit.*, p. 280.
    Paman left £500 to St John's College for the building of the old Stone Bridge which still exists. This legacy, a very sizeable one in the 17th century, heads the list of subscriptions. *The Eagle* (the magazine of St John's College, Cambridge) Vol. XLVII, 1932–1933 p. 69.
23. FL 550/11, SRO BSE.
24. Hervey, S. H. A. (ed.): *Suffolk Green Books*, No. XI, Vol. 13, Booth, Woodbridge, 1905 p. 73.
    Jones, A. G. E.: *Suffolk Hearth Tax Returns, 1674*, Suffolk Review, Vol. 2, March 1959 p. 31.
25. *PSIA:* Vol. XI, 1903 p. 1.
26. No. 87, CUL.
27. Redstone, V. B. (ed.): *The Ship Money Returns for the County of Suffolk, 1639–40*, PSIA, 1904.
28. Everitt, Alan (ed.): *Suffolk in the Great Rebellion, 1640–1660*, Suffolk Records Society, Vol. III, 1961 p. 8.
29. Hervey, Manners W.: *Annals of a Suffolk Village*, CUP, 1930 p. 58.

30. Gage, J.: *The History and Antiquities of Suffolk (Thingoe Hundred)*, John Deck, Bury St Edmunds, 1838 p. 203 and Gage, J.: *The History and Antiquities of Hengrave, in Suffolk*, London, 1822 p. 219, SRO BSE.
31. Everitt, A., *op. cit.*, p. 14.
32. *Ibid.*, p. 94.
33. Redstone, V. B.: *Presbyterian Church Government in Suffolk, 1645-1647*, PSIA, 1907-9 pp. 133-175, SRO BSE.
34. Everitt, A., *op. cit.*, p. 25.
35. Hervey, Manners W., *op. cit.*, p. 60.
36. Venn, I., *op. cit.*, p. 247.
37. Dymond, D. P.: *Suffolk and the Compton Census*, Suffolk Review, Vol. 3, Autumn 1966 p. 114.
    Henry Compton (1632-1713) was Bishop of London and the Census was ordered by the Archbishop of Canterbury. It was sent out by the Minister of the parish and churchwardens.
38. Duncan, J.: Suffolk Free Church History, Vol. I (typescript), *passim.*, 1961, SRO BSE.
39. Farmer, Thomas, of Wattisfield: *Account of Nonconformist Churches in Suffolk with additions*, 1774. Transcribed by Joseph Davy, 1846. MS in Dr. Williams Library, Gordon Square, London.
40. Whiting Street Records, FK3 502, SRO BSE.
41. *Ibid.*, p. 133.
42. *Ibid.*
43. Redstone, V. B.: *Suffolk Protestant Dissenters*, George Booth, 1912 p. 14.
44. *Ibid.*, p. 25.
45. Whiting Street Records, FK 3502/2, SRO BSE.
    Duncan, J.: The History of the Congregation in Bury St Edmunds (the first 150 years), (typescript), SRO BSE.
46. Gage, J., *op. cit.*, pp. 204 and 327 and 499/4/15 SRO BSE.
47. In 1642, Penelope married her third husband, Sir William Hervey of Ickworth, who had been married previously to Susan Jermyn of Rushbrooke. A daughter of that former marriage, Mary Hervey, married Lady Penelope's son, Sir Edward Gage, in 1648. Such complications indicate the very powerful influence of such families as the Gages, Jermyns and Herveys. According to Gage, *ibid.*, p. 206, Sir William Hervey, on his marriage to Penelope, moved with his entire family to Hengrave, 'and so many branches of the houses of Gage and Hervey were living there together, that it is said the establishment at this period consisted above a hundred persons in alliance with each other'.
48. *The Diary of John Hervey, First Earl of Bristol 1688-1742* with extracts from his book of expenses 1688-1742 and Appendices and Notes; Wells, Ernest Jackson, 5 High Street, 1894 p. 66, SRO BSE. ('Four Hundred guineas' amount to £420, not £430).
49. Ault, W. O.: *Open-field Farming in Medieval England*, George Allen & Unwin, 1972 p. 145.
50. Hervey, John, *op. cit.*, p. 38.
51. *Ibid.*, pp. 63-4.   52. *Ibid.*, pp. 65-6.   53. *Ibid.*, pp. 77-8.
54. *Ibid.*, p. 79.   55. *Ibid.*, p. 26.
56. Hervey, William: *Journal*, Suffolk Green Books, No. XIV: Ed. S. H. A. Hervey, 1906 p. XXXVIII, SRO BSE.
57. See *Department of Environment's List of Buildings of Architectural and Historical Interest*, Borough of Bury St Edmunds (entered in register 29-9-83), St Edmundsbury House, Bury St Edmunds for references to all houses mentioned here.
58. Venn, J. & J. A.: *Alumni Cantabrigiensis*, Part I, Vol. I, CUP p. 109.
59. PROB 11/504, PRO.
60. *Hengrave Hall*, Hengrave Hall Centre, Bury St Edmunds, p. 9.
61. Gage, T.: Remains of Antiquity in County of Suffolk, Vol. I, Hundred of Thingoe, CUP, 1813 p. 50.
62. The Diary of John Hervey, *op. cit.*, p. 66.
63. Venn, J. and J. A., *op. cit.*, Vol. 2 p. 271.
64. FL 550/3/2, SRO BSE.

65. 806/1/37, SRO BSE.
66. FCB/1, 1633-1736, NRO.
67. Gage, J., *op. cit.* p. 328.
68. 806/1/37, (1686), SRO BSE.
69. *Ibid.*, (1699), SRO BSE.
70. Brigg, W. (trans.), *Parish Registers of Chevington 1559-1812*, privately printed 1915 p. 54, SRO BSE.
71. 806/1/37, (1699), SRO BSE.   72. *Ibid.*, (1706).
73. *Ibid.*, (1709).   74. *Ibid.*, (1716).   75. *Ibid.*, (1723).
76. INV 78B/66, INV 78B/67, NRO.
77. Gage, J. *op. cit.* p. 332.
78. 806/1/37 (1706), SRO BSE.
79. *Ibid.*, 1729.
80. FL 550/11/1, SRO BSE.
81. FL 550/5/1, SRO BSE.
82. *Ibid.*
83. William White: 1855, *op. cit.*, p. 459.
84. Dalton VI, 334, SRO BSE.
85. Information given in a letter to me by the Records Officer of the National Society 23:VI:83.
86. *Ibid.*   87. *Ibid.*
88. Defoe, Daniel: *A tour through the whole Island of Great Britain*, first published 1721-26, published in Penguin English Library 1971, reprinted 1978 p. 77.
89. Gillingwater, Edmund: *An Historical and Descriptive Account of St. Edmund's Bury*, J. Rackham, Angel Hill, Saint Edmund's Bury, 1811 p. 215.
90. FL 550/11/1, SRO BSE.
91. *A list of subscribers for the purpose of building a ship of war*, Class 45.5 p. 9, SRO BSE.
92. Recruits in the District, 1808, 37904, F139 (additional 12), BL.
93. J 501/1/3, SRO BSE.

Chapter Three

1. White was Senior Wrangler* in 1765. He was elected Senior Fellow in 1774 and Dean of his College 1767-76. Venn, J.: *Biographical History of Gonville and Caius 1349-1897*, Cambridge University Press, 1898 p. 78.
2. 550/3/73-78, SRO BSE. White, William: *History, Gazetteer and Directory of Suffolk 1855*, p. 389, mentions a Robert Keable, Farmer of Kelsale (see a letter to Revd. Mr. White from James Bales of Westhall concerning land tax due upon estate at Calsale (Kelsale) and Westhall. 3 December 1798. 550/3/75, SRO BSE).
3. Deeds and papers concerning property in Westhall and Kelsale of Revd. John White. 550/3/31-78, SRO BSE. Details of lands specified in conveyances from Brewster to White 550/3/78, SRO BSE.
4. The Meeting House Green is shown on the Enclosure Award Map 1815.
5. This road joined the road leading to Little Saxham Church and to Bury St Edmunds.
6. 941/83/3, SRO BSE.
7. See Fothergill, Brian: *The Mitred Earl*, Faber & Faber, 1974, for a readable, but scholarly, account of Frederick, 4th Earl of Bristol. The National Trust publication: *Ickworth, Suffolk*, 1979, available at Ickworth, gives a short, but excellent, introduction to the Hervey family.
8. Young, Arthur: *General View of the Agriculture of the County of Suffolk*, David & Charles Reprints 1869 (first published 1813) p. 38.
9. 941/83/4, SRO BSE.
10. IR 26/209, p. 85, PRO; PROB 6/220, F370, PRO.
11. Venn, J.: *op. cit.*, p. 142.
12. Copinger, W. A.: *op. cit.*, narrates a case of Robert Underwood, parson, concerning payment.

13. White, William: *History, etc. of Suffolk*, 1844 p. 663.
    Under the Tithe Computation Act 1836 tithes could be commuted to a rent charge based on prevailing price of corn. However, by the Tithe Act 1936 all tithe rent charge was abolished.
14. Flint, Brian: *Suffolk Windmills*, Boydell Press, 1979 p. 132.
15. Wickhambrook Branch Quarterly Meeting Minute Book, 1857–71, CROC.
16. Account Book, 1857–73, CROC.
17. A Baptism Register Book for Wickhambrook Circuit, 1856–86, CROC.
18. The Account Book for Circuits, Branches and Missions in the Primitive Methodist Connection, CROC.
19. *Ibid*. The Account Book for Circuits etc.
20. Circuit Minutes, 1871–88, CROC.
21. Minutes of Quarterly Meetings of WN Circuit, 1871–88, CROC.
22. WN Quarterly Meeting Minutes Book, 1899–1917, CROC.
23. *Ibid*. Quarterly Meeting Minutes, CROC.
24. I am grateful to Miss Joscelyn, a grand-daughter of the Reverend John White III, of Manson House, Bury St Edmunds, for this written information.
25. *Op. cit*. Quarterly Meeting Minutes, CROC.
26. WN Quarterly Meeting Minutes Book, 1912–31, CROC.
27. WN Quarterly Meeting Minutes Book, 1917–29, CROC.
28. Prob. 11/1565 PRO. In 1815, General William Hervey, younger brother of the Earl Bishop, the builder of Ickworth, left £180 to nine annuitants and, after their death, to his nephew, who became the first Marquess of Bristol, for any subject of charity 'he might think proper'. The poor children of Rede, Horringer, Chedburgh and Chevington benefited from this bequest.
29. White, William: *History etc. of Suffolk*, 1855 p. 463.
30. Chevington Ed. 7/116 XP/4160, p. 2, PRO (Kew).
31. FL 550/12/3, SRO BSE.
32. Chevington School Ed. 21/16631, PRO (Kew).
33. See Reference 30.
34. Chevington School Minutes of Meetings. 13 July 1903, SRO BSE.
35. *Ibid*., 6 August 1904.
36. *Ibid*., 27 October 1908.
37. *Ibid*., 9 August 1910.
38. Ed. 21/16631. Inspector's Report. 26 October 1914, PRO (Kew).
39. Prob. 11, 2144 PRO.
40. Venn, J., *op. cit*., p. 438.
41. Venn, J., *op. cit*., p. 434.
    The Suffolk Green Book (the Bury St Edmunds Grammar School) gives details of Old Boys, SRO BSE.
42. White, William, 1855, *op. cit*., p. 44.
43. *Ibid*.
44. J 501/5/8, SRO I.
45. *Post Office London Directories*, 1861–90, GLL.
46. J 501/4/5, 1861, SRO I.
47. White William, 1855, *op. cit*., p. 149.
48. J. 501/4/5, SRO I.
49. *Ibid*.
50. I am grateful to the late Nell Copping, a nonagenarian of Chevington, for this information.
51. White William, 1855, *op. cit*., p. 207.
52. Mr. Joseph Raymond Smith, Eastbourne, Sussex, a great-grandson of William Henry Smith I, has kindly provided generous details of the Smiths of Bury St. Edmunds.
53. From the District Probate Registry, Bury St Edmunds. Mr Raymond Smith has kindly forwarded copies.
54. *Ibid*.
55. *Kelly's Directory of Suffolk*, Chevington, 1908, SRO I.
56. *Kelly's Directory of Suffolk*, Chevington, 1912, SRO I.

57. Undated newspaper report. Name of newspaper unknown.
58. Newspaper report, 2 February 1882. Name of newspaper unknown.
59. I am grateful to Mr. A. J. Keble-White, great-grandson of the Reverend John White III, for sending me letters from the College of Heralds and the Guildhall Library.
60. 941/83/9, SRO BSE.
61. J 501/5/8, SRO BSE.
62. Bristol Estate Book (Chevington) 114/1, SRO BSE.
63. Bristol Estate Book (Chevington) 187.4, SRO BSE.
64. Bristol Estate Book, 114/1 SRO BSE. (This was an account book in which landlords could keep their accounts for the purpose of Inland Revenue).
65. Report on Royal Commission of Labour, BPP 1893, XXXV, pp. 35-6 (and preparatory Report on Thingoe Union by Arthur Wilson Fox. Meeting at Chevington, 15 June 1892).
66. J 501/2/11, SRO BSE.
67. J 501/4/5, SRO BSE.
68. White, William, 1855, *op. cit.*, p. 266.
69. See Thirsk, J. and Imray, J.: *Suffolk Farming in the Nineteenth Century*, Suffolk Records Society, 1958 p. 31.
70. Howard of Britannia Iron Works, CRT 190/96A, BRO.
71. Supplement to Howard Pedigree, CRT 190/96C, BRO.
72. *Hall Farm, Chevington*. Agricultural Sale, printed by Free Press Works, Bury St Edmunds, 1919.
73. I am grateful to Rene Pettit, an octogenarian of Chevington, for lending me written extracts about the Village Hall, the Women's Institute, and the Ancient Order of Foresters.
74. Letter from R.H.N. to the Archdeacon of Sudbury, 30 July 1926.
    I am grateful to Mrs. Peggy Nottage and to her son, Christopher, for allowing me access to the correspondence.
75. Letter from R.H.N. to the Bishop, 13 September 1926.
76. Letter from the Bishop to the people of Chevington, 16 September 1926.
77. Nottage, R. H.: *The Village Eucharist*, Mowbray & Co. Ltd., 1930.
78. Over a 100 elms, mainly at Tan Office and Stonehouse Farms, died as a result of the recent Dutch elm disease.

Chapter Four

1. *Victoria History of the Counties of England: Suffolk*, Vol. 1: University of London Institute of Historical Research, 1911 pp. 588–89.
2. 'To the plough may be ascribed the destructive influence that has spared so few of those unrecorded landmarks. Some may be unknowingly extant, incorporated into later sites. Possibly this may be the case with the works of Chevington, but it can only be suggested by a study of the entrenchments, and is no way proven.' *Ibid.*, p. 583.
3. In some Suffolk parishes there is evidence of so-called 'gospel-bushes' around which early Christian worship took place and where Prayers were said during perambulations of the parish. Gage states: 'In a lease of the first year of Queen Elizabeth from Sir Clement Heigham of lands in Chevington occur one meadow called the New Mede, and one piece of ground being leye, next a bush called the *Gospel bush*'. Gage, J.: *History and Antiquities − Thingoe Hundred of Suffolk*, John Deck (B.S.E.), 1838 p. 334. The whereabouts of this bush are unknown.
4. *Ibid.*, p. 328.
5. White, W.: *History, Gazetteer and Directory of Suffolk* (David and Charles Reprints), 1844 p. 664.
6. Gage, J.: *op. cit.*, p. 325 (Bristol Evid.).
7. Chevington Parish Records, FL550 (1729), SRO BSE.

8. This house has been enlarged on several occasions by successive rectors. A glebe terrier of 1780 refers to the house as 'lately re-built'. The first allusion to the 'capital mansion house' being of 'brick and slated' was in 1827. The house, a Class II listed building, was sold into private ownership in 1978 when a new rectory was built on the Saxham Road.

9. *Observations upon Chevington Church 1828*, FL 550/5/30, SRO BSE

10. *Ibid.*   11. *Ibid.*   12. *Ibid.*   13. *Ibid.*

14. Atkinson, T. D.: *English Architecture* Methuen, 1904 p. 128.

15. *Faculty Books*: Book I 1633-1736, Class FCB/1, p. 294. NRO.

16. *Ibid.*

17. *Op. cit., Observations, 1828.*

18. Gage, J.: *The History and Antiquities of Suffolk*, John Deck, Bury St Edmunds 1838 p. 330.

19. Wills 1450-1575: Chevington, Baldwyne 64, SRO BSE.

20. *Ibid.*, Herveye 92.

21. *Ibid.*, Herveye 98.

22. *Ickworth Estate Accounts:* 941/83/3, SRO BSE.

23. The Honourable Augustus John Hervey, 3rd Earl of Bristol and Vice-Admiral of the Blue, visited Bury St Edmunds in 1758 as Captain Hervey, M.P. for Bury, from his home at Ickworth Lodge. 'I, therefore, went very early this morning, the bells of Horringer, Chevington and Bury ringing all the way as I passed, and three or four thousand people met me about one mile out of Bury with flags, morrice dancers, music and loud acclamations of joy.' Erskine, David (ed.): *Augustus Hervey's Journal*, William Kimber, London, 1953 p. 295.

24. Raven, J. J.: *The Church Bells of Suffolk*, Jarrold and Sons, Norwich, 1890 p. 100.

25. Cautley, H. M.: *Suffolk Churches & their Treasures*, Batsford, 1937 p. 48.

26. Raven, J. J.: *op. cit.*, p. 100.

27. Although no verse appears on the Chevington bell, at Ickworth the following couplet occurs:
                    Tho. Gardiner he did me cast
                    I'll sing his praise unto the last, 1711.
Clouston, R. W. M. and Pipe, G. J. N.: *Bells & Bellringing in Suffolk*, Suffolk Historical Church Trust, 1980 p. 33.

28. John White's name is inscribed on the bell together with those of A. Bridge and E. S. Farrow, churchwardens. A plaque in the vestry, on the ground floor of the tower, reads: 'To the Glory of God and in commemoration of the Golden Wedding of the Rev. John and Caroline Macdonnel White, the bells of this tower were rehung and the framework and masonry renewed and restored.'

29. Fred King, the schoolmaster, organist and choirmaster, was treble. 2nd Arthur Rolfe, insurance agent; 3rd Charles Bowers, blacksmith; 4th William H. Cooper, builder; Tenor and Conductor — Elijah Bradfield, farmer. They are referred to as the All Saints' Society, Chevington.

30. Wills 1450-1575: Chevington, Boner 80, SRO BSE.

31. Cautley, M.: *op. cit.*, p. 51.

32. Cautley, M., *op. cit.*, p. 241.

33. FL 550/5/30, SRO BSE.

34. Gage, Thomas: Remains of Antiquity in the County of Suffolk (Chevington) (privately printed), 1813.

35. *St Edmundsbury and Ipswich Faculty Book*, 7 October 1837, SRO BSE.

36. Tymms, S.: *PSIA* (2) 1854-1859, SRO BSE.

37. Chevington Wills. Baldwyn 27. SRO BSE.

38. *Ibid.* Herveye 92.

39. *Ibid.* Boner 80.

40. Cautley, M., *op. cit.*, p. 140.

41. Venn, J. & J. A.: *Alumni Cantabrigiensis*, CUP, 1897 p. 289.

42. FL 550/5/30, SRO BSE.

43. Gage, J.: *History and Antiquities – Thingoe Hundred of Suffolk*, John Deck (B.S.E.), 1838 p. 324.
Foster, R.: *Discovering English Churches*, B.B.C. 1981 p. 144.

44. Norwich Diocesan Registry: Faculty Books Bk. I 1638-1736. F.C.B./1, p. 294 NRO.

45. *Ibid*. Brydane 244.   46. *Ibid*. Boner 218.   47. *Ibid*. Herveye 92.
48. Gage, J.: *op. cit.*, p. 331.
49. Gage, Thomas: *op. cit.*, p. 55.
50. Agate, John: *Benches and Stalls in Suffolk Churches*, Suffolk Historic Church Trust, 1980 p. 17.
51. Cautley, H. M.: *Suffolk Churches and their Treasures*, Batsford, 1937 p. 241.
52. Munrow, David: *Instruments of the Middle Ages–Renaissance*, OUP, 1976 p. 12.

Chapter Five

1. Chevington School Log Book for the period, SRO BSE.
2. *Ibid*.   3. *Ibid*.
4. ED 21/40268, PRO (Kew).
5. Chevington School Log Book, *op. cit.*
6. ED 21/40268, PRO (Kew).
7. Chevington School Minute Book (Managers' Meetings), SRO BSE.
8. *Who Was Who, 1897–1915*, A. & C. Black, Ltd., 1935 p. 88.
9. *Ickworth*, The National Trust, 1978 p. 20.
10. Roy Strong *et al.*: *The Destruction of the Country House 1875–1975*, Thames and Hudson, 1974 p. 190.
11. Redstone, Lilian J.: *Suffolk*, Alfred A. Knoph, 1930 p. 95.
12. *Ickworth, op. cit.*, p. 33.
13. Stratton, J. M. and Brown, J. H. (ed. Whitlock, R.): *Agricultural Records A.D. 220–1977*, John Baker, 1978 (2nd edition) p. 139.
14. Fincham, P.: *The Suffolk we live in*, George Nobbs Publishing, 1976 p. 62.
15. Blythe, Ronald, *Akenfield*, Guild Publishing, 1980 p. 19.
16. I obtained these figures in 1936 when, as a student, I was preparing an essay on the Chevington Child. The Agricultural Wages (Reg.) Act 1924 was operative.
17. Trist, P. J. O.: *A Survey of Agriculture in Suffolk*, 1971 p. 188 (quoted by Scarfe, Norman: *The Suffolk Landscape*, Hodder and Stoughton, 1972 p. 238).
18. Blythe, *op. cit.*, p. 18.
19. School Log Book, *op. cit.*
20. *Ibid*.
21. I am grateful to the Reverend T. H. Bryant, Circuit Superintendent Minister, for sending me particulars. In addition, Chevington Chapel, CROC.
22. Minutes of the Annual Trustees Meeting, Chevington Chapel, 7 June 1960, CROC, and information from the Reverend T. H. Bryant to whom I am indebted.
23. *Bury Free Press*, Bury St Edmunds, 21 April 1978.
24. The 1841 Census Return, J 501/1/3 SRO BSE.
25. These are in my possession as indeed are the books of estimates, accounts and wages.
26. He was killed by lightning in 1918. Fred Pettingale, recently of Chevington, was with him at the time.
27. Evans, G. E.: *Ask the Fellows Who Cut the Hay*, Faber and Faber, 1965 p. 240.
28. Department of the Environment, *List of Buildings of Special Historical and Architectural Interest*, Borough of Bury St Edmunds, 1983.
29. *A Guide to the Legislation on the Listing of Historic Buildings*: privately circulated in the Royal Borough of Kensington and Chelsea.
30. Telling, A. E.: *Planning Law and Procedure*, Butterworth, 1982 p. 199.

APPENDIX I

An inventory of the main contents of the principal rooms and outbuildings at Chevington Rectory compiled in 1730 by the Commissioners of the Consistory Court after the death of the Reverend Doctor Edward Grove, Rector, 1726.

The Great Parlour
Hangings, a pair of glass sconces, two elbow chairs, a squab (a type of couch), a square table, eight cane chairs, an oval table, four pictures, a looking glass.

Total value = £4.47½p.

The Little Parlour
Four cane chairs, a cane squob, two cane elbow chairs, an escritoire (valued at £1 10s. 0d. (£1.50p.)), six Delph plates, a looking glass, a hand board, an oval table.

Total value = £6.

The Hall
One clock and case, two oval tables, ten leather chairs, two old guns (priced at 5s. 0d. (25p.)), two pairs of cob irons, Tongs and 'Doggs'.

Total value = £3.15p.

The Study
One clothes press, a brace of pistols, one square table, a fender, oval table, two chairs.

Total value = 50p.
(This is an unusually low estimate. Apparently all books had been removed).

Yellow Chamber
Bedstead and curtains, one clothes-press, chest of drawers, looking glass (old hangings not worth valuing).

Total value = £3.30p.

Blue Chamber
A bedstead, chest of drawers, a looking glass (old hangings not worth valuing), a square table, two pictures, one feather bed, bolster, a quilt, one blanket. (In the garret above: a pair of virginals, two writing desks.)

Total value = £4.80p.

Green Chamber and Closets
Green print hangings, rush chairs, square table, pictures, clothes press, 12 pictures and two

Green Chamber etc.—continued
maps, four blankets and one quilt, a feather bed and bolster, one bedstead with furniture and hangings.
(The closet and garret were nearby which contained a flock bed, bolster, six old chairs, two stools).

Total value = £5.10p.

The best chamber
Bedstead, hangings, three blue and white jars, one feather bed and bolster, cane elbow chair, 11 small ones.

Total value = £12.45p.

The Kitchen
Chain and weights, a jack, two cleavers, a candle box, two brass candlesticks, an iron dripping pan, tongs and poker, coal grate, 'horse doggs', six tubs, 'one maid to fry with', *(This is inexplicable; probably a maid's frying pan)*, two half hogsheads, one bushel, one ale stool.

Total value = £2.65p.

Brewhouse & Meathouse
A brass boiler, two skilletts, 'a maid to fry with', six tubs, two half hogsheads, a small brass kettle, a dripping pan, a kneading trough, part of old still.

Total value = £5.69p.

The Ale Cellar
One cupboard, one vessel, one ale stool.

Total value = 25p.

Small beer cellar
Two half-hogsheads, one ale stool.

Total value = 50p.

Nursery
A bedstead and curtains, a virginal case and two deal boxes, 'a slat-table', three old chairs.

Total value = 65p.

In the men's garrets
Two bedsteads, flock bed & bolster, feather bed & bolster, two old chairs, one table.

Total value = £2.50p.

The Coach house
An old chariot, harness, a pair of chariot fore-wheels.

Total value £9?
(unclear).

Corn garret
One barrel churn, one cheese rack, one bird cage.

Total value = 25p.

In the Servants' garret & other garret
Two old warming pans (one without a lid), old flock bed, a bolster, a feather bed, 'a mill to grind malt with', a linen horse, one coverlet.

Total value = £2.85p.

The Barn
A coach, an old cart, an old plough, a wheelbarrow, old copper, a knife, shovels.

A 'parcel of wheat' (sold for £7), two old coach horses valued at £6; the harness and two wheels, one rowel *(i.e. piece of leather with hole in centre inserted between horse's skin and flesh to discharge humours).*

Total value = £8.43p.

APPENDIX II

Extracts from probate inventories showing the value of personal possessions of people in Chevington in the late 17th and early 18th centuries during Sir Edward Gage's Lordship of the Manor.

Value of possessions

1660	John Wymarke, collarmaker[1]	£24 7s. 0d. (£24.35p.)
1678	John Langley, shoemaker[4]	£58 8s. 0d. (£58.40p.)
1709	E. Bell, husbandman[2]	£9 3s. 0d. (£9.15p.)
1710	'Marcy' Bangs, widow[3]	£19 13s. 10d. (£19.69p.)
1650	G. Sparrow, yeoman[5]	£103 19s. 0d. (£103.85p.)
1650	John Goodey, yeoman[6]	£249 10s. 0d. (£249.50p.)
1662	William Paman, yeoman[7]	£99 13s. 0d. (£99.65p.)
1665	Thomas Underwood, gent.[9]	£236 0s. 8d. (£236.3½p.)
1680	George Frost, gent.[8]	£77 0s. 0d. (£77)

Typical Domestic and Personal Possessions

Household linen: Bolsters, blankets, feather and flock beds, feather pillows, many linen and woollen goods.

Clothing: Coats and 'wearing apparel'. (John Wymarke's wearing apparel was valued at £2.)

Furniture: Kneading troughs, oval tables, square tables, long tables, hutches, beds (including pallet and boarded beds), chairs, livery cupboards, clocks.

Domestic items: Kettles, brass pots, pewter dishes, warming pans, candlesticks, frying pans, spits, cooking utensils, gridirons, porringers, silver *(yeoman and gentry only)*, copper, earthenware, barrels for beer, hour glasses.

Farm Vehicles and Utensils: Cart, tumbril, harness, milk churn, butter in dairy, ladders.

Animals: Bullocks, pigs, poultry, horses (and mares and ponies), cows, hogs, sheep.

Others: One and half-acre of wheat, barley, hay, loads of wood, books (John Gooday, yeoman, only), various tools. John Langley, the shoemaker, left £37 in his purse, 'Marcy' Bangs had 'money debts good and bad', totalling 1s. 2d. (6p.), George Frost, gentleman, was in credit to the value of £12 and Thomas Underwood, gent., owed £60 'in debt'.

References to Appendix II

1. 1C/500/3/5/138, SRO BSE
2. 1C/500/3/35, SRO BSE
3. 1C/500/3/36/65, SRO BSE
4. 1C/500/3/19/160, SRO BSE
5. 1C/500/3/3/137, SRO BSE
6. 1C/500/3/3/3/90, SRO BSE
7. 1C/500/3/7/100, SRO BSE
8. 1C/500/3/20/1 1, SRO BSE
9. 1C/500/3/11/22, SRO BSE

APPENDIX III

RECTORS OF CHEVINGTON

After the Dissolution of the Monastery of St Edmundsbury in 1539, no rector is known to have been appointed until:

1559–80	John Langley
1580–1630	Augustine Underwood
1630–90	Robert Underwood, M.A.(Cantab), son of Augustine
1690–92	Abraham Underwood, M.A.(Cantab), son of Robert. Rector of Ickworth, 1675–92
1693–1726	Edward Grove. M.A., D.D.(Cantab)
1726–34	John Giles Gipps, M.A.(Cantab). Rector of Brockley, 1726–34
1734–76	Edward Burch, M.A.(Cantab). Rector of Langham, 1728–76
1776–1818	John White I, M.A.(Cantab). Scholar and Senior Wrangler of Caius College, Cambridge. Fellow, Chaplain and Dean of the College, 1767–76. Master of the Perse School, Cambridge, 1768–76. Rector of Hargrave, 1799–1818
1819–51	John White II, M.A.(Cantab), son of John White I. Fellow of Caius College. Dean, 1812–17. Master of the Perse School, Cambridge, 1810–19. Rector of Hargrave, 1819–51
1853–1908	John White III, M.A.(Cantab), son of John White II
1908–26	Arthur Keble White, M.A.(Cantab), son of John White III
1926–34	Reginald Harry Nottage, B.A.(Lond)
1934–53	Arthur Kenneth Shrewsbury. Rural Dean of Horringer, 1950–53. Curate-in-Charge of Hargrave, 1947–53.
1954–67	Philip Seymour. Rector of Chevington with Hargrave, 1954–67.
1967–78	Mark Frederick James Shirley, B.A.(Lond). Rector of Chevington with Hargrave, 1967–78. Curate-in-Charge of Whepstead with Brockley, 1974–77.
1978–	Christopher Charles Kevill-Davies, A.K.C. Rector of Chevington with Hargrave, and Whepstead with Brockley, 1978–

PATRONS

The Institution Books, NRO, are confused at times in the mid-17th and early 18th centuries.

1559	The Countess of Bath (formerly Lady Kytson, wife of Sir Thomas Kytson I) and John, Earl of Bath.
1580	Sir Thomas Kytson II
1602	Lady Elizabeth Kytson (widow of Sir Thomas)

1630   Mary, Countess Rivers (the daughter of Lady Kytson)

According to Gage, 'the advowson of the church of Chevington was appendant to the manor until 1716 when, by purchase from Sir William Gage, it became the property of Edward Grove DD' who was then rector. If Gage is correct then, on the death of Mary, Countess Rivers in 1643, her daughter Lady Penelope became patron and remained patron until 1648 when she presented the manor of Chevington to her son, Sir Edward Gage. He was succeeded by his son, Sir William, who sold the advowson to Dr. Grove in 1716. Anne, Dr. Grove's daughter, would appear to have inherited the advowson which her son, Thomas Underwood, sold to the Reverend John White in 1770.

1776   Reverend John White I, Rector
1818   Reverend John White II, Rector
1853   Reverend John White III, Rector
1908   Helen Maud White (wife of the Reverend Arthur Keble White, rector)
1926   The Guild of All Souls which remains patron

GLOSSARY

Ale: a parish feast usually to commemorate the church's dedication when ale was sold to provide revenue for the church.

Advowson: the right of presenting a clergyman to a living.

Caracute: plough land which one plough team maintained in cultivation.

Cartulary: a record of lands and privileges granted by charter, sometimes in rolls, or book form.

Childwyt (Childwite): a fine paid to the lord for a child known to be illegitimate.

Classis: a judicatory committee of elders and pastors in a Presbyterian district.

Close Village: a village whose landlord discourages strangers to settle. Formerly it was difficult in such villages to obtain a settlement certificate under Poor Law regulations.

Copyholder: a tenant who held land upon the lord's will and who had to perform certain obligations. Scarcity of labour necessitated money payments instead of services. So called because evidence was in the form of copies of the court roll of the manor where all land transactions were entered.

Corbel: a projecting block, or brickwork, from a wall used as a support for certain features, e.g. vault, or arch.

Cottar: a peasant living in a cottage, sometimes with a smallholding of five to eight acres. Rent was paid in the form of labour, sometimes at a specified rate.

Crocket: a leaf-like decoration added to a pinnacle, or arch.

Customary Tenant: a tenant who held land by custom and not solely by the lord's authority.

Custos Rotulorum: Keeper of the Records. From earliest times a county was in the charge of a peer, or landowner, who usually was the Lord Lieutenant appointed by the Crown. From the 18th century, the Lord Lieutenant served as the official keeper of the Records which related to such subjects as crime, land, roads, rates and treatment of the poor and which are now housed in County Record Offices.

Demesne: the home farm. Land of the manor which the lord farmed himself upon which tenants gave free service.

Dog Tooth: tooth-like decoration of the late 12th and 13th centuries, placed diagonally in a moulding.

Early English: the prevailing English Gothic period of architecture throughout the 13th century.

Easter Sepulchre: a recess by the north wall of the chancel of a church, decorated at Easter.

Faculty: permission, or licence, to carry out work, e.g. alterations to a church, granted by the Bishop of a Diocese, or similar superior authority.

Freeholder: a holder of free tenure, i.e. tenure not subjected to custom, or to the lord's will.

Glebe: land belonging to a church living as part of the endowment of the church.

Glebe Terrier: inventories, or records, of church lands and property drawn up by the rector, or vicar, and his churchwardens.

Hereditaments: possessions which devolve on an heir, e.g. land, property, tithes.

Heriot: a fine, sometimes the best beast, payable to the lord on the death of a tenant by the tenant's heir. Later this was a money payment.

Homage: the jury which consisted originally of two, or three, freeholders. The term could refer to the tenant's pledge, or loyalty, to the lord, or to the body of tenants generally.

Merchet: a fine payable by a tenant on the marriage of his daughter.

Messuage: a house with the ancillary buildings and yard.

Modus: a payment in place of tithe made to the rector, or vicar.

Oxford Movement: a religious movement which began in Oxford in 1833 with the aim of returning to the fundamental character of the church.

Parish Clerk: the salaried parochial official, appointed by the rector, or vicar, who was responsible for the organisation of Baptisms, Communions and the church generally. He normally sat at the lowest stage of the pulpit and gave the responses at the church services.

Perpendicular: the prevailing English Gothic period of architecture, roughly 1350–1540.
Piscina: a recess near an altar with a basin (and drain) for washing vessels.
Poppyhead: a decorative finial on bench ends.
Probate Inventory: a list of movable property, including household goods, and their value, for proving and administering a will.
Propound: to put forward for consideration for membership of a society, or church demonination.
Rood Screen: screen which separated the nave from the chancel, on which was placed the rood, or cross, or crucifix.
Sacrist: the official responsible for keeping vessels and vestments.
Saddleback: a type of roof with two gables which gives the effect of a saddle surmounting the building.
Sankey's Hymns: hymns written by Ira Sankey, an American evangelist (1840–1908) who, with Dwight Moody, visited England at the beginning of the century.
Scantlings: the dimensions of the structure of the building, hence the proportions of the building.
Slit Window: a window with a narrow opening. If the side walls are cut diagonally the window is 'splayed'.
String Course: a protruding stone band built horizontally into a wall.
Tenements: strictly land, or a house, held in tenure. Sometimes large fields consisting of villagers' strips over which a rotation of crops was practised independently of the rotation in other tenements. In East Anglia there was likely to be a concentration of one holding in one area, i.e. land was held by an individual in 'severalty', as opposed to land held in common.
Vestry: a meeting to discuss parochial church affairs. Overseers of the Poor were appointed by the Vestry; later the vestry itself was responsible for the administration of the Poor Law. All ratepayers were eligible to attend an open vestry. Membership of a close vestry was determined by property qualification and restricted to co-opted members.
Villein: an unfree peasant who had a share in the organisation of a manor. He farmed strips on the common field. He was above the status of a serf, but he had to perform labour services at prescribed times. Some villeins had holdings about thirty acres, others considerably less.
Wrangler: a Cambridge University graduate in mathematics who obtained first-class honours. The graduates were formerly placed in order of merit, the Senior Wrangler was the first of those who had obtained first class honours, the Fourth Wrangler was placed fourth, etc.
Yeoman: usually a freeholder owning land.

Cowslip. (Paigle). *Primula veris.*

INDEX

LIST OF SUBSCRIBERS

C. J. Abrey
Frank Aldous
Susan & Anthony Aldous
Denise Aldridge
Shirley & Bob Allen
F. N. Anderson
Janet Carey Arbery
S. E. & M. Arbery
G. & J. Arbon
Iris & Bruce Ashton
Isla F. M. Ashton
Terence William Askew
William Askew
Mrs. S. A. Aston
Brenda Avis
H. F. Avis
Peter J. Bailey
J. C. Baker
Sid & Dorothy Baker
Thomas Selby Ballantine
Patrick Bermingham, MSc, DIC, CEng,
    MI Mech E
Mr. & Mrs. O. W. Bews
Lynne Binney
Victor H. Blake
Mary Greaves Blogg
Graham J. Bonson
Walter & Ivy Bottoms
Harold Ruskin Bowering
Ethel Bradfield
F. C. Bradfield
Frank Harry Bradfield
H. E. Bradfield
Dr. Hugh Bradfield
John R. G. Bradfield
Mary Lucy Bradfield
R. O. Bradfield
Ralph Bradfield
S. W. Bradfield
Wilfrid James Bradfield
Miss J. E. Bridge
Leslie Bridges
Stan Brinkley
His Excellency The Most Hon.
    Marquis of Bristol, GO St A, GCLJ
Mrs. D. Budd
V. & B. Budnik
Mr. & Mrs. R. J. Burton
Jean Bushell
Mrs. E. Cage
Joyce Carrick (nee Mayhew)
Jennifer Catterall
Clifford Charman
Mrs. C. Cherryman
Chevington V. C. P. School
Chevington Village Hall Committee
Charlie Clarke
Eric George Clarke
Geff Clarke

Mr. & Mrs. David Clarkson
Vanessa & Elizabeth Clarkson
A. O. G. Clarry
Geoffrey Clements, FSA
Margaret Clifford
Professor D. C. Coleman
J. F. J. Collett-White
Ann Cooper (Vancouver)
Anne Cooper
E. & G. Cooper
Giles H. Cooper
Mr. & Mrs. Giles Cooper
Mr. & Mrs. Henry Bradfield Cooper
Susan Cooper
David Cooper-Smith
A. G. Copping
D. J. Copping
Evelyn Copping
O. & G. Copping
Theresa Cork
The Corlett family
Dr. Peter J. Cox
Gordon Crysell
Mrs. K. M. Delefortrie
Roger C. Depper
Joy & Stan Deverell
Richard J. Dobbs
R. F. Dodson
Mrs. I. L. Doe
The Doyle family
C. J. Earl
Mrs. R. M. Edgeley
A. C. Edwards
Mrs. M. Edwards
D. Everitt
Peter & Elizabeth Farrance
Robert Stuart Fearnley
Mrs. J. Fincham
Sarah E. Fincham
Stanley Fincham
Mary Le Flem
Paul Ford
F. Frost
Mrs. E. M. Fuller
Mr. & Mrs. Gadsdon
Dr. & Mrs. Andrew Garrard
Mrs. M. B. Gibbs
Mildred Gray
Mr. & Mrs. P. Greenhalgh
Frank W. Gurling
Warner Haldane
C. C. G. Handscomb
Marguerite Hawkins
Mr. & Mrs. G. Hayward
S. J. Herod
J. A. Hey
R. A. Hey
Alfred C. Hicks
Mrs. Higgins

Michael & Frances Higgins
Enid Hill
Joan Hinxman
Mr. & Mrs. R. J. Hitchcock
Mrs. S. J. Howells
J. C. Hurrell
C. E. Illsley
Marilyn G. Ingle
Miss E. R. Jarvis
Mrs. B. Jordon
A. J. Keble-White
Kim Keble-White
Amy, Helen & Elizabeth Kemble-
    Taylor
Rev. Christopher Kevill-Davies
Alec & Peggy King
Bill King
D. King
Dorothy King
Mrs. G. King
R. M. King
B. C. Kingham
Mrs. J. M. Kingham
Mrs. J. E. M. Kramers
M. A. Lawfield
Kay & Jack Lees
Martin Lightfoot
G. J. Mackay
Mary MacRae
W. G. Marriott
F. I. Marshall
Geoffrey Martin
Glenda Martin
John & Stella Martin
K. C. & M. J. Martin
Oliver & Sophie Martin
Ian C. Mason
A. & M. McLaren
Mid-Essex Insurance Brokers
Mr. & Mrs. H. G. Miles
B. K. T. Von Möll
Montem Infant School, London N7
F. Morley
Nancy Mueller
Harry Murray
Mrs. D. Neame
Alf & Jean Newman
J. C. R. Newman
Professor R. J. Nicholson
Mr. & Mrs. D. Nobbs
Mrs. F. M. Nottage
Dorothy Nunn of Hargrave
Mr. & Mrs. G. Nye
Mr. & Mrs. Ollet
B. K. Ollett
Sir Richard Hyde Parker, Bt
E. Partridge
M. J. Partridge
F. W. Pawsey

F. D. Pearsall
Pat & Bill Pemberton
John Peters
Enid Grace Pettit
Ethel Irene Pettit
Gloria Pettit
O. C. Pettit
Susan Faith Pettit
R. C. Pewter
Mark Phillips
G. E. Pine
Mr. & Mrs. R. E. Place
Mrs. D. Pledger
J. A. N. & V. B. Post
J. G. Quantrill
K. A. Quantrill
Barbara Quigley
P. W. Ratcliffe
Mrs. G. Read
Mrs. S. Read
Mrs. Alexandra J. Reeve
James & Caroline Reid
S. E. Reynolds
E. Richardson
M. R. T. Richardson, MA
John W. Roberts
E. R. & B. M. Rolfe
The Mayor of St Edmundsbury
Jean Sangster

Ralph Sangster
D. Caroline Saxby
Norman Scarfe
Shenfield School
Mrs. M. F. J. Shirley
J. Raymond Smith
M. G. Smith
Mrs. M. H. Smith
Marion Smith
Mervyn Smith
Ethel L. Snellgrove
Geoffrey G. Sparrow
Mr. & Mrs. F. Spencer (Wales)
Lady Stirling
R. & E. Stocks
Mrs. D. M. Stuteley
Ellen Frances Stuteley
H. W. Stuteley (Bury St Edmunds)
K. C. Stuteley
S. R. Stuteley
W. J. Stuteley
J. Stutters
C. & J. Tabor
Jane P. Tapster
Mr. & Mrs. John Tapster
Mrs. B. L. Tate
Mr. & Mrs. Frederick Tate
The Marchioness of Tavistock
G. D. S. Taylor (nee Whiting)

Capt. C. J. L. & Mrs. P. J. Terrington
Gladys M. Theobald
Vyvian Thomas
M. Thomson
Mrs. L. Thurston
C. A. Tice
A. V. & P. C. Tomkins
Rev. Evelyn Turnbull
A. Turner
Rev. D. J. Turner
Alice M. Twyman
Veronica & Mel Vearncombe
F. & S. Wallace
Doreen Walladge
Alfred Watling
Ronald Webb
Westminster College, Cambridge
Mr. & Mrs. B. G. Weston
Eileen M. Whapham, MD, FRCS,
    FRCOG
E. H. White
Ian Thornley White
Matthew Thornley White
Richard A. White
Professor & Mrs. D. Wilkes
Sally B. Williams
Job Willis
Wilman & Griffith
Mrs. Helene Wreathall

ADDITIONAL SUBSCRIBERS: Penelope Colson
                                             Peter Gold New

These names arrived after the book had been sent to press and thus could not be included in the list.